ICONS
of
GARDEN DESIGN

ICONS
of
GARDEN DESIGN

Edited with an Introduction by

Caroline Holmes

With contributions by

Helena Attlee, Andrew Boorman, Peter Brimacombe, Susan Chamberlin, Peggy L. Cornett, David Crellin, Patrick Eyres, Godfrey Goodwin, Axel Griesinger, Caroline Holmes, David Jacques, Erik A. de Jong, Axel Klausmeier, Marcus Köhler, Susan Garrett Mason, Sue Minter, Magnus Olausson, Laurence Pattacini, David Radzinowicz, Jill Raggett, Michael Symes, Jan Woudstra

PRESTEL
MUNICH · LONDON · NEW YORK

Contents

Introduction

Caroline Holmes

'The basic plant bed, rectangular and conscribed solely for the need to attend to all its parts without stepping on its plants, gradually assumes more ornamental surrounds and forms, and at one period becomes pure design, completely eliminating plants in the most esoteric kinds of knot. Water conduits and basic irrigation led to decorated spouts and basins, to fountains and cascades, and finally to elaborate waterworks created entirely for their own sake. [...] The simple hedge is first clipped and finally emerges as topiary.'

ANTHONY HUXLEY
An Illustrated History of Gardening, (London: Paddington Press, 1978).

Viceroy's Garden, India.
See pp. 142–43.

Literature in every culture eulogises the garden as a place of sanctuary, an earthly paradise whose natural, organic constituency sets it apart from the wholly man-made realm. Today the world's most iconic gardens still offer more than just a functional approach to horticulture. Iconic garden design fulfils a promise of inspiration drawn from the roots of historical creations that nurture the vigorous new shoots of modern garden design. Formal garden design aims to perfect nature while informal design uses nature as art. Both display the initiator's status through civilised pleasure grounds, providing a showcase for the designer's taste and education as well as for conceits and humours. A brief tour of the history of garden design will show the close connections between gardens across the world and throughout the ages.

The earliest recorded gardens date back to the 7th century BC and emerge in Ancient Persia, whose influence spanned the East–West trade routes. The inspiration for these and other ancient gardens seems to be a mixture of topography and religion. For over a thousand years *qanats* channelled water from the mountains to succour Persia's *paradeisos* or walled gardens, and the forms of these sacred mountains were ritually imitated in the creation of ziggurats. In Islamic paradise there were also four rivers flowing with water, milk, wine and purified honey; gardens with rivers flowing beneath being an Islamic metaphor for the faithful. The quadripartite *chahar bagh* was divided by four water channels, centred on a pavilion or an octagonal pool, and designed to fulfil the promise of a sensual experience, a terrestrial paradise and a foretaste of heaven. For desert peoples water in the garden represented a living thread, its flow and return a metaphor for life, death and rebirth. The water-grid patterns became more stylised and the catchment pool ever more decorative. The Koran forbids the representation of human images in stone, so carved and applied calligraphy provided a decorative, contemplative and emotive fluidity. Islam and its gardens spread from the holy centre of Mecca eastwards into India, South-East Asia, Malaysia and Indonesia; westwards across North Africa into Spain and briefly southern France; and northwards into Eastern Europe and the southern Russian states. The influence of Persia can be seen in the designs of the ancient Medina Azahara near Cordoba, the Mogul gardens of Kashmir (sadly inaccessible at the time of writing) and Lutyens's Viceroy's Garden at New Delhi all of which offer the physical sanctuary of cooling shade and the sound of water.

Other ancient templates for garden design can be found in the Roman Empire and China whose creations display a profound love of landscape. The Romans gleaned, assimilated and perfected the green skills of Ancient Mesopotamia, Persia, Greece and

Egypt; their gardens are well preserved in mosaics, murals and archaelogical remains. Ancient Roman features such as colonnaded villa courtyards and garden peristyles echo through later garden designs as cloisters, arbours, *allées* and pergolas, as do 'furnishings' such as ornamental fencing and trelliswork; pools, basins and fountains; statuary and automata.

Archaelogical evidence for Roman garden design can be seen grandiosely at the Villa Adriana at Tivoli in Italy, or more modestly in Pompeii. The design of the John Paul Getty Museum in Malibu, California is based on the excavated Villa of the Papryi at Herculaneum. The Romans and Arabs traded with Serindib (Sri Lanka): the archaelogy at Sigiriya shows palatial gardens which combined the influences of the Hanging Gardens of Babylon, the water gardens of Ancient Rome and the boulder gardens of the East.

The Chinese used masters of *feng shui* to ensure sites were propitious and rich in *ch'i* or 'vital breath'. Places of religious importance were set high in the hills, and visitors took journeys along perilous paths to 'gardens' of unadorned natural beauty, reading the calligraphy carved on the living rocks. The word for landscape — *shan shui* — literally means 'mountains and water'. China was ruled for 3,000 years by a mandarin *élite* who created secret gardens with high white walls, such as the Garden of the Master of the Nets in Suzhou. Through the maze of walls and courtyards, the garden designer aimed to create, rather than represent, nature and thus to concentrate the natural forces. Pavilions, halls, bridges, covered galleries and summer-houses were carefully arranged overlooking small lakes and streams, all carefully aligned with selected rocks.

Chinese garden-makers such as Ji Cheng (1582–1624) and Zhang Lian (b. 1587) looked at nature with eyes educated by 1,000 years of landscape painting, layering their gardens and buildings with historical and symbolic associations. China had fascinated Europe from the 16th century onwards, its palaces and temples set around lakes and hills immortalised in the willow pattern. Sir William Temple wrote in his 1685 essay *Upon the Gardens of Epicurus* that Chinese gardens and landscapes employed *sharawadgi*, a studied irregularity of beauty. Engravings by Matteo Ripa, an Italian priest who had been at the Chinese court in 1713, also inspired French and English landscapers.

Ancient Japanese gardens derived from religious needs as well as practical agrarian traditions. The spiritual responses of Shinto were expressed in the selection of a natural object and its surroundings as a sacred place, as well as by Buddhism which was introduced from China via Korea in the 7th century. Japanese landscape design is in the Chinese tradition of 'lake and island' with artificial hills and rock-work laid out to resemble a rustic wilderness viewed from pavilions, terraces and arbours. Open courtyard gardens were designed for Buddhist temples, imperial and shogunal residences. The smaller *tsubo* garden occupied spaces between buildings, now often created as a light-well with minimalist arrangements of a few plants and stones and a ground-cover of moss, sand or bare earth. The tea garden or *roji* was designed to create *wabi* (rustic solitude); *yungen* (tranquility) and *sabi* (the patina of weathering). Stepping stones approached the tea house, a simple structure of refined rusticity, with a stone water basin for ritual hand cleansing in the tea ceremony. The greatest work of ancient Japanese garden design is *Sakuteiki* which was attributed to Tachibana-no Toshitsuna (1028–94; *Sakuteiki* republished 1735). It gives specific indications for garden design: for example waterfalls are classified and advice given on the placement of bridges and stones.

Greyer maritime climates transposed the limpid pools of the East into lawns, as at Hestercombe. The comparison between the Mogul miniatures of pool, canals, pavilion and maidens and the Cluny tapestries' depiction of a demure medieval maiden on a flowery mead amply illustrates the differences in Islamic and Christian medieval visions of the sensual delights of the garden. Later medieval gardens in illustrated manuscripts

Master of the Nets Garden, China.
See pp. 104–05.

feature courtly scenes, garden tasks or the landscapes beyond. The hortus conclusus with arbours and raised turf seats provided outdoor 'rooms'. Herbers were divided into four with specimen beds and raised benches in a flowery mead. Large moated herbers were created away from the main house as pleasure gardens, their designs providing the framework for the earliest Renaissance gardens. The Cloisters Museum, New York (originally designed and planted in 1938) has created three cloister herbers.

The Renaissance revived classical styles, rediscovered perspective and developed a revolutionary attitude to nature which was now seen as in many respects subordinate to the arts. Between 1450 and 1600 the Renaissance Garden developed in three stages: Humanist, High Renaissance and Mannerist, moving from enclosed inward-looking gardens to broader vistas and avenues. The Humanist Garden is illustrated in the allegory *Hypnerotomachia Poliphili* ('The Dream of Poliphilus'), written in 1467 by Francesco Colonna (1433–1527). The hero, Poliphilus, travels through forests, temples and ruins searching for wisdom and truth, which he finds embodied in the nymph Polia. In the Jardin d'Amour Poliphilus and Polia wash themselves clean of sin at the Fountain of Youth whose jets arc gently into a stone-edged basin under an arbour. The description of the garden also includes ornate trellises and an exedra seat. The lovers take a miraculous boat to the island of Cytherea which is described as a perfectly circular garden, bordered by a line of tall cypresses and divided into 20 equal sections, marked out by porticoes and covered with climbing plants. In imitation of Roman gardens topiary is used extravagantly, and the romance also includes a description of the first knot-garden design. The book was enjoyed both on a philosophical and allegorical level and as a practical source for the creative gardener. In 1545 Padua Botanical Garden in Italy was created as an almost exact imitation of the mythical isle of Cytherea.

Villandry, France.
See pp. 134–35.

High Renaissance styles have had lasting design impact. The gardens were planned architecturally with grand steps and terraces in symmetry with the house and the contours of the land. This is epitomized in the Villa Belvedere, where Bramante's (1444–1514) vistas move out into the landscape and are adorned with statues in niches, gushing fountains and grottoes. In 1495 the French abandoned Naples, returning with Italian garden craftsmen who transformed French garden design. Jacques Androuet du Cerceau (c.1515/20–c. 1584) published *Les plus excellents bâtiments de France* (1576/79) with detailed plans, dates, and the names of the designers of France's finest 16th-century gardens. The Amboise plan shows ornate compartmented gardens but the disposition and inward planning of the enclosed garden space remained medieval in style. The basket-weave rectangular beds could perhaps be interpreted as early knots and the intricate *parquets* as ornamental *parterres*. High Renaissance designs inspired re-creations such as Biltmore in 1891 and Villandry in 1906.

In Scotland Edzell Castle gardens, created in 1604, epitomise Renaissance education. The south wall has niches for statues and plaques illustrating the Liberal Arts i.e. the elementary Trivium: Grammatica, Rhetorica and Dialectica and the higher studies Quadrivium: Geometria, Musica, Arithmetica and Astronomia. Such gardens are testament to an education that enabled the conception and justification of designs with mathematical precision as well as a knowledge of the stars and musical harmony.

The grandest Renaissance style, Mannerism, required an architect and hydraulic engineer to design gardens that symbolised an earthly paradise and contained allegorical and moral instruction. The garden should be suitable for courtly dalliance, philosophical discussion and meditation while displaying the owner's collections of antique sculpture alongside horticultural 'exoticks' and stupendous water effects. The finest example is Pirro Ligorio's (1500–83) design for the Villa d'Este which encapsulates Mannerist hydraulics and iconography.

Etienne du Perac (1544–1601) introduced Mannerist designs to France but Claude Mollet (c. 1564–c. 1648) and Jacques Boyceau (c. 1565–c. 1633), were the first to lay down rules of symmetry and proportion. They applied the laws of optics and perspective to the principal avenues, for example the sculpted green palissades lining the *allées* should be no higher than two-thirds the width of the walk. Sculpture and fountains were used to 'mark and divide up the spaces detaining the sight, forcing the eye to stop in order to consider the relief and hence make the viewer aware of other works which these relief elements surround' (J. Boyceau, *Traité du jardinage selon les raisons de la nature et de l'art*, 1638).

Away from the Italianate terraces, *parterres* were created on flat ground in elaborate geometric and flowing patterns using dwarf box. The *compartiment* and *broderie parterres* evolved from Renaissance knot gardens and are created as a unified design in reflecting boxed compartments. Boyceau and Mollet created the first *parterres de broderie* which were to be viewed along one axis only, preferably from the house. Mollet redesigned the royal gardens for Henri IV and at the Tuileries in Paris where he worked with Pierre Le Nôtre (active c. 1570–1610), grandfather of André Le Nôtre (1613–1700). A third-generation Renaissance royal gardener, André studied a panoply of skills: painting, tapestry design, science of perspective, ancient mythologies and Cartesian laws of optics.

In the 17th century French cultural and aesthetic style dominated Europe, both in theory and in practice. Baroque landscaping was introduced at Vaux-le-Vicomte where Le Nôtre's designs manipulated the expanses of space, allowing a sense of pattern to form along an undulating landscape. These innovative designs provided the template for Versailles whose avenues and vistas drew in the outer landscape. Versailles was at the hub of European court style and Le Nôtre gardens formed a 'crown of jewels' around Paris. His legacy is echoed in the designs of Daniel Marot (1661–1752) at Het Loo and Hampton Court Palace; George London (d. 1714) and Henry Wise (1653–1738) at Chatsworth; and Jean-Baptiste Le Blond (1679–1719) at Peterhof.

Giverny, France.
See pp. 126–27.

The rolling of lawns for bowling-greens (or in French *boulingrins*) and the *parterre à l'anglaise* revealed an *entente cordiale* between the English love of turf and the French love of patterns. *Parterres de pièces coupées pour les fleurs* were glorified flowerbeds whose vibrant colours would brighten a dull day: they are the parents of today's bedding schemes. The *plates-bandes* were formed in carp's-back beds edged with boards to raise them and create specimen flowerbeds, a style imitated by Monet in the Grande Allée at Giverny. Water *parterres* started as ornate cascades and steps in Italy, that developed into mirrors of water and pools in geometric and symmetric designs that reflected the garden. In England George London and Henry Wise laid out Le Nôtre-style gardens with hallmark symmetry in *parterres*, waterworks and wildernesses which radiated from the house. The gardens also incorporated walks and rides which were captured in Johannes Kip's and Leonard Knyff's detailed bird's-eye views between 1697 and 1707.

In England the revolt against formal garden design was officially sounded in 1712 by Joseph Addison in his article in the *Spectator*: 'Why may not a whole Estate be thrown into a kind of Garden by frequent Plantation, that may turn as much to the Profit as the Pleasure of the Owner? A marsh overgrown with Willows, great Mountains shaded with Oaks, are not only more beautiful, but more beneficial, than when they lie bare and unadorned. Fields of Corn make a pleasant Prospect, ... a Man might make a pretty Landskip of his own Possessions' (The *Spectator*, no. 414, 25 June 1712). The challenge was taken up between 1716 and 1781 by John Aislabie (d. 1742) and his son William (d. 1781) who created the landscape around Studley Royal, set in the wild wooded valley of the River Skell in North Yorkshire. Its design of still water, lawns and temples set against a dark background of trees is the perfect fusion of wild landscape (the 'sublime') and polished 18th-century planning (the 'beautiful').

William Kent (1685–1748), first commissioned by Lord Burlington, guided noblemen returning from the Grand Tour initially as an artist and architect, then as a landscaper. Lancelot 'Capability' Brown (1716–83) learned landscaping from Kent at Stowe, beginning a career which ruthlessly swept away the old formal gardens in favour of naturalistic 'landskip' — a vision of England that has been copied worldwide. He perfected the serpentine style with its outer belt of 'sublime' trees which shielded the estate and provided a circuitous route to the house so that one could glimpse vistas through clumps of trees across 'beautiful' glades of grass and sinuous lakes. Humphry Repton (1752–1818) was in many ways heir to Brown but his landscaping encompassed picturesque villages and flower and rose gardens around the house. Repton presented his clients with a Red Book, (so-called because they were usually bound in red morocco leather): the watercolours and plans showed unflattering views of the garden before and more pleasing ones after his proposed designs by means of lift-up flaps.

Stowe, England.
See pp. 84–85.

With the expansion of the British empire under Queen Victoria, the British created nostalgic formal rose gardens and parks around the world, regardless of the climates. They were also avid and adventurous plant hunters, creating botanic gardens around the world, linked to the Royal Botanic Gardens at Kew. The Great Exhibition in London of 1851 brought design ideas (and visitors) from all parts of the British Empire; later the Exposition Universelle de Paris of 1889, the Columbian Exhibition, Chicago of 1892 and the Anglo-Japanese Exhibition, London of 1910 demonstrated fashionable Japanese garden styles.

In 19th-century Britain Italianate gardens were still popular, often designed by Sir Charles Barry (1795–1860) or William Andrews Nesfield (1793–1881). As the century moved on, in East-Coast America, England and Scotland designs for grand houses drew more and more widely from Italy and France. Formal gardens appeared on upper and lower terraces, magnificent conservatories were built, vistas spread across the landscape, and specialist Japanese or rockery gardens, and tennis or croquet lawns were created. In 1909 Sir Reginald Blomfield (1856–1942) was engaged to layout gardens at Mellerstain near Gordon in the Scottish Borders. The grandiose scheme, inspired by Le Nôtre, merged the architectural garden into the blue of the horizon. In *The Formal Garden in England* first published in 1882 Blomfield had written: 'The formal treatment of gardens ought, perhaps, to be called the architectural treatment of gardens, for it consists in the extension of the principles of design which govern the house to the grounds which surround it'.

At the turn of the century the Arts and Crafts movement, inspired by medieval skills, advocated craftsmanship and informality in gardens vociferously supported by William Robinson (1838–1935) who was a regular traveller to France and America. His garden at Gravetye Manor in Sussex was filled with native trees, shrubs and flowers complemented by hardy American introductions. He planted drifts of springtime bulbs under his trees, a style inspired by wild flowers and now emulated worldwide. The formal versus informal design debate between Blomfield and Robinson was observed by Frederick Law Olmsted (1822–1903), the founder of American landscape architecture. Olmsted said in 1892: 'A complete return to the old formal gardening is to be desired rather than that the present contradictory hash of formal-natural gardening should continue.'

Robinson's influence can be seen in the work of Gertrude Jekyll (1843–1932). Between 1894 and 1912 Jekyll and Edwin Lutyens (1869–1944) undertook some 70 garden designs, Jekyll's plantings softening Lutyens often stark Wrenaissance architecture. Terraces and courtyards were filled with flowers leading to pergolas and arches, down steps, alongside rills and pools to specialist gardens for every season. Jekyll rejected regimentation, creating what she called 'drifts' of colour. She had specific views on the effects of colour: with orange 'the effect is bright and hot, sufficient to visually warm up any grey day, so the oranges veer towards red not yellow'; for grey, 'the effect is grey-green and silver grey with flowers of white, pastel pink and blues'; for blue, 'blues veer towards white and grey, not purple'; for green, 'shades, shape and texture of foliage with white flowers'. The best formal European styles influenced landscape architect Beatrix Farrand (1872–1959), who travelled around Europe with her aunt, the novelist Edith Wharton, and went on to create American gardens such as Dumbarton Oaks.

Modernist styles, mixed with more ancient influences, revolutionised approaches to garden design in the 20th century, in the architecture of Antonio Gaudí (1852–1926) in Barcelona and Frank Lloyd Wright (1867–1959) in Chicago for example.

Gaudí's Parque Güell echoes the sense of baroque multitude and ingenious Moorish use of water, clothed in rough rendering and *trencadis*. Lloyd Wright did not consider himself a landscape architect but his response to nature and the landscape was intuitive. His 'Prairie' style echoes the long, flat landscape: the gardens merged and the houses themselves were softened with planters inside and out. His masterpiece, Fallingwater in Pennsylvania, was inspired by the contrasts of his native Wisconsin landscape and a Hokusai print showing a farmhouse on a knoll above a plunging waterfall. In 1937, inspired by an article on Fallingwater and having lived in Japan for a year, Alvar Aalto (1898–1976) was commissioned to design the Villa Mairea and was visited by Thomas Church (1902–78). Both men developed a relaxed, curvilinear form that absorbed the swimming pool into modern gardens.

Dumbarton Oaks, USA.
See pp. 144–45.

The Arts and Crafts influences continued under Lawrence Johnston (1871–1958) at Hidcote Manor and La Serre de la Madone, and with Vita Sackville-West (1892–1962) and Harold Nicolson at Sissinghurst. Classic designers in the Italian tradition such as Harold Peto (1854–1933) and the collaborations of Russell Page (1906–85) and Geoffrey Jellicoe (1900–96) retained symmetry and proportion in European gardens. In 1929 Christopher Tunnard (1910–79) came to England, and before going to Yale in 1939 he published *Gardens in the Modern Landscape*. Tunnard was inspired by the spirituality and simplicity of Japanese gardens. The Japanese notion of the sliding door radically altered the transition from house to garden, so Tunnard sought a starker, simpler look with low maintenance and plants that looked good all the year round. In Brazil Roberto Burle Marx (1909–94) shook off the formal European influence on South American gardens, using bold blocks of Miró-style colour. His swirling public and private landscapes are filled with tropical grasses, flowers and shrubs. The effect is boisterous, harmonious and innovative.

The elements of garden design which have been mixed up over the centuries — architecture, water, plants and rocks, as well as religion and philosophy — should not, however, overshadow the sensual promises of the garden. Evocative sounds and movement, such as birdsong or the effects of wind and waves, are a vital design element. Contrast the rustle of silk and murmuring water sitting in an enclosed Islamic garden with the noise of baroque crowds assembled for court masques, mock sea battles and fireworks in the vast spaces of Versailles. Just as important as the symbolic meanings of gardens and their inspiration from mythology or literature is their constant refinement according to the sensual and emotional needs of society. Today's art and craft of garden design echo the innate desire to recover Paradise, while evoking a desire to understand and trace its history, and to develop its arts further. Today, garden design can enhance a house, palace or cottage. In a naturalistic landscape the house can graze; framed by formal terraces it can dine; while modern urban dwellings can drink through a long straw, enjoying their landscapes from rooftops, windows and doorways.

Sigiriya

SRI LANKA

'From Paradise to Taprobane is forty leagues; there may be heard the sound of the Fountains of Paradise'

TRADITIONAL
reported by Friar Marignolli in 1335, and cited in the Foreword to Arthur C. Clarke's *Fountains of Paradise.*

An aerial view of the site.

3rd century BC: Buddhist monastery and resumed until fourteenth century AD.
484 AD Kassapa moves into completed palace with broad moats and walls.
16th–17th centuries AD: Becomes distant garrison of Kandyan kings.
19th-century: Archaelogical investigations undertaken by British.
1980s Designated part of UNESCO Cultural Triangle project.

Sigiriya in Sri Lanka (from 'Sigiri' meaning Lion Rock) has been described as the eighth wonder of the world with its unique history, topography and geology. Sri Lanka has many ancient names: among them the Roman 'Taprobane' and the Arab 'Serendib' which inspired Horace Walpole to coin the word serendipity and formed the Chinese 'Si-Lan' [Land of Delights]. The design of Sigiriya's gardens echoes these names.

King Kassapa (reigned 477–495) transformed the 1.2-mile rock into a recumbent lion by the addition of a brick and stucco upper body. Visitors entered through the lion's mouth to start the frescoed ascent to a courtly paradise of elegant pavilions, gardens and pools covering 3 acres which overlooked terraced, water and boulder gardens. Water was taken from the *wewa* (huge 'tanks' or artificial lakes to store water during the rainy season) to the south-east of the base, cranked to the summit by a series of pulleys, and supplemented by the stored rainwater which created decorative and bathing pools. The only flowers to have survived decorate the frescoes of the 'Cloud Damsels' and the graffiti describing them says: 'Hail! gold-coloured one on the mountainside, whose resplendent rosy hand bore a blue water-lily...'. Today the visitor still enters through the stone carved paws whose claws seem menacing as one starts the long climb past the few remaining frescoes.

The boulder, terrace and water gardens cut out of tropical forest lie to the west of the rock. The boulder gardens predated Kassapa as a third century B.C. Buddhist monastery complex and are typically Chinese in design. A network of winding pathways and paved passages create a spiritual journey around 'natural' rock boulders of varying sizes decorated with carvings. The boulders created caves, some with painted ceilings, and provided support to tiered platforms. *Shan shui* (Chinese for mountains and water but commonly used to mean a 'natural' designed landscape) is encapsulated in the transition from boulder to water gardens by an octagonal pool sheltered by a 45-foot boulder. A brick-lined path with flights of limestone steps cuts a central axis through the terrace gardens, rising away from the rock base through the boulder gardens to the Royal Bathing Pools. The terraces were contained by rubble walls, each providing a formally planted area in Babylonian ziggurat style. The visitor could walk to the *wewa* (now half its original size) and stroll around its margins enjoying the sheet of colourful blue waterlilies. The complex hydraulics that ran underground for decorative and utilitarian needs demonstrate sophisticated ingenuity. The water gardens lay within a walled enclosure entered by elaborate gatehouses: there one found pools, running water and fountains, their gentle cooling properties brightened by tropical birds, trees and aquatic plants. Near the western entrance there is an intricate layout of tiled and marble-floored buildings with winding and corbelled water courses interspersed with shallow reflecting pools. The court could then approach four moated islands, two with 'cool water palaces': fountains gushed under gravitational pressure through perforated and patterned limestone. Finally, the Royal Bathing Pools, four L-shaped smooth-sided pools

surrounded a large pavilion which were linked by terraces and steps. All this takes place under the dominating Sigiriya Rock which was perhaps symbolic of Alakamunda, the Himalayan mountain paradise of Kuvera, God of Riches. Symbolically and in reality, both then and now, this is a landscape designed for power and pleasure which also inspired Arthur C. Clarke's *Fountains of Paradise*. C.H.

Sigiriya rock fortress and gardens.

Byodo-in

UJI, JAPAN

'Anyone who wants a vision of paradise must visit the temple at Uji.'

Old saying quoted in *Sakuteiki.*

The Phoenix Hall 'floats' on the Heian era pond.

The Byodo-in at Uji, south of Kyoto, is the finest surviving example of a Pure Land villa-temple, created during the Heian period (794–1185). The famous Phoenix Hall was built on the site of a villa owned by Fujiwara Michigan (966–1027), who played a powerful role in the Imperial Court by acting as an intermediary between the Emperor and court officials. He was succeeded by his son Fujiwara Yorimichi (922–1074) who built an extensive palace, Byodo-in. This palace was converted into a temple in 1052 and the Phoenix Hall, which has survived until today, was completed in 1053. The central hall houses the temple's statue of Amida Buddha, which gazes out over the lake and garden. The Phoenix Hall — named for the mythical bird reborn from the ashes of a fire — derives the appellation from the layout of the buildings, outstretched wings being provided by the flanking corridors and the central hall representing the body. The imagery of the Phoenix Hall gives an insight into Heian court society where imagery and metaphor were central: they are not only found in the building but also in the garden which is a representation of the Western Paradise of Amida Buddha, the traditional design imagery for gardens in the Heian period.

The lake west of the Phoenix Hall is formed from what was once an inlet of the River Uji, and may well be a remnant of an earlier and larger lake. The gardens of the Heian period were part of a highly developed court culture where officials had to display a refined aesthetic sensitivity in all aspects of their lives from the selection of appropriately coloured kimonos to reflect the season, to the ability to write a well composed poem. The gardens of this era were a vital setting for the activities of the aristocracy and are depicted in the *Tale of Genji*, a novel written in the Heian era. The major feature of a Heian garden was the lake, as at Byodo-in, which often occupied the majority of the garden space. It would contain at least one island and be connected to the shore by a bridge. The lakes were a performance space for musicians, who crossed the water in dragon- or phoenix-prowed boats, while the owners and their guests could observe the gardens from the adjacent buildings. The gardens were planted with a wide range of flowering herbaceous plants and shrubs, so making the gardens more colourful than those of later periods. The earliest manual of garden design known, the *Sakuteiki*, written in mid- to late-11th-century Japan is attributed to Tachibana-no Toshitsuna (1028–94) whose father is credited with building of the garden at Byodo-in; this work must surely have been influenced by the garden.

Though the garden at Byodo-in has suffered with the passing of the centuries its most vital feature, the lake, remains, although possibly reduced from its former size. The major value of the lake at Byodo-in is that it provides a canvas for the perfect reflection of the Phoenix Hall. This wonderful building, with the strong horizontal lines of the central hall and symmetrical corridors, is reflected in the water's so the garden and building unite to recall for the viewer the 'Pure Land' or Western Paradise of the Amida Buddha, as was surely the intention of the original designer. *J.R.*

c. 1000 Existing villa built for Fujiwara Michigan.
1053 Creation of the main temple buildings and possible alterations or construction of the garden.
1336 Majority of palace buildings destroyed.
1999 Restoration work on the lake in front of the Phoenix Hall.

The corridor wings of the Phoenix Hall.

The Phoenix Hall was completed in 1053.

Alhambra

GRANADA, SPAIN

'Come when the shadows of evening temper the brightness of the court and throw a gloom into the surrounding halls. Then nothing can be more serenely melancholy or more in harmony with [a] tale of departed grandeur.'

WASHINGTON IRVING
The Alhambra, 1832

View of the Generalife from the Alhambra.

The Alhambra tops the Sabika Hill like a boat moored on the fertile plains below the Sierra Nevada. It comprises the Alcazaba, Palacios, Medina and Generalife but is famed for its patios in the Palacios and Generalife. The Moorish Nasrid dynasty (1237–1492) designed palaces around patios whose inner (spiritual) beauty contrasted with plain exteriors. Entry was through small courts and circuitous passageways. In 1526 this complex was incorporated into a Renaissance palace for Carlos V. The Patio de los Arrayanes has a long rectangular pool fed with two circular bubbling fountains, representing the circle of life, death and rebirth. Two clipped myrtle hedges edge the plain reflective pool marking the transition to the rich carvings on the surrounding colonnades. The kaleidoscope of colours in stucco, mosaics and fabrics has gone but the swallows, swooping in this open courtyard, provide sound and movement.

The Patio de los Leones typifies the Persian *chahar bagh*, quartered by four rills, each with two circular bubbling fountains feeding the central fountain supported by twelve lions within a forest of pillars supporting the colonnade and two pavilions. The rills transport the garden design into the inner rooms as well as reflections from the courtyard and a means of cooling the air. Marble floors extend from within, framing the rills, the lions fountain and the sunken quarters which were originally planted with orange trees. The simple layout and columns rise into a sumptuous canopy of stucco intricately carved with calligraphy and patterns. Seated on Granada silks and brocades the visitor was in a sensuous paradise — the design and poetry of the garden to look at; heady scents; cool, smooth and carved textures to touch; the sound of water, chatter, and song and sweet luscious fruits.

A mirador with views over the garden.

Carlos V remodelled the Patio de Lindaraja with a central fountain and four box-edged beds and the Patio de la Reja where he placed a beautiful fountain from the Mexuar (Moorish entrance); finally, the Partal, a mirador recreated early in the 20th century with a rectangular pool, clipped myrtle hedges and terraces. The hairpin walk to the Generalife overlooks the terraced orchards and vegetable plots along the intervening ravine. The Generalife was restored as a summer residence by Sultan Ismail in 1315, and predates the surviving developments.

En route new gardens have been designed with quartered rills and arched cypresses until you reach a small courtyard and climb narrow stairs to be assailed by a cacophony of gushing water. The arcing jets in the Patio de la Acequia were originally in the sides of the canal leaving a path between water and beds. The patio was designed to be an intimate, inward looking garden, the cruciform water channels with lotus bowl fountains at each end and quartered flowering beds enclosed by an ornately carved colonnade and pavilions. This garden leads to the Patio del Cipres de la Sultana but the final Moorish water feature is reached through later box *parterres*. The water staircase rises in three flights with a central round bubbling pool at each level, and the tile-lined handrail holds a rivulet of icy water, an idea which predates the Villa d'Este by about 300 years. *C.H.*

9th century: Red Citadel al Qalah al-Hamra built on original foundations.

1319 Sultan Ismael restores Generalife (Jinnah al-Arif = garden of the architect) as a royal summer residence.

1377 Patio de los Leones begun.

1526 Carlos V, Moorish palaces and gardens absorbed into new palace complex.

1654 Patio de la Reja created.

1931 Restoration and creation of garden labyrinth leading to Generalife.

1951 Pieto Moreno designs the Nuevos Jardines.

An aerial view of the Patio de la Acequia.

The Patio de los Leones.

Alcázar Palace SEVILLE, SPAIN

'How everything seems disquieted in this palace, as if its very silence poses a question, offering an ever-present enigma to the wandering souls that people its ancient courtyard just as its babbling waters seem to be speaking to our soul.'

ROGELIO PEREZ OLIVARES
Alcázar de Sevilla, Madrid, 1943

The Myrtle Maze.

The fountain with Mercury statue.

The origins of the Alcázar in Seville date back many centuries to the Moorish conquest of Spain. The Moors occupied Andalusia for nearly 800 years during which time they created palaces, mosques and other fine buildings and gardens of exquisite beauty, the most famous being in Granada, but also at Cordoba and Seville.

The Moors elevated gardening to an art form — graceful, elegant, yet both innovative and directional. Moorish gardens had spiritual as well as artistic significance: the Koran depicts the Islamic afterlife as a heavenly garden whose inhabitants enjoy the soothing sound of water amidst lush greenery. Thus the Moors created gardens as an earthly paradise of cool courtyards, tinkling fountains, tranquil pools and tall trees, conceived on a scale and with a degree of sophistication not to be found elsewhere in medieval Europe at that time. The pools, fountains and contrasting shadows cast by huge palms in the Jardines de los Reales Alcázares symbolise the Moorish garden as a welcome oasis amid the stifling heat of an Andalusian summer — Seville is well known as the 'cauldron of Europe'. Bougainvillea stands out brightly against dark green myrtle and cypress, the smell of orange blossom and jasmine lingers everywhere. The Moorish gardens possess a wonderful ability to exploit the senses, providing the visitor with a soothing yet sensual experience.

Muslim influence in garden design was destined to be profound and long-lasting. Twentieth-century English designers such as Edwin Lutyens, Geoffrey Jellicoe and Harold Peto were particularly impressed, as were the Spanish, long time enemies of the Moors. The Alcázar Palace and gardens which exist in Seville today were created in the Mudejar style, using Muslim craftsmen, more than 100 years after the Spanish had recaptured Seville in the mid 13th century. The present palace was initially constructed by Peter the Cruel within the 10th-century walls of the former Moorish palace, and an orange tree reputedly planted during his reign still flourishes in the gardens today. Garden features such as the Charles V Pavilion, finely domed in cedar wood, the beautiful bronze fountain and statue depicting Mercury, and the original Myrtle Maze, date from the 16th century, when Spain was at the zenith of its powers. The gardens cover almost 40 acres, divided into 18 distinctive areas such as the Garden of Mercury's Pool and the secluded Poet's Garden. Nearby are the Patio de las Banderas and Patio de los Naranjos, the latter being a relic of the Moorish occupation.

The Alcázar Palace and gardens are significant because they portray Spain at the peak of its achievement, but still conscious of its Moorish past. The Alhambra and the Generalife in Granada depict Muslim culture at its finest but Seville's Alcázar represents an intriguing fusion of Islamic and Christian ideals, like the extraordinary mosque/cathedral in Cordoba and the city's Arab-style gardens. It is conceivable that the blend of savagery and sophistication that characterised the Moors appealed to the Spanish as, long after the Moors had been expelled, their influence lingers on at Granada, Seville and Cordoba, three outstanding European gardens. *P.B.*

711 AD The Moors invade Spain.
712 The Moors capture Seville.
1236 Cordoba re-captured by the Spanish.
1248 Seville re-captured by the Spanish.
1362 Peter the Cruel builds the Alcázar at Seville on the site of the former Moorish palace and gardens.
1492 Granada re-captured by the Spanish.
1492 Columbus discovers the New World. On his return he recounted his adventures to King Ferdinand and Queen Isabella in the Salon De Los Embajadores in the Alcázar Palace.
1516–56 Reign of Charles V.
1556–98 Reign of Philip II (Spain's golden age.)
1928 The French landscape designer J.C.N. Forestier (1861–1930) carries out replanting work.
1991 Extensive garden restoration programme.

Joaquin Sorola y Bastida (1863–1923), The Alcázar Garden in Seville*, Museo Sorolla, Madrid.*

The Alcázar Gardens. *Engraving, c. 1890 after a drawing by Richard Püttner (1842–1913).*

The front of the palace with its triple loggia. The garden was designed to be seen from the first floor.

Palazzo Piccolomini

PIENZA, ITALY

'I do not think it necessary for the gentleman's house to stand in the most fruitful part of his whole estate, but rather in the most honourable, where he can uncontrolled enjoy all the pleasures and conveniences of Air, Sun and fine prospects....'

LEON BATTISTA ALBERTI
Ten Books on Architecture.

This small, 15th-century hanging garden is one of the earliest to have survived, almost unchanged, since its creation in 1458. Built for Pope Pius II, the garden is a perfect embodiment of Leon Battista Alberti's (1404–72) architectural principles. Alberti was a humanist scholar who wrote a treatise reinterpreting the architectural precepts of ancient Greece and Rome. His words served first to determine the form taken by the Tuscan gardens of the early Renaissance and then became a blueprint which influenced the whole of Europe.

Alberti was not concerned so much with the layout of the garden as its situation. He recommended a site on the side of a hill as it would afford the combined advantages of views and cool breezes. The views that he preferred were 'over the city, the owner's land, the sea or a great plain and familiar hills and mountains'. In the foreground there should be 'the delicacy of gardens'. The garden of Palazzo Piccolomini is the perfect embodiment of these rules.

Pius II was passionate about classical architecture and Alberti was his personal friend. On his election to the papacy he decided to rebuilt his native village of Corsignano as an 'ideal' town, using Alberti as his advisor. The design for his new palace was modelled on that of Palazzo Rucellai, a building designed by Alberti in Florence. As a theorist rather than a practical architect, Alberti used his pupil Bernardo Rossellino to execute his designs in Florence. The Pope followed his example, commissioning Rossellino in 1459 to build him a palace and garden.

The new palace was sited to take advantage of a magnificent view over the Val d'Orcia and, as Alberti recommended, the 'familiar mountains' beyond it. A triple loggia on the first floor allowed the Pope to enjoy the view and also to look down on the intimate hanging garden laid out immediately below.

The garden was made in the space between the palace and the edge of a cliff. The original layout, which was extemely simple, is still intact. It consists of four *parterres*, with raised beds running along three of the garden walls. The beds are edged in stone that is thought to be original. A well head at the centre of the space is decorated with urns, shells, acanthus leaves and the Piccolomini crest. The true genius of the design lies in the relationship between the small, enclosed garden and the vast, sunny expanse of the Val d'Orcia stretching away beyond it. A high hedge forms a screen between the intimate garden room and the massive expanse of the horizon. The hedge is pierced by three arches which frame the view. Beyond them is a sheer cliff face, making this a true 'hanging' garden. *H.A.*

1458 Aeneus Silvius Piccolomini elected to the papacy as Pius II.
1459 Bernardo Rossellino commissioned to design the Piccolomini palace and garden.
1463 Both the palace and garden completed.
1978 Last Piccolomini dies and property passes to a trust.

The garden seen from the first-floor loggia. The magnificent view of the Val d'Orcia is screened at ground level. The layout of the garden is unchanged since 1459.

Topkapi

ISTANBUL, TURKEY

'Nor indeed doth a Turk, at any time, shew himself to be so truly pleased and satisfied in his senses as he doth in the Summer time, when he is in a pleasant garden; for he is no sooner come into it [...] but he outs off his uppermost coat, and lays it aside, and upon that his Turban, then turns up his sleeves and unbuttoned himself, turning his breast to the wind.'

A Description of the Grand Seigneur's Seraglio or Turkish Emperor's Court (ed. John Greaves), London, 1653 [translation by John Withers from the Venetian Ambassadorial Relazione by Ottavino Bon].

The Palace of the Gun Gate, Topkapisaray, was built by Mehmet II, the conqueror of Constantinople, in the 15th century and it grew continually until the 19th. The Second or Divan Court was famous for its trees of which a few survive, protected by walls against the gazelles, which were allowed to graze freely. Most of the trees have been planted or replanted since the coming of the Republic and this is true of the Third Court which was that of the College where the leaders of the Empire were trained.

Beyond this are the private terraces and kiosks of the sultan. In part this was his private garden which extends to the great terrace with its fountain and pool. In the 18th century for three days and nights all these areas overflowed with flowers when Nevsehirli Ibrahim Pasha created the equivalent of a Chelsea Flower Show for Ahmet III. Flowers flowed into the pavilions and everywhere was lit by tortoises with lanterns on their backs while overhead was cage upon cage of singing birds. The sultans' private terrace or hanging garden still exists but is newly designed. In the 16th century bulbs were ordered especially from eastern Anatolia: a convoy of 40,000 narcissus bulbs was not exceptional. At least half died during a journey that could take two months.

Extensive woodland surrounds the palace filled with carefully selected trees. The finest of these would be encircled with bulbs in their honour. They included arbutus, hornbeam, elm, lime, various species of oak, plane, terebinth, wild pear and mulberry. This park was walled off from the palace on its high terraces. Between them was a series of now neglected individual gardens. The Harem Garden bears the most romantic name, but the 50 or so girls used it for games and there is no record of flowering shrubs or flowers. Beyond it is the boxwood garden with a large boating pool where Murat III, whose mother was Venetian, enjoyed pushing in mutes and dwarfs — and even grander courtiers — to cool off. Past a ruined kiosk are the large elephant lawns, necessarily

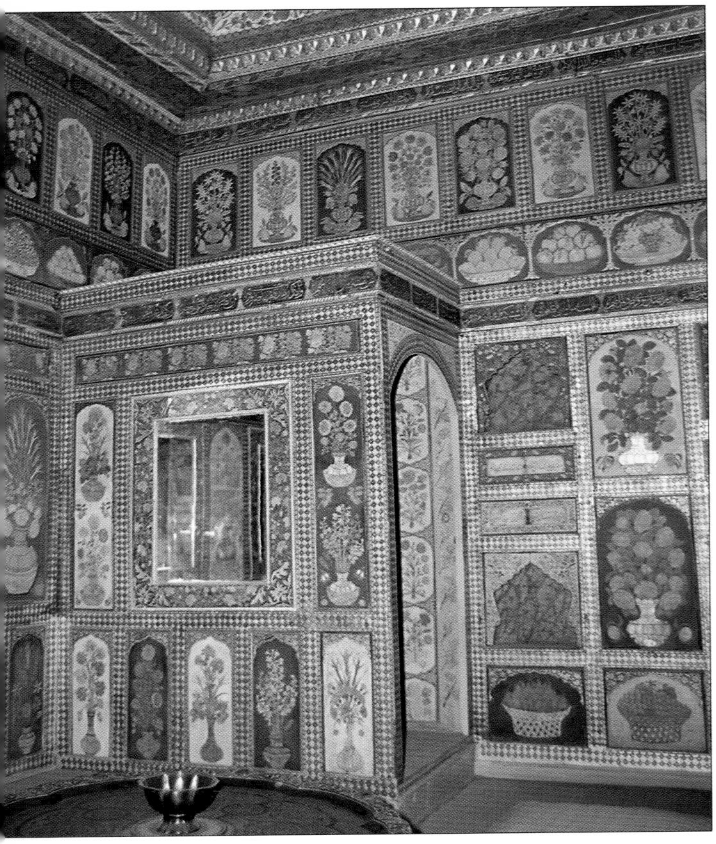

The fruit and flower room.

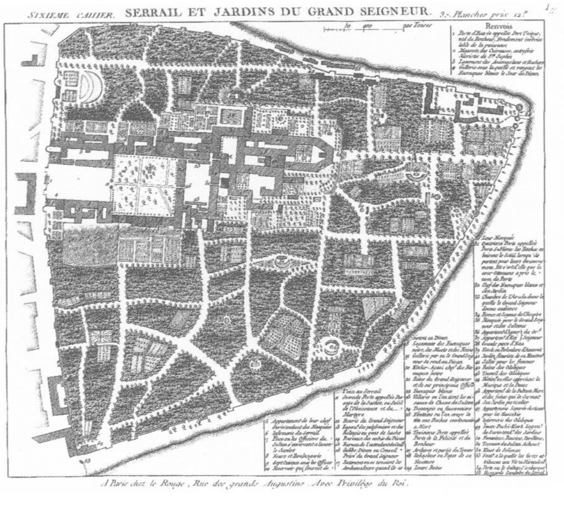

The Seraglio and Gardens of the Grand Seigneur, c. 1774–76. Engraving, Paris (Le Rouge). From Plans de Jardins.

The Rivan pavilion.

The Baghdad pavilion.

reached via a slope. There the only flowers were weeds. Taking a right-angle turn beneath the greatest kiosk that celebrates Murat IV's reconquest of Baghdad, one discovers among its lofty supporting arches that there was once a cascade in the Italian manner. Beyond one can trace the ghost of a once magnificent *parterre* in the Persian manner each side of a long dry pool that no longer mirrors the sky, the symbol of heaven. Beyond, below the pavilion of the royal garden — and Mehmet II and other sultans gardened with their own hands — is now a small park.

The gardens flourished in the spring and so their flowers were mainly bulbs as can be seen in miniatures and tiles. They included narcissus, crocuses, daffodils (of which there were 99 listed varieties), roses, jasmine and double violets (before those of Parma were known). There was also an extensive market garden near the Gate of Majesty to the First Court whose products supplied the palace kitchens and were also sold to the public — but no longer.

G.G.

1470s Work on gardens begins.

early 18th century: Topkapi hosts tulip festivals.

Heian pond seen on route to the kare-san-sui *garden at the temple.*

The autumn colours of the trees are edged with traditional bamboo fencing.

Ryoan-ji

KYOTO, JAPAN

'What silent words does this garden contain?'

FRANÇOIS BERTHIER, 1997.

The enigmatic *kare-san-sui* [dry-mountain-water] garden is the most well known of the gardens surrounding the Rinzai Zen temple of Ryoan-ji, in the historic city of Kyoto. Yet the origins of this dry landscape garden are a mystery and the designer remains unknown, although the garden has been attributed to the artist Soami (1480?–1525). The dry landscape garden of rocks and gravel was probably built shortly after 1499 when the *hojo* [abbot's hall], was replaced following a fire. The garden occupies an area of little more than 240 square yards adjacent to the temple and is designed to be viewed from a seated position within the building rather than by the physical act of walking around a prescribed path.

The garden consists of fifteen rocks, set in groups of five, three and two, and it is the careful distribution of these to create balance and harmony which gives Ryoan-ji such distinction. The grouping of the stones is a fine example of asymmetrical balance for which Japanese gardens are so well respected. The rocks are enhanced mainly by the raked white gravel, while the use of space has been much admired over the centuries. However, there is more to the scene than rocks and gravel: the area is delineated by a durable earthen wall, made from loam mixed with rape-seed oil and roofed with shingle, thus forming a backdrop for the monochrome rocks. It is reminiscent of the Chinese ink-wash landscape paintings so popular in the Japanese Muromachi period (1333–1568 AD) when the garden was created.

The dry landscape garden of Ryoan-ji is not devoid of plants: moss encircles the stone groupings and changes colour with the seasons, being brown in the hot Kyoto summers and rich green in the damper autumn and winters. In addition, beyond the earthen wall, the various greens supplied by a variety of trees provide a contrast with the stark nature of the monochromatic scene and are a vital component of the whole subtly changing picture.

The original meaning of the garden, like the designer, remains unknown, but many explanations have been forthcoming. Significance has been given to the uneven number of rocks which in Japanese culture is considered propitious; the rocks have been thought to depict the Chinese character for the word 'heart'; they have been seen as an interpretation of a story concerning a tigress carrying her cubs across water; and at the simplest, the rocks have been described as islands in the sea or mountains through the clouds. The garden challenges each viewer to devise their own interpretation, as in the use of a *koan* in Zen Buddhism, where a puzzling statement is used to aid enlightenment.

The simplicity of materials and their careful use in the dry landscape gardens of Japan, and particularly Ryoan-ji, have had a profound effect on the work of contemporary artists, including garden designers. The gardens of the American sculptor Isamu Noguchi reflect the use of natural stone materials and minimal planting, while the role of the Zen priest as garden designer is continued by Shumyo Masuno, who believes the garden is a spiritual place 'in which the mind dwells'. Surely the very essence of Ryoan-ji. *J.R.*

c.1150 Creation of Kyoyochi pond in the late Heian period, preceding the foundation of the temple.
1450 Ryoan-ji temple built.
1470 Original temple destroyed in the Onin War.
1499 Earliest date for the creation of the kare-san-sui garden, when the hojo was constructed.
1797 Hojo and Buddha hall destroyed by fire, replaced by the hojo of a minor temple.
1977 Restoration of shingle to the wall surrounding the kare-san-sui garden to replace tiles which were considered historically inaccurate.
1994 Ryoan-ji added to the UNESCO World Heritage List.

'Island' rocks amid the 'sea' of gravel.

Water basin near the kare-san-sui *garden, which reads 'I learn only to be content'.*

Daisen-in

KYOTO, JAPAN

The gravel cones in the Ocean of Nothingness.

'The garden is an attempt to represent the innermost essence of water, without actually using water and to represent it at that even more profoundly than would be possible with real water.'

YOSHINBOU YOSHINAGA
Composition and Expression in Traditional Japanese Gardens, Tokyo: Shôkokusha, 1962.

The Daisen-in sub-temple of the Rinzai Zen School of Buddhism, in the Daitoku-ji complex of Kyoto, is surrounded by a famous allegorical *kare-san-sui* [dry landscape] garden. The garden was created in the period following the building of the temple around 1510, towards the end of the Muromachi period (1333–1568). However, like the other masterpiece Ryoan-ji, the history of the design and building of the Daisen-in garden is shrouded in mystery.

At Daisen-in the creation of the garden is most often credited to the founder of the temple Kogaku Soko (1464–1548), who may have been assisted by the artist Soami (1480?–1525) whose landscape paintings of the four seasons decorate the sliding doors of the abbot's quarters. Some texts suggest that the garden could have been bought from the estate of a samurai, while the labourers who set out the garden have been credited with the placing of stones at Kinkaku-ji and Ryoan-ji.

The Daisen-in dry landscape garden embodies in its design many of the influences of Muromachi gardens: unlike Ryoan-ji, there is the restrained use of shrubs and trees, but the major components are rocks and gravel. Since the totality of the garden cannot be viewed at one time it resembles the sequences of monochromatic ink scroll paintings, popular during the era of the garden's creation.

The garden also reflects the teaching of Zen Buddhism by the allegorical nature of its design which expresses the Buddhist quest for enlightenment. The *hojo* [abbot's hall] is surrounded by the dry landscape garden; the north-eastern corner — only 10 feet wide and yet encapsulating mountainous scenery with a raging river — is considered by Eastern geomancy to be in need of defence, often by a mountain. This area of weakness is defended by large rocks evoking the image of tall mountains, while terraces of white gravel represent a waterfall, the source of life or truth. The gravel river which flows from the mountains then develops in two directions: north of the temple, building along stone 'cliffs' to a natural hand-washing stone, a feature which was later to be developed in tea gardens; and south through rocks arranged as crane and tortoise islands, both representing longevity derived from the stories of the mythical Mount Horai (clipped camellia trees form the shapes of distant mountains). The islands interrupting the flow of the river represent the trials of everyday life.

Bell-shaped window on to the garden.

The scene is punctuated by a corridor which crosses the garden; here the gravel area supports a stone in the shape of a junk, known as the 'treasure ship', laden with the experiences of life. A rock arrangement nearby is a young turtle swimming against the river's flow, and represents the futility of man's efforts to return to the past. The largest portion of the garden is to the south of the *hojo* and is composed of a simple rectangular area of raked white quartz — the Ocean of Nothingness.

Daisen-in is a garden with many symbolic landscape features and its allegorical content does not detract from the beautiful placing of rocks and controlled planting.

J.R.

c. 1510 Creation of the main temple buildings and the garden.
post-1945 Temple buildings restored and moss covering the sand removed.
1961 Corridor and associated bell-shaped window reintroduced to the garden.

The beginning of the allegorical journey — the stone waterfall.

Hampton Court Palace

MIDDLESEX, ENGLAND

'There were all manner of shapes, men and women, half-men and half-horse, sirens, serving-maids with baskets [...] made from dry twigs bound together and the aforesaid evergreen quickset shrubs, or entirely of rosemary, all true to the life, and so cleverly and amusingly interwoven, mingled and grown together, trimmed and arranged picture-wise, that their equal would be difficult to find.'

THOMAS PLATTER OF BASEL
in 1599 cited by Laurence Fleming & Alan Gore, *The English Garden*, London: Michael Joseph, 1979.

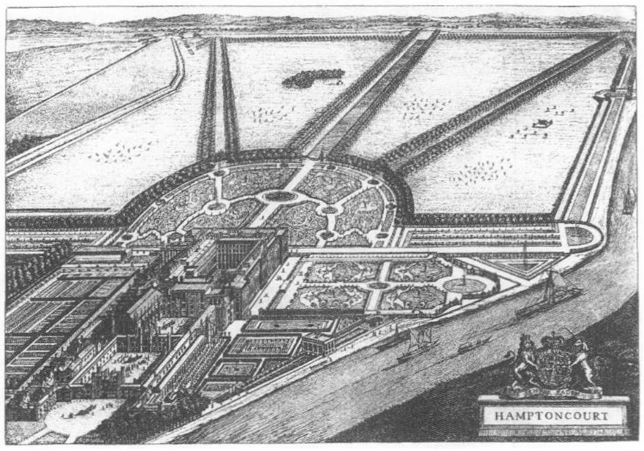

Leonard Knyff (1650–1721), View of Hampton Court Palace showing avenues, canal and the location on the Thames.

1525 Henry VIII forces Cardinal Wolsey to relinquish Hampton Court to him.
1660s Charles II introduces canal and avenues.
1690s William IV's garden designer Daniel Marot creates maze and other European features.
1840s Gardens opened to public.
1982 Modern restoration begins after an historical survey.

During the 1530s Henry VIII made Hampton Court into the top garden in the kingdom. His interest in medieval chivalry gave the gardens a special air, as scores of richly painted 'King's Beasts', derived from heraldry, were set up on the walls. South of the palace a huge triangle down to the Thames was fortified and divided into: the Privy Garden, set out in compartments; a triangle containing a mount topped with a glazed banqueting house; and another triangle containing ornamental stew-ponds. Northwards as far as the park wall were a tiltyard, to invoke jousting tournaments, and a Great Orchard. To the east was the House Park with a deer course, and nearby were further parks. Later in the 16th century the Privy Garden, famous for its topiaried hedges was created.

Charles II planted avenue systems, laid out according to Dutch principles with a canal down the middle walk (in St James's Park) and a larger scale version in the House Park at Hampton Court in 1661. Until the canal at Versailles was dug, the canal at Hampton Court was briefly the longest anywhere. Similar grand avenues were installed at other places connected with the court, for example Cobham Hall and Twickenham Park, but otherwise the English fashion was for avenues on the approach to houses, not to the rear, of houses. William of Orange, succeeding to the throne in 1689 with his English wife Mary, chose Hampton Court as his favourite palace for indulging his interests in sculpture, water and fine gardening. They had created gardens at Het Loo and elsewhere, and William imported many of his team, including Daniel Marot (1661–1752) as designer, and his head gardeners. William Talman, the Comptroller of the King's Works, and George London (d. 1714), the Royal Gardener, joined them in creating a layout of European

The Knot Garden.

The Dutch Garden

importance. Mary's outstanding plant collection was transported from Honselaersdijk and installed in new 'glass cases'.

William wanted a new approach across Bushy Park, but turning the whole palace through ninety degrees proved too ambitious, though the avenue was planted by Henry Wise (1653–1738). The Fountain Garden was designed by Marot, and maybe the wilderness, with its maze. In 1699 William commenced a wholly new Privy Garden with scrollwork borders with the grass plats and a view of the Thames, but died at its completion. It was widely copied over the next decade. Queen Anne simplified the Fountain Garden, planting the yews that remain, and dug the canals around it. The gardens were at the time the largest in England, at the high point of formality in English gardens. For twenty-five years Hampton Court was indisputably the finest garden in England. For precisely this reason, succeeding generations interested in promoting the natural style, derided it as the cynosure of bad taste, and its reputation hit a low in the late 18th century.

From 1840 parts of the gardens were opened to the public, which generated magnificent bedding-out schemes in the Fountain Garden. From the 1880s a resident, Ernest Law, published the history of the palace. Garden names were changed, and then the gardens themselves, to give a more Tudor feel in the Pond Yard. Limes were replanted in the Fountain Garden in 1987, and in 1994–95 the Privy Garden was excavated and reconstructed as close as the evidence permitted to its form in the heyday in the 1700s. *D.J.*

The Privy Garden.

Villa Medici

FLORENCE, ITALY

'The most rich, magnificent and ornamental garden in Europe.'

G. VASARI, 1568.

Garden façade of the villa.

A niche in the grotto.

The Villa Medici at Castello was laid out initially by Niccolò Tribolo (1500–50) from 1538 and later by others including the sculptor-designers Bartolommeo Ammannati (1511–92) and Bernardo Buontalenti (1531–1608). The elaborate iconographical programme, drawn up by the historian Benedetto Varchi, celebrated the triumph of the Medici family and was devised for Cosimo, the first grand duke of Tuscany (1519–74). Two upper fountains represented the two mountains whence the Rivers Arno and Mugnone flowed, and Ammannati's memorable bronze sculpture of Winter (sometimes called the Apennines), huddled and shivering on a rock in a pool, also suggests the mountain as the source of water. The lower fountain of Venus, by Giambologna (1529–1608) (now elsewhere), portrays the goddess wringing her hair: she is both Venus and the city of Florence, dependent on the river running through it. Water descended from Winter through the grotto to the River Fountains, then via Venus to the lowest fountain, depicting Hercules and Antaeus. Hercules squeezes water from Antaeus' mouth just as in the myth he squeezed the life out of the giant. This may refer to Cosimo bringing water out of the mountains, which he did by aqueduct to the garden.

The garden slopes upwards from the (rather plain) villa. First is a large *parterre* garden laid out on the slant of the hill, with the Hercules fountain in the central path. This area is now all open whereas originally a large cypress grove or labyrinth in concentric circles filled much of the space. To the sides are an orangery and a lemon-house. A wall terminates this part of the garden. In the centre recess a grotto dating from 1546 onwards is full of symbolism. The niches contain sculptures of animals in coloured or painted marble which appear to emerge from the surrounding rock. Shells, coral, *spugne* and tufa decorate the grotto. Water spouts from some of the animals, continuing

1538 Garden design begins.
c. 1780 Renovations in neo-classical style, fountains moved.
c. 1830 Wood at top replanted, paths created in the English style.

The statue of Winter.

the theme of Cosimo's control and power over water. Some of the animals have real horns or tusks. A multitude of animals, and birds too, originally inhabited the grotto but many have been removed to the Bargello Museum in Florence. The unicorn was said by legend to purify poisoned waters, making it safe for other animals to drink. In political terms the unicorn was Cosimo, presented as benevolent uniter and protector of the Florentine people. Above the grotto is a terrace which is essentially a grove, of ilex, fir, cypress and laurel. In the middle of the grove is the pool where Winter crouches.

Much has been lost at Castello, especially in plantings. Original walled enclosures and secret gardens for herbs, fruit-trees and exotic plants and shrubs have disappeared or been altered beyond recognition.

M.S.

Boboli

FLORENCE, ITALY

'On the 29 May of the year 1620 at 14 hours and 11 minutes, a time thought favourable and propitious by Giovanni Peroni, Cosmographer and Mathematician to Cosimo II de' Medici, was laid its first stone on the north side, the which had previously been blessed by Ser. Antonio Zucchetti, Chaplain and Master of Ceremonies [...] with Holy Water [...and who] also blessed a stone casket filled with medallions and gold, silver and bronze coins that was placed in the foundations....'

'MEMORIE MS' ON THE REBUILDING OF THE PALACE WINGS cited in Gaetano Cambiagi, *Descrizione dell'Imperiale Giardino di Boboli,* Florence, 1757.

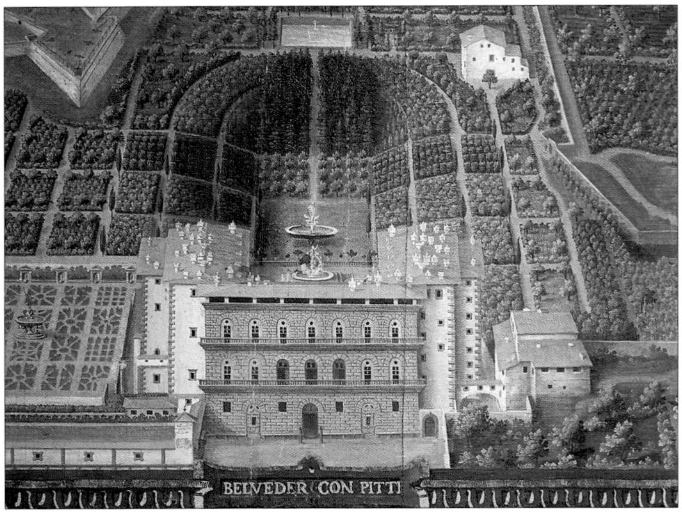

Giusto Utens, Lunette view of Palazzo Pitti and the Boboli gardens. Tempera on canvas, 1599. Museo Firenze com'era, Florence.

1453	Luca Pitti commissions Filippo Brunelleschi to build the Palazzo Pitti.
1549	Eleanora de' Medici, wife of Cosimo I, buys the unfinished palace and hillside behind it. Il Tribolo is commissioned to design the gardens.
1550	Il Tribolo dies.
1560	Eleanora and family move into the Palazzo Pitti.
1583	Buontalenti's grotto is completed.
1618	Alfonso Parigi's Isolotto is built.
1637	Amphitheatre and courtyard are built by Giulio Parigi.

The Boboli gardens stretch across the hillside behind the Palazzo Pitti in Florence. Their history begins in 1549, when Eleanora de' Medici, wife to Cosimo I, purchased a half-built palace from the Pitti family. Niccolò Pericoli (1500–58), a famous architect and sculptor known as Il Tribolo, was instantly engaged to design a garden that would provide a suitable setting for civic events and celebrations. Although it has passed through many phases of change and adaptation, Boboli still serves as a perfect example of a garden designed to display the power and wealth of its owner. Il Tribolo's first task was to arrange for the rough hillside to be levelled, covered in a thick mulch of manure and then planted with ilex, cypress and fir trees. Unfortunately, Il Tribolo died in 1550, only a year after beginning work. It is said that he died of exhaustion. This seems entirely credible as he was already at work on Cosimo's large garden at Castello, outside Florence. The task of developing Boboli thus fell to Bernardo Buontalenti and Bartolommeo Ammanati. Today, Boboli is a rich concoction of features from different periods and designers. Much of it was lost long ago, giving the site a fragmented feel. Among the finest features is Buontalenti's magnificent grotto, which has recently been restored. Built in 1583, its richly decorated interior contains Giambologna's *Venus* and a copy of one of Michelangelo's *Slaves*. Behind the palace, a natural hollow was made into an amphitheatre by Giulio Parigi in 1637. The design took the form of a simple semicircle lined with six tiers of stone benches. It was a marvelous setting for the festivities mounted to mark every civic occasion. In 1661, for example, Cosimo III de' Medici was married to Louise d'Orleans. There was a performance of *Il Mondo Festeggiante* in the amphitheatre to mark the occasion. Part masque, part pageant and part equestrian ballet, the performers played to an audience of 20,000. Sadly, the new bride remained unimpressed — despite her husband's appearance as Hercules in jewel studded armour.

Perhaps the most appealing area of the garden is the Isolotto, designed by Giulio Parigi's brother, Alfonso, in 1618. It consists of an island in a large, oval pool. Bridges lined with pots of lemons link the island to the shore. Wrought-iron gates closing the bridges are decorated with goats — a reference to Cosimo III's star sign. Il Tribolo's first fountain, *Oceanus*, the source of all seas and rivers, stands at the centre of the island. Executed by Giambologna, the statue is supported by the three greatest rivers known at the time — the Ganges, the Euphrates and the Nile — and stands in a 30-foot circle of granite which had to be brought to Florence from the island of Elba. There is also a dramatic Perseus riding through the water to rescue Andromeda, who is chained to her rock at the far end of the pool. All the fountains in the gardens celebrate Cosimo I's magnificent achievement of bringing fresh water to Florence. *H.A.*

The Isolotto with Cosimo III's Capricorn goats adorning the gates.

Below: The grotto.

Bottom: One of the Isolotto's linking bridges.

Villa d'Este

TIVOLI, ITALY

'All the jets being turned inwards and facing one another discharge the water into the tank [...] the sun falling in the same produces on the surface of the basin, in the air, a rainbow so marked and so like nature that it in no way falls short of the bow seen in the sky. I saw nought to equal it elsewhere.'

THE JOURNAL OF MONTAIGNE'S TRAVELS IN ITALY IN 1580 AND 1581.

Top: The Path of the One Hundred Fountains.
Centre: The Fountain of Nature.
Bottom: Fountain and statuary originally from Hadrian's Villa.

The Villa d'Este at Tivoli, 19 miles from Rome, was one of the most magnificent of all Italian Renaissance gardens. Created by Cardinal Ippolito II d'Este on a west-facing hill, it had views across the plain to Rome. The steepness of the site necessitated the construction of a series of terraces, with the villa at the top and the great central axis delineated by a stairway. A number of cross-axes stretched along terrace walks with features alongside and at each end. The entire garden was related physically and conceptually to the antiquities of Hadrian's Villa and a number of temples nearby, so that lines within the garden can be extended on a map to link with some of these classical features.

The most astonishing and spectacular element of the garden was its water effects, ranging from *giochi d'acqua* to water-powered automata (birds singing, an owl hooting), which have disappeared. One of the cross-walks was called the Path of the One Hundred Fountains, in serried rows, each a small fan-spray, accompanied by one hundred reliefs taken from Ovid's *Metamorphoses*. The Fountain of the Organ was originally played by water, which would also power the cannon mechanism which detonated in the Fountain of Dragons. The fountains varied from mighty waterfalls to a steady rain which created a rainbow in the sunshine.

There was an elaborate iconographical programme, centred around Hercules and Hippolytus (chastity). Hercules is faced with a choice at the Fountain of Dragons between the steep path to virtue (Grotto of Diana) and the easy path to pleasure or vice (Grotto of Venus) — a similar statue can be found at Stourhead. There are a number of other themes such as the Muses and the creativity of art; the fecundity of Nature, expressed in the multi-breasted Fountain of Nature (based on Diana of Ephesus); and the coming of Christ as apparently foretold by one of the classical Sibyls and as represented by the Fountain of the Tiburtine Sibyl. Rometta, a tableau of the buildings of ancient Rome in miniature, included the statue of the Lion Tearing the Horse (copied at Rousham), which symbolised the subjugation of Tivoli by Rome. The programme is difficult to interpret fully, not least because most of the statuary (taken originally from Hadrian's Villa) was removed in the 18th century.

In a hundred years the water mechanisms had largely failed, and decay set in. A further century on, Hubert Robert and Fragonard painted the gardens in a state of neglect and romantic disarray. There is now an ongoing process of restoration: the state has owned the villa and garden since World War I.

The importance of the Villa d'Este was as an expression of power and control over nature, water in particular. The variety of its water effects inspired others in Italy to create their own aqueous marvels, and the influence of fountains and water-power spread to France and to England in the 17th century. *M.S.*

The Villa d'Este still offers a stunning spectacle of fountains.

1550s Work starts on gardens.

1575 Gardens substantially complete.

From late 17th century: Decline and decay.

1918 Gardens become property of Italian state.

Engraving by Piranesi showing the gardens in decay.

Chenonceaux

INDRE-ET-LOIRE
FRANCE

Parterres *quartered around a central pool.*

'The Queen Mother then threw her banquet at Chenonceaux which it has been said cost her more than one hundred thousand livres that was raised on a loan from the more prosperous of the King's servants [&] and at this fine banquet, the most beautiful and noble ladies half-naked and their hair loose in the way of married women were employed to do the serving...' 15 May 1577.

THE JOURNAL DU RÈGNE DE HENRI III
in *Notice historique sur les châteaux de Chenonceaux,* Tours, 1845

In ancient hunting woods, by the calm waters of the Cher and in the gentle climate of the Loire Valley, the château of Chenonceaux has a magical setting. In 1547 Henri II gave this domain to his mistress, the intelligent and gifted Diane de Poitiers. Diane's first, and still existing, rectangular garden was a massive separate, self-contained unit with no visual or spatial relationship to the château and was typical of early French Renaissance designs. The layout was four rectangles subdivided into six squares each, a fruit and vegetable garden ornamented with various figures, knots and a labyrinth, a design echoed today in the potager at Villandry. The broad perimeter *levée* offered views both across the river and over the fruit trees and seasonal vegetables. The patterned squares were planted with herbs and borders of violets, lilies and roses.

Philibert de l'Orme, who had designed the château at Anet for Diane built a bridge to link Chenonceaux to the far bank of the Cher. The axis from the bridge formed a central path between two square gardens (now lost), one quartered around a central pool and the other quadripartite and quartered — a pattern used in the restoration of Diane's first garden. After Henri's death in 1559, his wife Catherine de' Medici demanded the return of

Diane de Poitiers's garden.

1551	Diane de Poitiers creates first 2.5 acre garden.
1556	Philibert de l'Orme builds bridge to other bank enabling creation of further two gardens (now lost).
1559–89	Catherine de' Medici regains Chenonceaux — temporary and permanent elaboration of gardens for magnificences.
1890s	Restoration of gardens.

Chenonceaux. She celebrated it by using the gardens for elaborate fireworks, water spectacles and masques. Catherine's *magnificences* were an integral part of her political policy. In 1563 the royal party advanced up the tree-lined avenue to be met by singing sirens who were answered by wood nymphs. Satyrs entered and tried to carry off the wood nymphs who were rescued by knights. It is possible there was also a crescent moon and deer in the woods symbolising Diane's early reign.

Inspired by the Humanist *Hypnerotomachia Poliphili* Catherine commissioned Bernard Palissy (c. 1510–90), an eccentric potter, naturalist and garden designer, to design the Fontaine du Rocher which represented the mountain of the muses, Parnassus. Streams of water poured from this artificial rough-surfaced mount into a large basin and dark grottoes adorned with Palissy's glazed earthenware. Using plans recommended by Philibert de L'Orme, Catherine, under the guidance of the architect, Jacques Androuet du Cerceau (c. 1515/20–84), built a two-storey gallery above the bridge. In 1559–65 he drew a birds-eye view of these gardens in his work *Les plus excellents bâtiments de France*.

Chenonceaux lapsed into obscurity with one brief note of interest. Claude Dupin employed Jean-Jacques Rousseau who recorded: 'One had such a fine time in this beautiful setting.... We played music, and acted dramas. I composed some lines entitled "The avenue de Sylvie" after an avenue in the park looking on to the Cher'. In the 19th century the Menier family commissioned Achille Duchêne (1866–1947) and his father Henri (1841–1902) to restore the gardens of Diane and Catherine. The scrolling *broderie* hedges of santolina with plats of hibiscus and yew trees underplanted with bedding plants in the former are effective but not authentic. The dramatic approach through ancient groves, the massive garden platforms and the château spanning the river evoke the early Renaissance in their combination of art and nature. *C.H.*

The broderie *hedges.*

Sacro Bosco BOMARZO, ITALY

'Children walked about startled, going from one group [of statues] to another, asking questions of the teams of workmen, shouting and pointing as if they were [...] in some fabulous amusement park, in some strange Luna Park of stone.'

MANUEL MUIJICA-LAINEZ,
Bomarzo, 1969.

The temple in the meadow at the garden's highest level.

One of the huge sculptures — the warrior and the woodcutter.

The Bear — emblem of the Orsini family.

The Sacro Bosco, or 'sacred grove', takes the Renaissance passion for garden symbolism to a climax. It is a bizarre collection of statues and architectural follies in a wood close to the border between Umbria and Lazio. Pier Francesco 'Vicino' Orsini, who designed the grove between 1552 and his death in 1584, was an important figure in the intellectual circles of Rome and the Vatican. His working life was spent as a soldier in Pope Paul III's army.

Visitors to the Sacro Bosco would have been able to 'read' Orsini's creation rather as we read a book today. The statues carved from lumps of tufa strewn about the site give three-dimensional expression to the theme of Man's journey through the snares and passions of life to an understanding of divine love. Orsini could explore this theme very effectively in relation to the events of his own life, both as an intellectual and as a soldier on the battlefields of Europe. As a result, the grove doubled as a form of visual autobiography and a personal monument.

In 1552 Orsini planted the trees that would create his sacred grove — *sacro bosco* — on a rocky site some distance from his villa. Fifteen years later, when the trees were already quite mature, he retired from the army and devoted himself to the creation of the park. The site was laid out on three levels. It was made up of a combination of bizarre buildings, statues, fountains and carved inscriptions. The first tableau facing contemporary visitors was that of two struggling giants. Ariosto's *Orlando Furioso* (1532) was a source of inspiration for Orsini and the scene represents Orlando in his madness, rending the body of a woodcutter in two. Beyond them a huge, moss-covered tortoise supports a statue of Fame blowing a trumpet. This would have been seen at once as a symbol of *festina lente*, or 'make haste slowly'. As so often in the Renaissance garden, it was in the juxtaposition of figures — the tortoise, the figure of Fame and the statue of Pegasus beyond them — that the crux of Orsini's message lay. Many rich patrons used Pegasus, the horse connected in classical mythology to creativity and the Muses, in their gardens. This was a means of drawing attention to their own role as intellectuals and patrons of the arts. By placing Pegasus in juxtaposition to the tortoise, Orsini succeeded in mocking this pompous tradition.

The Hell Mouth, which is probably the most famous of Orsini's monuments, was a crucial part of the allegory of human existence played out in the park. It forms part of a monstrous face with flared nostrils and staring eyes. A flight of steps leads into the open mouth, above which are inscribed the words 'Abandon hope all ye who enter here', from Dante's *Inferno*. The mouth is carefully designed to amplify and distort sound. It is said that the voice of anyone inside it can be heard all over the park.

After Orsini's death the Sacro Bosco fell rapidly into obscurity. Only when it was rediscovered by Salvador Dalí did the park come back into the public gaze. Years of patient restoration by the current owner have ensured the survival of this unique place.

H.A.

1552 Work begins on the Sacro Bosco.

1567 Orsini retires from the army and devotes himself to creating the Sacro Bosco.

1584 Orsini dies.

1645 The Sacro Bosco sold to the della Rovere family.

1845 Sold by the della Rovere to the Borghese family.

1949 Salvador Dalí's visit brings Bomarzo back into the public eye.

1954 The park is bought by Signor Bettoni and restored.

The floors inside the Crooked House are built horizontally despite the alarming tilt of the whole building.

The Hell Mouth.

Palazzo Farnese

CAPRAROLA, ITALY

'Perhaps the highest example of restrained majesty which secular architecture has achieved.'

JAKOB BURCKHARDT
The Renaissance in Italy, 1860.

Mosaic paving to the rear of the casino *links inside and outside.*

The Farnese Palace at Caprarola is the quintessential villa and garden of the high Renaissance. Giacomo Barozzi da Vignola, Rome's principal architect, was also employed by Cardinal Gambara at Villa Lante in Bagnaia, and there are many similarities between the two gardens.

The massive walls of the Farnese Palace tower over the town, and at first sight it is difficult to imagine a garden that would not be crushed into insignificance against a background of such overwhelming grandeur. The solution found to this problem was brilliantly simple. The principal garden was laid out at a considerable distance from the palazzo. In this way any conflict between the garden and the building was avoided.

Vignola was commissioned in 1556 by Cardinal Alessandro Farnese to transform his grandfather's part-built fortress at Caprarola into a luxurious palace. When the architect died in 1573 one of the two secret gardens was complete and the palace itself was almost finished.

Inside the palace the Cardinal had two sets of apartments, one facing south for winter use, and the other north facing for use during the heat of the summer. Each set of rooms was designed to overlook its own garden, linked to it by a wooden bridge over the moat that surrounds the palazzo. The winter garden contains four *parterre* beds surrounded by hedges of box, holly and laurel. A central avenue leads to the Fountain of the Rain in a grotto. The summer garden was planted with flowers and fruit trees. A nymphaeum at the far end contained the Fountain of Venus.

There are no records to prove that the main garden was planned by Vignola. It is linked to the palazzo by a path through the ancient hunting wood. In a clearing cut from the dark trees there is a *casino* that was probably designed by Giacomo della Duca. It is a two-storey building with a triple-arcaded loggia at the centre of each floor. It stands at the top of a slope and is reached by a flight of shallow steps that run between rusticated walls. A water staircase made of intertwined dolphins runs down the centre of the steps. Grottoes are set into the retaining walls on either side.

A small grassy piazza opens out at the top of the water staircase. Here there is a large fountain made up of a massive urn flanked by two enormous tritons bearing cornucopias. Curved steps lead up to another piazza, beyond which lies the large terrace surrounding the *casino*. The terrace is planted as a formal *parterre* garden. The low wall surrounding it is decorated with herm-satyrs, each with a vase on its head. It is said that each of the 28 figures is a portrait of one of the workmen who was employed in the construction of the garden. Sadly, this is an unlikely tale as the statues date from Girolamo Rainaldi's alterations to the site in about 1620.

H.A.

Fantastical herms in a grotto.

1530 Antonio da Sangallo and Baldassare Peruzzi begin to build a fortress in Caprarola for Alessandro Farnese.

1534 Alessandro Farnese becomes Pope Paul III and building work ceases.

1556 Alessandro Farnese the Younger, the Pope's grandson, commissions Vignola to transform the fortress into a palace.

1557 Work begins on the secret gardens behind the palace.

1573 Vignola dies.

1584 *Casino* and gardens built.

1620 The gardens around the *casino* are redesigned by Rainaldi.

Herm-satyrs surrounding the parterre.

Stone dolphins form the water staircase.

Villa Lante BAGNAIA, LAZIO, ITALY

'One of the most richly ornamented places I ever saw. It is so well provided with fountains, that in this respect it not only equals but surpasses, both Pratolino and Tivoli.'

MONTAIGNE
Journey [travelling in 1581], trans. W. Hazlitt, 1859.

Above left: Giambologna's Pegasus and the Muses.

Above centre: The catena d'acqua.

Above right: The Fountain of the Giants.

1568 Gardens started.
1656 Gardens rented by Pope to Lante della Rovere family — changes in box design on ramped *parterre* and high hedges.
1953 Purchased by the Società Villa Lante: major restoration work.
1973 Gardens given into care of Italian state.

The Villa Lante, near Rome, has been described on more than one occasion as the most perfect of all gardens. The reasons for this are its atmosphere, its intimacy and above all an immensely satisfying and rounded design. Created for Cardinal Gambara from 1568 by the architect Giacomo Barozzi da Vignola (1507–73), the garden consists of a flat *parterre* (the *quadrato*) in front of the villa, which is split into two *casini* with a gap in between, and, behind, a series of three level terraces cut into the hillside, with a linking slope between two of the terraces. The garden represents a narrative of transition from primitive times at the top to Renaissance civilisation at the bottom. To one side of, and above, this garden is another, a woodland park which has lost most of its architectural features except for a magnificent fountain group of Pegasus and the Muses by Giambologna, representing the arts and poetic inspiration.

At the summit of the garden, backed by the woodland park, is the Fountain of the Deluge, a grotto obscured by moss and fern which furnishes the water for the garden. On this highest of the terraces two Houses of the Muses reinforce the theme of classical and primitive times, the source of life (water) and of art (the Muses). The Fountain of the Dolphins, surrounded by stone seats, helps the water on its onward and downward journey. At this top level plane trees provide shade and indeed announce the presence of the *bosco*, integrated into the garden rather than as a separate area — this helps to produce the intimate effect of the garden as the planes accompany the visitor all the way down. The linking slope to the next terrace is dominated by the famous *catena d'acqua*, the water chain. Its sides are in the form of the limbs of a crayfish, the emblem of the Cardinal's family (*gambero* = crayfish). Descending to the middle terrace, the visitor encounters first the Fountain of the Giants, two River Gods with cornucopias, which

receives its water from the claws of the crayfish, while jets of water issue from vases set along the balustrade. The centrepiece of this terrace is a large stone table with a central trough through which water flows to cool wine and fruit. The lowest terrace is reached at the Fountain of Candles or Fountain of Lights, a concave tiered fountain with multiple jets of water, some in the form of candlesticks. The steps on each side have surprise jets, the *giochi d'acqua* beloved of Italian garden designers. On each side of the fountain there are grottoes dedicated to Neptune and Venus respectively, set into the retaining wall of the second terrace. Between the *casini* there is a ramped box *parterre* and in front of them spreads the final display representing the advanced state of civilisation. The *quadrato* contains beds embroidered in box and a square lake. In the four compartments of the lake are stone gondolas, and the Fountain of the Moors stands in the middle. *M.S.*

The quadrato.

The Fountain of Candles.

Tsarskoe Selo

ST PETERSBURG
RUSSIA

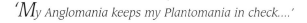

The Creaking Pavilion.

1710 Catherine I becomes Tsarina and begins work on Tsarskoe Selo.
1743–46 Palace façade extended to take up entire width of site.
1762 Catherine II accedes to the throne.
1771 She appoints Johann Busch as court gardener.
1783–84 Babolovski Palace built, park designed by Busch.
1785 Ionic colonnade, the Cameron Gallery, built.
1792–96 Alexander Palace bulit for Catherine II's grandson, with small gardens by Ilia Neelov.

'My Anglomania keeps my Plantomania in check....'

CATHERINE THE GREAT TO VOLTAIRE.

Shortly after the wife of Peter the Great, Catherine, became Tsarina in 1710, Peter presented her with a small wooden country house in Tsarskoe Selo. She began to rebuild the house in stone and had the gardener Jan Rosin lay out a small garden with greenhouses and an orangery. A short time later Jan Roozen (Rosin), a gardener who was also active in the Summer Garden in St Petersburg, provided a first plan, which was carried out by Johann Voght. By 1720 the terraced garden seen today had been completed, soon followed by the basins and formal beds. In 1723, the architect Förster built a pleasure seat in the lake, as well as the Old Orangery. At the commencement of the approach to this small pleasance there was a deer park.

The second key construction phase in Tsarskoe Selo began under Peter´s daughter, Empress Elizabeth Petrovna (1709–61). An impression of its size is conveyed by a mid-18th-century engraving, probably by the architect Bartolomeo Rastrelli. The square deer park, or New Garden, in front of the palace was adorned in 1748 with a Monplaisir pleasance, a work by Rastrelli, as was the Hermitage, built in the new *bosquet* area added to the existing gardens in 1744–54. On the lakeshore, the empress had a grotto erected in 1749–61, and in 1754–57, to the south-west of the palace, a Roller Coaster (Flying Mountain) by Rastrelli was completed.

The conversion of the original, small country seat into a royal summer residence was the work of architects such as Bronstein (fl. 1718–24), S.I. Tchevakinski (1745–48), and Rastrelli (from 1752). The garden proper, whose enclosed configuration was oriented more towards Dutch and German than French models, grew into a superb baroque garden that appeared to reflect more a consciousness of status than a pleasure in aesthetics.

The garden remained largely unchanged until the end of the 1760s. Like her mother-in-law Elizabeth, however, Catherine II wished the garden to make an impression, this time not in terms of the outmoded forms of the rococo but in the modern ones of the emergent English landscape garden. To study such gardens, which were unknown in Russia, Catherine sent the gardener Andrei Ekleben and the architect Vassili Neelov (1722–82), with his sons Ilia (1745–93) and Piotr, to England in 1769–70. As the plans they submitted were deemed unsatisfactory, she appointed a new court gardener in 1771: Johann Busch (d. 1795), a gardener and plant dealer of German origin who was active in London. Although he worked according to Neelov´s plans until 1785, the empress convinced Busch to adopt many of her suggestions, so that the French traveller Paul Sivigne could justly write in 1816: 'Instructed by her, the renowned Busch has artfully transformed the regular gardens into an English garden'. Catherine was indeed an ardent amateur gardener, and she translated into Russian and provided notes to works such as William Chambers´ *Designs on Chinese Buildings* (1757) and re-edited Thomas Whately´s *Observation on Modern Gardening* (1770). Closest to her heart, however, were architectural features. In the 1770s she erected — much as in Stowe — many monuments in commemoration of military victories, in Chios (Tchesme Column), Moldavia (Morea Column), and the Kagul Obelisk. Initially responsible for the

architecture were Antonio Rinaldi and Neelov, but in 1779 new appointments were made. Being the historical successor of the emperor of Constantinople, Catherine desired to see this status reflected in her garden. Under the northern Italian architect Giacomo Quarenghi (1744–1828) and the Englishman Charles Cameron (1736–1812), the village of Sophia, the Agate Baths, an antique temple ruin were added, and Greek architectural elements found entry into the scheme. The empress even went so far as to challenge the Chinese emperor by constructing the largest park village in the Chinese style in Europe. And as if this were not enough, she quoted Emperor Hadrian, who had conjured up his world empire at his villa in Tivoli, by doing the same in Tsarskoe Selo. Due to the numerous park buildings that went up, as early as 1772 Catherine could tell Voltaire that her garden resembled a ninepins-alley. This changed when Busch returned to Isleworth in 1789, where he died on 22 May 1795. The garden was simplified and plainer structures were created, which were so harmonious that they were largely retained during reconstruction after the ravages of World War II.

M.K.

The parterres *in front of the palace.*

Rostral Column and Turkish Bath.

Aldobrandini

FRASCATI, ITALY

'In one of these Theatres of Water, is an Atlas spouting up the streame to an incredible height, and another monster which make a terrible roaring with an horn; but above all the representation of a storm is most naturall, with such fury of raine, wind and Thunder as one would imagine ones selfe in some extreame Tempest.'

JOHN EVELYN
Diary, 4–5 May 1645.

Top: The water theatre.

Above: Saracin's Atlas in the water theatre.

Villa Aldobrandini towers over the little town of Frascati, to the east of Rome. As soon as the magnificent house and the dramatic gardens surrounding it were completed in 1604, descriptions of them began to find their way into the letters and journals of 17th- and 18th-century travellers from all over Europe. The villa was built in 1598 for Cardinal Pietro Aldobrandini. The intitial design was by Giacomo della Porta, an architect from Lombardy who worked in the Mannerist style. The site, which commands long views over the surrounding countryside, was given to the Cardinal by Pope Clement VIII, who was his uncle, in return for ousting the Este family from Ferrara in northern Italy and restoring the city to Papal rule. Giacomo della Porta designed a building only one room thick, and it is said that during the Cardinal's lifetime it was like a jewel box, filled with precious things. In 1602 della Porta died unexpectedly *en route* to Rome, following a lavish feast of ice cream and melon provided by the Cardinal, who was famously hospitable. Carlo Maderno, another Lombard architect, was appointed in his place and he managed to complete the villa the following year. Meanwhile, the Cardinal had bought water rights from a neighbour and built 8 miles of aqueduct and canal. It is said that Cardinal Gambara spent 70 thousand *scudi* on Villa Lante, which was famous for the quantity of fresh water used in its garden. This was a far smaller sum than Cardinal Aldobrandini spent in his determined attempt to outdo him.

Water is the key feature of the difficult site behind the villa. In the narrow space between the rear of the building and the steep hillside is a magnificent water theatre which is one of the most lavish Renaissance water features to have survived anywhere in Europe. It was designed by Maderno, who used Giovanni Fontana as his technician. Fontana was often employed by the papacy and was considered the chief authority on hydraulics in Rome at the time. At the centre of the theatre stands Atlas, sculpted by Jacques Saracin, bowed beneath the weight of the globe. At his feet the titan Enceladus struggles for freedom. In niches to either side of the theatre are Pan and a centaur playing a horn. These are all that remains of an extraordinary water-powered orchestra.

To either side of the central pool are two buildings: a chapel dedicated to Saint Sebastian and the Temple of the Winds. The temple originally contained a representation of Mount Parnassus, home of the Muses, and a statue of Pegasus. John Evelyn, the 17th-century diarist, described 'a copper ball that continually dances about three foot above the pavement by virtue of a wind conveyed secretly to a hole beneath it'.

Above the theatre a water staircase climbs the steep hill. This part of the garden was designed to be viewed from the first floor of the villa. Part of the way up the staircase is flanked by two stone columns. Water originally spurted from the top of the columns and raced down channels cut into their sides. The staircase becomes progressively more rustic as it ascends the hill, and at its top, water issues from the heart of a rough stone grotto. *H.A.*

The main façade gives no clue to the extraordinary use of water behind the villa.

1598	Cardinal Pietro Aldobrandini commissions Giacomo della Porta to design and build a garden around his villa.
1602	Della Porta dies.
1603	Main garden completed under the guidance of Carlo Maderno.
1604	Pope Clement VIII gives Cardinal Aldobrandini 50 thousand *scudi* to build a water theatre.
1621	Cardinal Aldobrandini dies, property passed to his cousins.

This façade of the villa gives spectacular views of the water theatre.

The pine tree carefully trained to resemble a boat.

The moss ground-cover beneath the trees surrounding the lake.

c. 1220 The Saion-ji family build a villa and temple on the site, but these decline as the family's power wanes.

c. 1398 Ashikaga Yoshimitsu purchases the site from the Saion-ji family and begins the construction of the Golden Pavilion.

1408 Emperor Gokomatsu visits the pavilion and lavish celebrations are held in his honour.

1467–77 The Onin Wars. The majority of the temple compound is destroyed but the Golden Pavilion and the lake survive.

c. 1610 The main temple buildings, tea house and its garden are created by Emperor Gomizuno.

1904 The original bronze phoenix which had adorned the roof of the Golden Pavilion is removed.

1950 1 July: The original Golden Pavilion is destroyed by arson.

1955 An exact replica of The Golden Pavilion is constructed with the support of the Japanese people.

Right: The foliage of maple trees frames the view across the lake to the Golden Pavilion, the distance enhanced by the use of an island.

Kinkaku-ji

KYOTO, JAPAN

'The reflection of the night sky gave a dim whiteness to the surface of the pond. The dense duckweed made it look as if it were solid land and it was only from the occasional interstices between this thick covering that one could tell that water lay beneath.'

YUKIO MISHIMA
The Temple of the Golden Pavilion, (tr. Ivan Morris), London: Everyman's Library, 1994 [1959].

In the north-west district of Kyoto lies the Rokuon-ji [Deer Park Temple], named for the deer park in India where the Buddha gave his first sermon on enlightenment. Within this park is one of the most famous garden buildings in Japan, the Temple of the Golden Pavilion, Kinkaku-ji. Each storey of the pavilion represents a different style of Japanese architecture used in the Muromachi period (1333–1568); displaying the power that its creator, Ashikaga Yoshimitsu, the third Ashikaga shogun, had over all aspects of life. The garden of Kinkaku-ji is a testament to the grand garden building of the Ashikaga shoguns and such large landscapes were rare until the Edo period (1600–1868).

Yoshimitsu was enamoured with all things Chinese, particularly from the Sung Dynasty. He was a patron of both the arts and Zen Buddhism, and the Golden Pavilion became a Zen temple when he died in 1408. Another influence on the garden may well have been the design and rock-work of the temple gardens of Saiho-ji and Tenryu-ji, which were appreciated by the Ashikaga shoguns.

The Golden Pavilion is sited so that it projects into the bordering lake, Kyoko-chi. As in earlier Heian period gardens the lake was used for boating parties and is interspersed with carefully placed islands, each surrounded with rock-work and planted with shaped pine trees. There are turtle and crane islands (symbols of longevity), created by the placement of the surrounding stones. Near a small boating jetty adjacent to the Pavilion two turtle islands represent arrival and departure, depicted by the placement of each turtle-head's stone. These islands and projections of land into the lake are a design technique to enhance the perceived scale of the lake whose major role is to provide a stunning reflection for the Golden Pavilion. (It must be remembered that the garden was also designed to be appreciated from the pavilion looking out across the islands on the lake.) All three storeys of the building are now richly covered with gold leaf following restoration after the original was destroyed by fire.

Trees with a moss-carpeted ground-cover form the major planting surrounding the scene, and act as a calming influence after the drama of the Golden Pavilion. Near the temple buildings there is a famous pine pruned into the representation of a boat. Behind the pavilion, to the east, the ground rises and the Dragon Gate waterfall splashes onto the famous 'carp stone'. Originally from a garden in Kamakura built by Saion-ji Kitsune, the stone represents a carp struggling against the water flow; in legend a carp who can succeeded in gaining the top of the waterfall would become a dragon, thus the stone carp can also represent the struggle for enlightenment.

There is a higher lake beyond the waterfall which is thought to date from the earliest villa complex on the site. Still higher is a later addition of a tea house and associated garden. From the high point of the garden path there is a fine view over the roof of the Golden Pavilion which is adorned with a statue of the mythical phoenix.

J.R.

Hellbrunn

SALZBURG, AUSTRIA

'In this park I lose myself, more than in a labyrinth. In these waters, Venice is embodied, and the buildings give me an impression of Rome. Hellbrunn is a maze of waters, a play of Naiads, a theatre of flowers, a capitol of statues, a museum of the Graces.'

DOMENICO GHISBERTI
Court Poet to the House of Wittelsbach, 1670.

Right: A stag's head spouting water.

Below: The mechanical theatre.

Bottom: Donato Mascagni, Portrait of Archbishop Markus Sittikus, 1619 (detail).

The gardens of this *villa suburbana* were laid out in accordance with the ideas of Markus Sittikus von Hohenems (1574–1619), Archbishop of Salzburg from 1612 to 1619, shortly before the outbreak of the Thirty Years´ War. In his youth Markus Sittikus had lived with his uncle, Cardinal Marco Sittico Altemps, in Rome, and spent the summers in his villa in Frascati. He was familiar with the latest in Italian garden design, and was especially intrigued by the hydraulic water follies at villas in Pratolino, Frascati, and Terra Ferma outside Venice. The *giardino segreto* at Hellbrunn with its hydraulic follies is among the best-preserved Mannerist gardens in Europe. Under the supervision of the Italian architect Santino Solari, Markus Sittikus had an Italianate villa with ground-floor grotto rooms erected. The rooms include a Mirror Grotto, a Rain Grotto with concealed water follies, and a Bird Grotto, in which a hydraulic apparatus produces imitations of bird songs.

These grottoes, refreshingly cool in summer, were directly linked with the surrounding garden areas, grouped loosely around the palace along a waterway axis known as the Prince's Way. This area forms the first part of the garden plan, the *giardino segreto*. At the beginning of the north-west axis lies the Roman Amphitheatre, where there is a stone table with a water-bearing channel once used to cool drinks. The model for this table is found in the garden of Villa Lante, outside Rome. The stone stools around the table contain hidden water jets, which were turned on when the Archbishop felt his guests needed 'refreshment'. The water axis that begins here expands at regular intervals into square or round ponds and ends in the western water *parterre*, the second section of the garden, whose mid-point is marked by an island. The island originally featured a lookout hill topped by a round pavilion.

The informal succession of features along the Prince's Way, its diverse grottoes, pavilions and fountains — and occasionally quite risqué *giochi d'acqua* — was augmented by a further curiosity in 1752: the Mechanical Theatre, which replaced a grotto that had gone into disrepair. Designed by F. A. Danreiter, this hydraulic theatre represents life in a small baroque town: over 100 figures moving to the strains of a water organ present an incomparable spectacle. The music may possibly have been composed by Leopold Mozart.

The Animal Enclosure forms the third section of the park. Located to the west, like all park areas it is surrounded by walls. On a stretch of high ground, the Little Month´s Palace [Monatsschlösschen], was built in 1615. This *casino*, said to have been finished in only a month, was reputedly erected by Markus Sittikus in honour of a Bavarian duke who was passing through Salzburg. From here a forest path leads to the Rock Theatre [Felsentheater], one of the oldest open-air theatres in Europe. Here, on 31 August 1617, Monteverdi´s Orpheus became the first Italian opera to be performed north of the Alps. Annual concerts maintain the tradition to this day. In the vicinity of the theatre there were originally several hermit´s retreats with chapels, and a game reserve. *A.G.*

1425 Creation of a deer park with fishponds for the Prince-Bishops of Salzburg.

1613–15 Palace building by architect Santino Solari for Markus Sittikus von Hohenems; layout of gardens with grotto architectures and *giochi d'acqua*.

1615 Erection of Monatsschlösschen.

1615 First open-air opera performances north of the Alps at the Felsentheater.

1730s Simplification of gardens by Danreiter.

1750 Mechanical Theatre by Danreiter.

Late 18th century: Partial redesign of park in the landscape-garden style.

The Roman Amphitheatre (1615) with giochi d'acqua.

The Orpheus Grotto.

Katsura Rikyu Imperial Villa

KYOTO, JAPAN

The Cycas revoluta *in summer.*

'I have said that the whole expanse of this spacious garden and its large central pond could be viewed in one unbroken sweep, but the truth is that I only thought this to be so [...] As we strolled along the stone-paved path, climbed to the summits of the artificial hills and descended again to the brink of the pond, the scene changed constantly.'

YASUSHI INOUE, 'The Villa, the Garden and the Prince', alluding to the *Tale of Genji*, in Teiji Itoh (ed.), *Imperial Gardens of Japan*, New York/Tokyo/Kyoto: Weatherhill/Tankosha, 1970.

Stones are placed with care to regulate the visitor's journey.

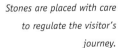

The stroll garden of Katsura Rikyu Imperial Villa lies to the south-west of Kyoto and was created during the Edo period (1600–1868) when Japan was closed to almost all foreign trade. At the heart of the complex is an irregularly shaped lake with islands and promontories around which winds a path. The design of the garden has in the past been attributed to the designer Kobori Enshu (1579–1647), though it is now considered that he may only have acted as a consultant and that the artistically able Prince Toshihito and his son, with the aid of skilled workmen, were responsible for the garden's layout.

The main house, perhaps the finest example of Japanese Sukiya Shoin architectural style, has three major parts which are stepped in a diagonal alignment, known as the 'geese-in-flight-formation'. The garden is intended to be admired both from the major buildings and by the act of walking around the garden on a prescribed path which circles the lake in a clockwise direction. The stability of the Edo period allowed the larger stroll gardens to develop and these were designed with the intention of concealing and revealing scenes to the viewer as they walked along a path, with progress often being set on the diagonal, as with the villa design, thus making the garden seem larger. Sensitivity

c. 1000 The area of Katsura Rikyu is owned by the Fujiwara family.

c. 1200 The Konoe family takes possession of the area of Katsura Rikyu.

c. 1600 The land of Katsura Rikyu comes into the ownership of Prince Toshihito (1579–1629), brother of the Emperor Goyozei (1571–1617).

1615 Prince Toshihito begins construction of the Katsura Rikyu Imperial Villa.

c. 1645 Prince Toshihito's son, Prince Toshitada (1619–62) makes additions to the buildings and grounds, following a financially advantageous marriage to the daughter of a *daimyo* [feudal lord].

1663 The retired Emperor Gomizuno (1596–1680) visits Katsura Rikyu; additions may well have been made in preparation for the visit.

1881 The family line of inheritance for Katsura Rikyu comes to an end with the death of Princess Sumiko.

1883 Katsura Rikyu Imperial Villa comes under the control of the Department of the Imperial Household.

was shown not only to the views, the seasons and the type of material used underfoot but also the visitor's intellect: the historical, literary and geographical allusion were designed to be understood by the well-educated Japanese elite.

Left and above: Views of the garden change as the viewer moves around the central lake.

Prince Toshihito studied the classical literature of both Japan and China, including the *Tale of Genji*, which contains descriptions of Heian period (794–1185) gardens. In his travels he was so impressed with the beauty of the famous shoreline peninsula of Ama-no-hashidate, the 'Bridge to Heaven', that a stylised representation is included at Katsura Rikyu. The *wabi-sabi* aesthetic, an appreciation of simplicity and the patina of age, had been developed in the tea ceremony of the preceding Momoyama period (1568–1600) and the garden contains five rustic tea houses for use during the different seasons. The Pavilion of Admired Blossoms resembles the type of tea pavilion that might be found in the countryside and so conveys the idea of walking far beyond the confines of the garden.

As in other Japanese gardens the planting at Katsura Rikyu is carefully controlled. One of the most well-known plant groups faces a thatched shelter, where visitors can rest prior to being invited to enter the garden for a tea ceremony. This grouping consists of a stand of *Cycas revoluta* planted on a raised hillock. Their fern-like fronds strike an exotic note in summer, while in the winter they are decoratively wrapped with straw for protection against the cold. In August visitors can view the full moon from a specially designed platform, surrounded by a lake, islands and the soft illumination of stone lanterns. *J.R.*

Isola Bella LAKE MAGGIORE, ITALY

'Groves of oranges and pomegranates and large bowers of lemon and citrons all covered with fruit. It is like a little bit of the Garden of Hesperides had been wafted to this enchanted spot.'

SELECTED LETTERS OF CHARLES DE BROSSES
1739, trans. Lord Ronald Sutherland Gower, London, 1897.

François Flameng (1856–1923), Bonaparte's Reception on the Island of Bella in the 5th year of the Republic, *oil on wood.*

The raised, terraced gardens enjoy a precipitous view over the lake.

Isola Bella, an island transformed into a garden on Lake Maggiore, is one of the most striking gardens imaginable. Created for Count Carlo Borromeo out of bare rock, the garden isle appears like a spectacular galleon breasting the waters of the lake. One end (the poop so to speak) rises in ten terraces, with the palace at the prow end. Although the name conveys the obvious meaning of 'beautiful island', in fact it is an abbreviation of the original, 'Isola Isabella', which commemorated the count's wife. Work continued for forty years under the count and his sons. During this period the principal architects involved were Angelo Crivelli, Carlo Fontana (1638–1714) and Francesco Castelli.

The shape of the island precluded an axial design aligned with the palace, though the plan is nonetheless formal and geometrical. From the palace a rectangular garden culminates in the Theatre of Hercules, prominently displaying a statue of that hero. A large *parterre* leads to the principal feature, a five-tier water theatre surmounted by a figure on a unicorn, the symbol of the Borromeo family. The theatre conceals a cistern which feeds the water effects and provides water for the garden. Statuary tops square columns faced with pebbles and stands in niches decorated with scallop shells. The tableau is pure baroque display: the unicorn may possess a heraldic meaning but otherwise the effect is sheer spectacle. On the other side of the water theatre ten terraces step down to the lake. They are decorated with plume-capped obelisks: on the main terrace is a formal garden with four *parterres de broderie*. Originally, and ironically, one planted motto visible from the palace reads 'Humilitas'.

A print of 1726 shows the garden as relatively bare and architectural. Subsequent growth and plantings have considerably softened the austere lines and enriched the overall colour. In the large *parterre* are to be found camellias, magnolias, roses, jasmine, pomegranates and citrus trees, patrolled by a flock of white peacocks. *M.S.*

c. 1630 Work begins commissioned by Count Carlo Borromeo.
1670 Gardens completed.

The Water Theatre.

Magnolia and cherry blossom bring colour to the stone terraces.

Flower reliefs on the mausoleum walls.

Exterior view of the mausoleum.

Taj Mahal

AGRA, INDIA

'But O thou soul at peace
Return thou unto thy Lord well-pleased and well-pleasing,
Enter though among thy servants
And enter thou My Paradise.'

HOLY KORAN SUTRA 89
inscribed on Main Gate.

In 1526, when Emperor Babur led his army out to defeat Ibrahim Lodi, he did more than found the Mogul dynasty: a tradition of garden building was established that was designed to delight the senses and house the constantly moving court. The Moguls also built mausoleum garden complexes, of which the Taj Mahal is the last and most sublime. Situated on the banks of the River Jumna at Agra, it was completed in 1648 after 22 years of construction. One of the world's greatest buildings was sited in a paradise garden that in its heyday was one of the finest examples of the Mogul garden art. Regardless of whether the Taj Mahal is Shah Jahan's memorial to his beloved wife Mumtaz Mahal or not, it is truly a glimpse of heaven.

Arab khalifs in Iraq around 860 AD built the first Koran gardens, but Paradise was added to an already ancient type. Inspired by the Koran to shape a paradise on earth, the creators of Mogul gardens also included a rich layer of symbolism to create perfectly

balanced formal compositions of space, water, architecture and vegetation. The word paradise derives from the Assyrian *pairidaeza*, meaning hunting park or garden. Using the Persian *chahar bagh* as a model, the Moguls added a unique quality by blending Islamic, Hindu and Sufic influences.

Time has not been kind to Mogul gardens: even where the fabric is in place, much of the planting has been lost or replaced inappropriately. The Taj Mahal is no exception, as the present trees, flowerbeds and lawns are Westernised 18th-century informal parkland. The *chahar bagh* layout is intact but departs from tradition as it has a central pool, rather than a viewing pavilion or tomb. In this pool, we see a perfect reflection of the mausoleum. Water channels, symbols of the four Rivers of Paradise, quarter the area into the four Gardens of Paradise. Raised paths are then used to further divide the quartiles into sixteen, which are then further sub-divided into *parterres*. Colonel Hodgson's plan of 1828 shows this clearly and locates the trees that define the formal layout, but gives no detail. The Moguls chronicled their plants and used diverse fruits, flowers and shade trees, most of which have been identified. François Berrier, travelling in India 1658–84, refers to the Taj as having 'many *parterres* filled with flowers'.

Could we re-create the Taj Mahal plantings as they would have appeared in 1648? Possibly: recent research indicates that the layout could be based on The Plan of Assembly on the Day of Judgement, a drawing by the Sufi mystic Ibn al' Arabi. In this case, the tomb would signify the Throne of Allah and the gardens would contain additional symbolism, including the plants. Intriguingly a second garden complex has been discovered, aligned to the Taj on the opposite bank of the river. Tempting as a re-creation seems, it is probably too early and maybe inappropriate at this time. *A.B.*

1592 Shah Jahan born to Jahangir, fourth Mogul Emperor and Jagat Gosayini, a Rajput Princess. Given the name Prince Khurram.

1612 Married Arjumand Banu who adopted the name Mumtaz Mahal on her marriage.

1618 His son and successor Aurangzeb is born.

1626 Possible start date for the Taj Mahal.

1627–28 Jahangir dies and Khurram becomes Emperor after a year's struggle. Becomes known as Shah Jahan.

1631 Mumtaz Mahal dies giving birth to their fourteenth child. Alternative start date for the Taj Mahal.

1648 Taj Mahal completed (some authorities suggest the later date of 1652).

1639–48 Red Fort and Palace, Delhi, built; two of the many architectural projects completed by Shah Jahan.

1658 Deposed by his son Aurangzeb in a coup. Imprisoned in the Agra Fort, where he was cared for by his daughter Jahanara.

1666 Dies of an overdose of aphrodisiacs on 31 January aged 74. Buried in the Taj Mahal alongside Mumtaz Mahal.

Villa Garzoni

COLLODI, ITALY

'The sun broke from its clouds, and lifted up the green of the vegetation; at the same time spangling the waters that pour copiously down a succession of rocky terraces.'

DIARY OF WILLIAM BECKFORD, 1780.

At the foot of the balustrade lie charming parterres de broderie.

A dinosaur in the topiary menagerie.

1652 The Garzoni family begins alterations to the existing house and garden.
1786 Diodati commissioned to embellish the garden laid out from 1652.
1945 Property bought by the present owner.

The water staircase that forms the main axis of the garden.

The balustraded double staircase originally had giochi d'acqua *set into each retaining wall.*

The garden of Villa Garzoni in Tuscany is one of the most extravagent examples of baroque garden design anywhere in Italy. Unlike the Renaissance gardens of the area, which were typically built as a series of intimate enclosures, Garzoni reveals its full splendour at first glance.

The Garzoni family bought the ancient fortress of Collodi at the beginning of the 17th century. Although they were able to transform the austere building into a villa, they could do nothing about its impractical position. The site on a rocky outcrop had been ideal for a medieval castle, but it presented extreme practical difficulties in more settled times. Chief among these was the absence of any area close to the house level enough for a garden. The architect, whose name has unfortunately been lost, found an ingenious solution to the problem. He designed a bridge to span the gorge that lay to the east of the new building. In this way he created access to a steep slope beyond the gorge and some level ground below it. This was the site of the new garden.

Very little is known about the first phase of garden making at Garzoni. In 1562 Francesco Sbarra wrote a poem in praise of 'the splendours of Collodi', and his description suggests that the gardens were complete by this time. Over a century later the garden entered a new phase of development. The Garzoni family commissioned Ottavio Diodati, an architect, to add to the existing structure.

The foreground of the garden consists of a circular space enclosed by yew tunnels. A bizarre topiary menagerie includes a peacock, a dinosaur and an elephant. The impression of having entered a strange zoo is heightened by the cages of exotic game birds that stand in the shade at the edges of the garden. Beyond them are the swirling arabesques of *parterres de broderie*.

The steep hillside beyond the lower garden is cut into a series of terraces. These are linked by immensely elaborate balustraded steps and terraces decorated with terracotta statues of monkeys. Like all of the terracotta statues in the garden, the monkeys were Diodati's addition. The first terrace leads to Diodati's pretty green theatre, cut from hedges of yew and box.

The design culminates in a spectacular water staircase that scales the hill at an extraordinary angle. At its head there is a massive statue representing Fame. At this level there is also a little bath house which was once furnished with marble baths, dressing rooms and a discretely screened musicians' gallery.

Today we enter the garden at its lowest level and are presented almost at once with the full glory of the massive water staircase. The Garzonis' guests would have reached the garden by crossing the bridge over the gorge. This oblique approach meant that first-time visitors stumbled across the water staircase quite unexpectedly, arriving at a mid-point, and seeing it only from one side. It is very rare that the practicalities of opening a garden to the public serve to increase our enjoyment in this way. *H.A.*

Tuileries

PARIS, FRANCE

'André Le Nôtre ..... endowed the garden with the climactic burst into space of its central axis, so creating the very soul of French urbanism and the major symbol of modern France: the Champs-Elysées.'

VINCENT SCULLY
The Designs of André Le Nôtre: French Royal Gardens.

1564 Catherine de' Medici commissions new palace and gardens.
1577 Jacques Androuet du Cerceau (c. 1515/20–c. 1584) draws up plans showing regular symmetrical layout (probably not fully implemented).
1600–09 Claude Mollet parterres completed.
1637 André Le Nôtre appointed Premier Jardinier au Grand Jardin des Tuileries to Louis XIII, succeeding his father.
1643 André Le Nôtre named Dessinateur des Parterres de Tous les Jardins du Roi. Louis XIII dies.
1649 Le Nôtre appointed Jardiniste du Roi.
1668 Le Nôtre lays out Champs-Elysées, main axis of the Tuileries.
1889 Tuileries gardens extended with Carrousel gardens over site of palace.
1989 Completion of Grand Cour of Louvre and Avenue du General-Lemonnier underground.
1991–95 Restoration programme by designers Pascal Cribier, Louis Benech and Jacques Wirtz.

The Good Samaritan by François Sicard (1862–1934).

On 12 March 1613 André Le Nôtre was born on Faubourg Saint-Honoré next to the Tuileries royal palace. His grandfather Pierre (c. 1517–c. 1610) had been superintendent of the gardens' original great *parterres* and his father, Jean (d. 1655), had been Premier Jardinier au Grand Jardin des Tuileries to Louis XIII. Both men had worked on the intricacies of the *parterre* designs with Claude Mollet but the dynamic axis that stretches from the Tuileries through Paris's Elysian Fields, now Avenue des Champs-Elysées, was to be the baroque brainchild of André.

The cloistered palace gardens created for Catherine de' Medici, over a former tile and brick works, introduced the Italian Mannerist style for fashionable promenades, juxtaposed with a theatre, menagerie, aviary and a grotto designed by Bernard Palissy (c. 1510–90). Then Henri IV commissioned Claude Mollet to design parterres de compartiments which he created with Pierre Le Nôtre. In 1651 André Mollet (1600–65) published *Le Jardin de Plaisir* which André Le Nôtre used when he redesigned the old gardens, and Louis Le Vau used when working on the palace. The central axis was maintained but two sets of ornamented *parterres de compartiments* enlivened by two large basins were introduced.

This model pleasure garden in three parts — the ornate Grand Carré; the wooded quincunxes and the octagonal pool — epitomises the 'garden as theatre'. Le Nôtre included an open-air theatre and his designs set the trend of opening out the gardens edges and drawing in surrounding nature as part of the stage setting. He extended the vista from the Tuileries to the westerly horizon, manipulating the length and width of *allées* and walks so that the sky itself entered the garden theatre. Le Nôtre translated Descartes's optical theories ('the purest lights of the optiques and the most regular perspectives') into practical landscape design. The parallel flanking raised walks of the Terrasse du Bord de l'Eau by the Seine terminating at the Musée de l'Orangerie (enlarged

The Seine and the Marne by Nicolas Coustou (1658–1733).

in 1853) and the Terrasse du Jeu de Paume and, later, Terrasse des Feuillants running beside the Rue de Rivoli still appear as much a part of Paris beyond as of the gardens.

By Le Nôtre's death in 1700 lack of funds meant that nature had begun to mask the garden's geometry with overgrown trees and weeds. Fashion favoured naturalistic *jardins anglo-chinois*, revolutions and wars wrought further damage; and after fires the buildings were finally demolished. The Carrousel gardens were designed between the surviving Pavillon de Marsan and Pavillon de Flore, verdantly captured on canvas by Monet.

In 1989 with the Avenue du General-Lemonnier underground, a restoration programme was initiated 'to regive life and coherence to the ancient elements that formed the gardens, at the same time allowing an aesthetically pleasing contemporary landscape for the needs of nature, freedom and promenaders. ...However a new coherence will be created between ... the Terrasse des Tuileries and the Carrousel ...'. The successful outcome links the Louvre to the Champs-Elysées with 69 acres of broad *allées*, flowery *parterres*, dramatic water basins and stands of trees re-creating Le Nôtre's vision of symmetry, water and theatre, as well as a sumptuous array of statuary dating from Louis XIV to the present day.

C.H.

Claude Monet, Les Tuileries, *1876, oil on canvas, 54 x 73 cm. Paris, Musée Marmottan.*

Jean Joseph Sulpis (1826–1911), Historic topography of old Paris. Undated engraving after a drawing by A. Berty.

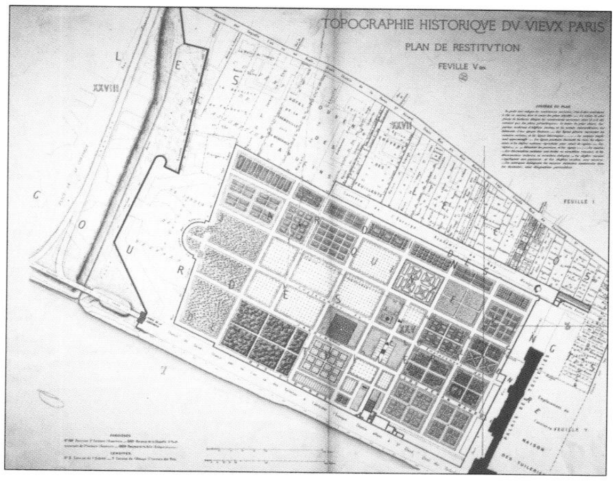

Vaux-le-Vicomte

SEINE-ET-MARNE, FRANCE

'The essential element to grasp about Vaux or Versailles or Chantilly or any of the other great classic French gardens is that they were not the creation of one artist's vision or execution, but instead were the result of a complex and carefully tuned, collective effort by many talented men brought together to transform and shape nature into an acceptable work of art. The creation of a great garden in the seventeenth century was rather like the organization of contemporary productions of the new Italian opera or the French Ballet de Cour'.

WILLIAM HOWARD ADAMS.

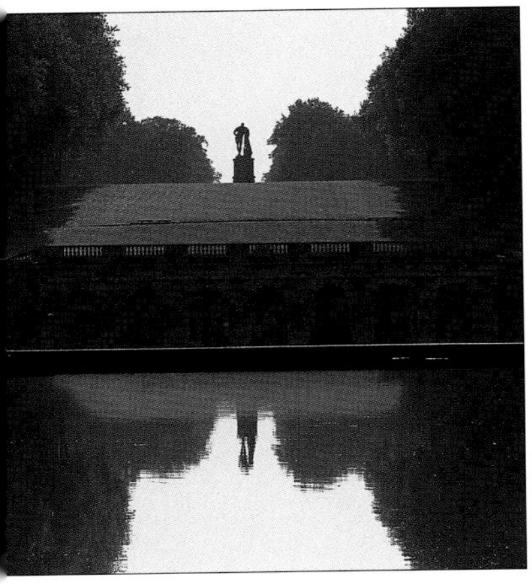

The Grande Allée with framed statue of Hercules.

In 1652 Charles de Sercy published Claude Mollet's *Théâtre des plans et jardinages* with a dedication to Nicolas Fouquet (1615–80) praising his 'superbes jardins de Vaux-le-Vicomte'. Although this predates André Le Nôtre's (1613–1700) involvement, it is likely that extensive tree planting would have been done prior to the latter's collaboration with architect Louis le Vau (1612–70) and artist Charles le Brun (1619–90).

Fouquet, Louis XIV's immensely wealthy finance minister, was one of the most influential cultural forces in mid-17th-century France and the work he sponsored at Vaux-le-Vicomte was at the vanguard of French Baroque style. Three villages were swept away to create a generous landscape geometricized so that accidents of nature were perfected. Descending terraces are decorated with *parterres* and mirror pools. Tree planting on a massive scale orchestrated shady walks and rides into the adjoining forest.

Le Nôtre took over the landscaping, modelling it not on Italy but on the rich, flat fields of France. He created a complex work of art aided by *fontainier* Claude Robillard, the stonemason Villedo, head gardener Antoine Trumel and sculptors Nicolas Poussin, Anguier, Lespaynander, Poissant, Girardon and Legendre.The baroque theatre of Le Nôtre's designs was his mastery of perspective, foreshortened by increasing the distance between the cross-axial walks and manipulated by trees, hedges, pools and fountains with the light filtered or reflected. Unexpected gardens and the grotto appear along the walk, providing an element of fantasy and unreality — excursions enhanced by the wooded backdrop.

The sculpture at Vaux reflects Fouquet's aspirations to regal status.

The central Grande Allée is flanked initially by *parterres de broderie*. Then comes the first deception: the smooth *parterres de l'Angloisse* leading to the Fontaine de la Couronne on the left are actually twice the size of those 'coupées pour les fleurs' on the right. Two canals act as 'water gates' to the circular pool after which the third terrace can be seen to dramatically descend into the amphitheatre and River Gods grotto. This involved canalising 0.6 miles of the River Anqueuil. A rectangular pool mirrors the château from afar as a double stone stairway descends by the Grandes Cascades. A long walk or gentle row leads to the River Gods Tiber and Anqueuil, who gaze powerfully through the play of the Petites Cascades. Towards the horizon the Allée is broken by the vertical accents of a single jet of water and the statue of Hercules is framed by the narrowing wall of trees. The avenue-lined Rampe rises appropriately to frame a copy of Farnese's Hercules resting after his labours, before disappearing over the horizon.

On 17 August 1661 Louis XIV, his mother, wife and mistress attended a lavish *fête* to celebrate Vaux-le-Vicomte, and horrified by such blatant display of riches the king

1641 Nicolas Fouquet purchases estate of Vaux-le-Vicomte.

1656–61 Le Nôtre, Le Vau and Le Brun design new gardens and château.

1661 17 August: Fouquet hosts a sumptuous reception invoking the wrath and envy of Louis XIV; three weeks later Fouquet is arrested, imprisoned and exiled.

1875 Alfred Sommier purchases Vaux-le-Vicomte.

1880 onwards: Alfred Sommier replaces lost statuary, commissioning Henri Duchêne (1841–1902) and his son, Achille (1866–1947) as well as new sculptors (Hiolle, Gardet, Peynot and Lanson).

1908 Death of Alfred Sommier. Garden restoration completed by his son Edme and daughter-in-law, Germaine.

1919 Gardens open to the public.

1929 Château and gardens classified as historic monuments.

The parterres de broderie.

The circular pool.

ordered Fouquet's imprisonment. The designers, most of the statues and 1,200 trees were transplanted away from Vaux and into the Herculean task of Versailles.

In 1875 Alfred Sommier bought the ruins of Vaux, and after the château was restored, the re-creation of the gardens was undertaken with the help of the Duchênes, and completed by his son, Edme. The moated symmetry of the château sets the tone for this first example of *pourtraiture* where the geometry is adjusted to the actual dimensions of the ground and the *broderie* of the *parterres* is designed to give a vast visual expanse.

C.H.

Versailles

YVELINES, FRANCE

'Versailles ...a web spun of palace, dependencies and gardens... The supreme example of character and contrast in gardenwork is fairly represented by the palace of Versailles, and the humblest by the peasant's cottage that nestles under a thatched roof. The one is more pronounced than the other, but the relation to nature is the same in principle. The formal house extends to meet its wild surroundings, and the two discuss their differences in the garden.'

GEOFFREY JELLICOE

The Studies of a Landscape Designer over 80 Years, vol. 1.

Jacques Rigaud (c. 1681–after 1753), Les Bains d'Apollon, *copper engraving, later coloured.*

The modest gardens of Louis XIII's hunting lodge at Versailles had been designed by Jacques Menours with longitudinal and transverse axes radiating from a central *allée* leading to a large basin. From 1662 André le Nôtre (1613–1700) and his team from Vaux-le-Vicomte redesigned them in the new Baroque style, retaining the axes and *parterres* (albeit with a more austere refinement) and remodelling the basin into the Bassin d'Apollon. Versailles thus became the outward manifestation of the power of the *roi soleil*, Louis XIV, his authority as monarch and warrior symbolised by the sun and the sun-god Apollo. The gardens reverberated with magnificent water displays. Stone and marble proclaiming the sun-god theme echoed into *bosquet* theatres, botanical treasure houses and pleasure grounds for the courtly multitude. Despite appalling soil and parlous water supplies the gardens lived up to the king's conceit of creating a horticultural wonder of the world.

Le Nôtre ingeniously extended the main axis with transversal lines which grew organically in a spreading geometry of circles and squares that retained a sense of proportion and balance. The château dominates the imposing baroque terrace of large open *parterres*, and basins mirror its splendours. The Royal Avenue leads to the Bassin de Latone, representing the mother of Apollo and Diana protecting her children, then draws the eye over the *tapis vert* to Jean-Baptiste Tuby's magnificent Apollo on his Chariot rising powerfully from the waters (1670).

The Cent Marches descended from 'heaven' to the ordered earthly paradise of Jean-

1631–34 Louis XIII enlarges hunting lodge at Versailles, Jacques Menours and his uncle, Jacques Boyceau (d. c. 1633) designed a few acres of gardens.
1661 Inspired by Vaux-le-Vicomte, Louis XIV decides to enlarge Versailles.
1662 André Le Nôtre starts work.
1665 Petit Parc established.
1674 Grand Commission for 24 marble statues based either on drawings by Charles Le Brun (1619–90) or ancient statues.
1682 Seat of French court and government transferred to Versailles.
1693 Louis XIV stops work on gardens and park.
1715 Death of Louis XIV at Versailles.
1750 Claude II Richard (1705–84) designs a botanical garden for Louis XV at the New or Petit Trianon.
1775 Richard Mique redesigns Louis XV's botanical garden into an anglo-chinois landscape.
1778 Mique designs The Temple of Love.
1783 Mique designs Le Hameau de la Reine.
1789 French Revolution
1830 Louis-Philippe declares Versailles a museum 'to all the glories of France'.

The magnificent Apollo fountain framed by the receding avenue of the patte d'oie.

This canopy of trees would have been decorated for Versailles' many grands divertissements.

Marie-Antoinette's farm at the Hameau.

Baptiste de la Quintinie's (1626–88) Potager du Roi, an image underlined by the clipped citrus (1,000 orange trees were taken from Vaux) as well as palms radiating from the earthly pool in the Parterre de l'Orangerie. Wooded groves recapture the spirit of ancient myths, a living backdrop for plays, concerts and *grands divertissements* elaborated with rock work, shells, fountains and statuary. For festivities the trees would be hung with oranges, peaches, currants and plums. The vast Grand Canal reflecting the distant sky stretches away widening at the far end and releasing the view while symbolically drawing the whole of France back to its hub — Versailles. The court rode through the park in carriages but Louis preferred to walk through gardens that spread over hundreds of acres on axes leading from the King's Apartments, and surrounded by 16,000 acres of hunting park. The transverse canal leads to the Grand Trianon, Louis XIV's intimate peristyled palace whose *parterres* might even have their flowers changed during lunch.

French rulers continued to use the Trianon until 1848, reworking the gardens according to the contemporary fashions. Napoleon built a bridge to the Petit Trianon, originally created as a botanical garden by Louis XV then landscaped by Marie Antoinette in the anglo-chinois style with *fabriques* such as the Rock Pavilion or Belvedere. From the Temple of Love a sinuous stream and path lead to her Hameau (1785) inspired by the Hameau at Chantilly. Around the lake Richard Mique designed a dozen rustic thatched roof houses which, unlike their forerunners, all had a farming purpose. *C.H.*

Veitshöchheim

VEITSHÖCHHEIM
NEAR WÜRZBURG
GERMANY

'Within a mere ten years and without disturbing the earlier arrangement Adam Friedrich von Seinsheim introduced intimate spaces in the rococo taste and decorated the garden with a wealth of sculpture.'

HELMUT REINHARDT
in *The History of Garden Design*, edited by Monique Mosser and Georges Teyssot.

Partial view of Bossi's Grotto House.

Tietz's Indian Pavilion, 1768.

Tietz's statue of the Kaiser (1766) in the Circus.

Despite its relatively small dimensions (262 by 437 yards), the originality of Veitshöchheim's complex spatial scheme and the quality of its garden sculptures (once numbering 200) lend this park a special charm. Importantly, it has survived the last 250 years almost unspoilt.

The originally humble gardens of the summer house of the Prince-Bishops of Würzburg were converted into a baroque pleasure garden at the beginning of the 18th century. However, the most significant change came with the rococo period. Prince-Bishop Adam Friedrich von Seinsheim entrusted his Court Gardeners Johann Prokop Maier and Joseph Orth with the redesign (1763–79), and commissioned one of the best rococo sculptors, Ferdinand Tietz of Bohemia, to execute the figures (1765–68), which were originally polychrome.

Disregarding the conventions of the day, Veitshöchheim is entirely self-referential — the result of a continual adaptation to existing structures. The palace does not stand in the centre of the park nor do its vistas extend to the surrounding landscape. The park is encompassed by a high wall dating from the first phase of the layout, and opens only at one point to provide a view into the countryside. The palace lies on a raised terrace at the extreme edge of the garden and is surrounded by formal floral *parterres*. An axial *allée* of trees links the palace with the main entrance.

The garden to the south of the palace consists of three main parts. The first, known as the Lake Region, is populated by figure groups representing the gods and the arts. Its centre is occupied by a large, oval lake in whose middle a Parnassus, crowned by a winged horse, was erected. The lake adjoins a hedged zone, which is criss-crossed by transverse and diagonal paths, and has fruit orchards. The Lake Region is separated by an avenue of lindens from the arbour area in the middle of the garden. The focus of this area is formed by a circular plaza known as the Circus. This is divided by high hedges into 32 compartments which are decorated with sculptures representing a courtly party. Dancers, musicians and vases adorned with musical instruments lend this area a delightful atmosphere. Along both sides run pergolas which end in round pavilions, the Temples of Autumn and Spring. Oval windows in the pavilions and corresponding peepholes cut into the hedges behind playfully draw the eye to vistas that extend through the entire section. An avenue of firs demarcates the wooded region in the eastern part of the garden. This is the realm of the animals. The area is divided into three main sections: the Hedge Theatre to the north; south of it the Source Axis with two Chinese pavilions; and the Hedge Hall with sculpture groups based on the fables of La Fontaine.

Along the garden wall there are a few autonomous garden structures which form the focus of key vistas. The Grand Cascade, destroyed during World War II, served as the

1619 Two small palaces acquired by the Bishopric of Würzburg.
1680–82 Construction of a Summer or Pleasure House at the behest of Prince-Bishop Peter Philipp von Dernbach.
1702 Under Prince-Bishop Johann Philipp von Greiffenklau, conversion of the grounds into a stately baroque garden. Addition of large lake, main paths and peripheral walls.
1749–54 Execution of first figure cycle by Johann Wolfgang von Auvera.
1753 Annex to Summer House by Balthasar Neumann.
1772–80 Ornamental figures by J.P. Wagner.
1772–73 The Belvedere, a grotto structure by Materno Bossi.
1776 Opening of the park to the public.
1802 End of the Bishopric of Würzburg. In the 19th century the park serves as summer residence of the Bavarian royal family.
1927 First measures taken to maintain the historical site.
1945 Architectural features partially destroyed.
1952–66 First extensive restoration. Over the past 40 years the sculptures have been replaced by copies. The originals are in the Mainfränkisches Museum, Würzburg.

View out of the northern pavilion (1765) and through the peepholes cut in the line of hedges.

point of departure of the garden´s true main axis. This runs through all three areas to culminate in the Temple of the Muses in the large pond.

At the south-east corner of the wall we come upon the picturesque Grotto House, also known as the Belvedere. The lower floor consists of a tufa grotto ornamented with sea-shell sculptures of animals. A semicircular outside stairway leads up to an octagonal pavilion. The walls of the pavilion are likewise covered in sea-shells, coloured stones, glass and other materials. From here one has a wonderful view over the entire garden.

A.G.

Het Loo

APELDOORN, HOLLAND

Natural springs are the source of the garden's many fountains.

Orange trees in pots are an ever-present reminder of Het Loo's royal patron.

'The Gardens are most Sumptuous and Magnificent, adorned with great variety of most Noble Fountains, Cascades, Parterres, Gravel-walks and Green walks, Groves, Statues, Urns, Paintings, Seats, and pleasant Prospects into the Country.'

WALTER HARRIS
A Description of the King's Royal Palace and Gardens at Loo, London, 1699.

The present-day visitor to the gardens of Het Loo may easily forget that he is walking through an environment reconstructed by the Dutch State and finished as recently as 1984. Its rebuilding resulted from controversial political decisions to recreate the former dynastic glory in honour of the present-day House of Orange. Unknowingly, that decision echoed the political meaning these gardens held for their original patron, William III (1650–1702).

The construction of Het Loo is closely associated with William's career. Purchasing terrains near Apeldoorn in the east of Holland as a *stadholder* in 1684, William III intended Het Loo to be a personal project that would represent his passion for both hunting and gardening. Building started in 1686, but was soon interrupted by the political events that led up to the Glorious Revolution, when William and Mary took over the English throne in the spring of 1689. After this event, work at Het Loo began under the supervision of Hans Willem Bentinck, Duke of Portland and Romeyn de Hooghe, the artist responsible for William III's propaganda machine. Daniel Marot (1661–1752), for long seen as the designer of the gardens, in fact contributed decorative elements only.

In 1691, William III showed off his creation to his international allies against the French: thus the garden formed part of his political propaganda. This also explains why he ordered the garden to be enlarged from 1691 to 1699 — it had to match his royal status. William III normally eschewed the grand and spatious, preferring the refined and enclosed, much in keeping with his documented admiration for Trianon-like structures. Yet, the many prints of Het Loo seem to confirm that Het Loo should not been seen as an imitation of but as an answer to the gardens of his great French rival.

Statues, plants and fountains, fed from natural springs, played an important part in this theatre of art, nature and politics. River and nature gods give the gardens symbolism as a *locus amoenus* in the sandy and heather-covered Veluwe region. Four large urns representing Holland, England, Scotland and Ireland referred to William's empire. Globes of heaven and earth added a macrocosmic order to the garden, whose symmetrical arrangement was thus an allegory of political order. With Venus on the central fountain, the garden reflected a new golden age of prosperity and fertility under the government of William and Mary. An exquisite collection of flowers in the *plate-bandes* and of exotics in the orangery-garden, enhanced this representation of the richness of natural creation.

Cascades of Arion and Narcissus symbolised the virtues of William III, more particularly as the leader who defended Protestantism and saved his people against foreign intruders. A Hercules fountain introduced an international princely emblem, symbolizing strength and innate virtue: Hercules reigns not at Versailles, but at Het Loo. A wooden pyramid at the end of the main axis was emblematic of princely fame and glory. These virtues were also reflected in the many orange trees in the garden, living emblems of the garden of the Hesperides, a reward for the Herculean efforts of a Prince of Orange. In all these aspects, large and small, the garden functioned as a *theatrum politicum* for a great European prince, William III.

E.A. de J.

1684 William III purchases existing medieval castle and land at Het Loo; initial work is carried out on a new house with gardens.

1688–89 Due to political events work is abandoned.

1691 Gardens and house of Het Loo finished (first phase).

1691 William orders Het Loo to be enlarged to reflect his royal status.

1699 Het Loo (second phase) is finished and celebrated by many prints and a text by Walter Harris, *A Description of the King's Royal Palace and Gardens at Loo*, London, 1699.

1699 Claude Desgots (d. 1732), nephew of Le Nôtre, draws up a new plan for the gardens, which is not executed due to the untimely death of William III in 1702.

The Globe of the Heavens.

Chatsworth DERBYSHIRE, ENGLAND

'By the Grove stands a fine Willow tree, the leaves, barkes and all looks very naturall, and all on a sudden by turning a sluice it raines from each leafe and from the branches like a shower, it being made of brass and pipes to each leafe nut in appearance it is exactly like any Willow.'

CELIA FIENNES, *Journal*
cited by Laurence Fleming and Alan Gore in *The English Garden*, London: Michael Joseph, 1979.

Wellington Rock dominates the Strid.

From 1686 onwards Chatsworth was radically remodelled by the 1st Duke of Devonshire to create an English Versailles. George London and Henry Wise designed vast geometrical gardens with intricate *parterres* by the house and *allées* around formal wildernesses fanning away towards Stand Wood. Water was channelled from Stand Wood, appearing under and across the stepped roof of the Cascade House, designed by Thomas Archer (1668–1743), to feed the magnificent cascade, designed by Grillet, a pupil of Le Nôtre. Varying sounds are produced when the water flows over different lengths and widths of the paving stones, and 24 groups of steps. The 1698 Greenhouse acts as a camellia house today with a formal rose garden replacing the pond. The earliest survivor is the 1692 'willow tree', (not the original as it was replaced twice and restored once). It is created out of copper and lead and in winter resembles other deciduous trees — until it weeps water.

During the 1760s 'Capability' Brown transformed the setting of the house and its gardens by planting a belt of trees around the moorland horizon. This was arranged in wedge-shaped plantings so that sections could be felled without changing the skyline. The formal terraces were landscaped into five acres of grass called 'The Great Slope' which today form The Salisbury Lawns, sprinkled with wild flowers and grasses. The village of Edensor was razed, clumps of native trees were planted, the course of the River Derwent altered and the architect James Paine (1716–89) designed new stables, a mill and an upstream bridge.

Formality was reintroduced by architect Jeffry Wyatville who extended the Broad Walk parallel to the East Front for a third of a mile and created elaborate stone-edged flowerbeds in the West Garden. Joseph Paxton was appointed Head Gardener in 1826 and his knowledge and enthusiasm inspired the 6th Duke. Plant-hunting expeditions were sponsored, resulting in the Arboretum, Pinetum and many exotic glasshouse plants. Paxton's most famous achievement was the Great Conservatory (demolished in 1920), which was constructed in wood, iron and glass. It covered three-quarters of an acre and it was here he coaxed the first *Victoria amazonica* into flower, named at the time *Victoria regia* as the link between the Queen and an amazon was considered inappropriate.

The 327-foot 'Conservative Wall' still exists bearing tender fruits and camellias. The Cascade was realigned to the Broad Walk and four reservoir lakes were dug to supply the Cascade and new Emperor Fountain, inspired by Peterhof — its jet in the Canal Pond can still reach 276 feet. The 46-foot Wellington Rock was hauled into position to dominate the Strid with other boulders that formed The Rockeries (now mostly planted). In 1960 geometric patterns of box and golden yew were introduced into Wyatville's beds. The round pond matches the size of Chiswick House's dome, so in this way the latter's Palladian ground plan has been recreated in golden box. Water, an integral part of Chatsworth's history, features in Angela Conner's recent water sculpture, *Revelation*. C.H.

1688 George London and Henry Wise commissioned to design and layout formal gardens.

1760 'Capability' Brown commissioned to landscape the gardens.

1826 Joseph Paxton (1803–65) appointed Head Gardener.

1960 West Garden replanted with box and yew in Wyatville stone beds, copying a central feature of Chiswick House's ground plan.

1998 Angela Conner's sculpture *Revelation*: the dull metal exterior opens to reveal a golden orb.

The rose garden.

The 'willow tree'.

Bird's-eye view of Chatsworth House and Park. Engaving by I. Kip after a drawing by Leendert Knijff (1650–1721).

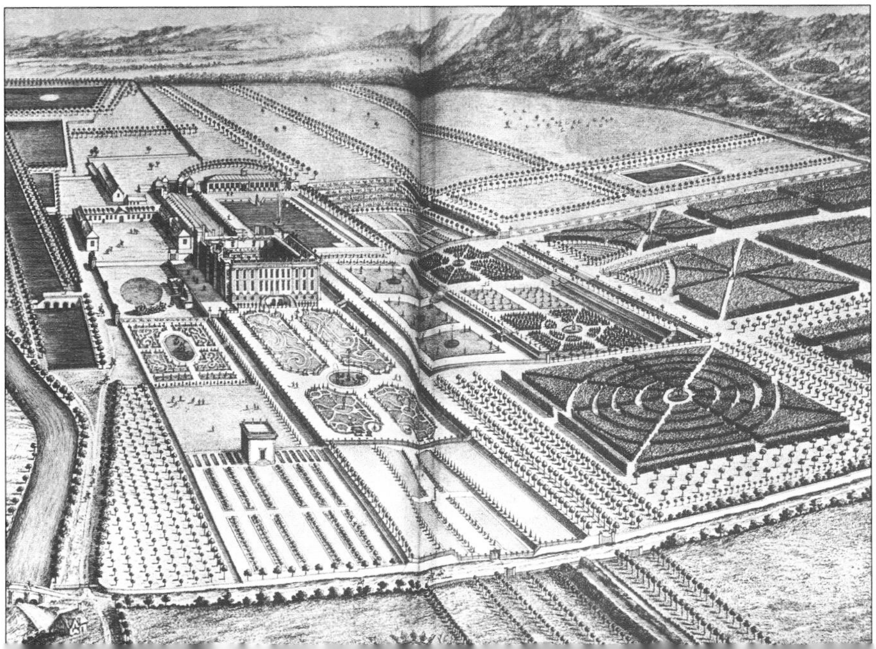

Yew topiary in the form of chess pieces.

c.1250/1300 Original pele tower and hall constructed.
c.1570/1590 Fortified house converted into more comfortable residence.
1688 Colonel Grahme moves to Levens Hall.
1694 Guillaume Beaumont creates the gardens.
c. 1800 Bagot family acquire Levens Hall.
1994 Tercentenary of gardens.
1994 Levens Hall receives the Garden of the Year Award from the Historic Houses Association.

Levens Hall

WESTMORLAND
ENGLAND

'We will endeavour to shew how the aire and genious of Gardens operate upon humane spirits towards virtue and sancitie, I meane in a remote, preparatory and instrumentall working. How Caves, Grotts, Mounts, and irregular ornaments of Gardens do contribute to contemplative and philosophicall Enthusiasms; [...] for these expedients do influence the soule and spirits of man, and prepare them for converse with good Angells.'

John Evelyn
friend of Colonel Grahme, in a letter to Sir Thomas Browne, 1657.

William III's succession to the English throne in 1688 inevitably led to changes at the Royal Court. Colonel James Grahme, hitherto Keeper of the King's Buckhounds, retired to Levens Hall, his newly acquired northern estate, accompanied by Guillaume Beaumont, erstwhile royal gardener at Hampton Court, whose services were also no longer required by the new regime.

Together they redefined and developed this garden and park on the southern fringe of the Lake District in a manner that attracted admirers from many miles around, in spite of the primitive communications prevailing towards the end of the 17th century. Indeed it was largely due to its isolated location that Levens Hall subsequently remained immune to changing fashion in garden design and today continues much as it was more than three hundred years ago.

Topiary is the key feature at Levens Hall, which was rumoured to have been won by Colonel Grahme in a card game. The garden design which Beaumont initiated in 1694 remains largely the same, together with the trees and bushes which he planted. Inevitably topiary more than three centuries old has grown out of all proportion, despite vigorous annual clipping. More than 90 giant yews now loom high over visitors' heads; an intricately shaped crowd of peacocks, chess pieces, large umbrellas and other wondrous shapes that contrive to make any other English topiary garden appear a trifle ordinary.

Guillaume Beaumont was a man of considerable taste and style in a particularly stylish age. It was a time of change in both architectural and garden design, as French flamboyance gave way to small scale, understated Dutch elegance. Ironically, this Frenchman, forced to seek fresh employment by a Dutch king, fashioned a perfect English garden in the Dutch style.

Dark green and golden yew together with box bushes are surrounded by low box hedging forming a *parterre* with contrasting planting, ranging from gleaming white tulips in late spring to yellow and white daisies, vibena and heliotrope in high summer. Levens Hall is truly a garden for all seasons, and is particularly striking in winter after flower beds have disappeared under a blanket of snow and dark yews become flecked with white. At this time the garden acquires a unique abstract quality which is quite exceptional. The entire history of Levens Hall has seen only ten head gardeners and they have ensured the continuity of Beaumont's concepts, considerably furthered by the care and diligence of the Bagot family, the owners for more than two centuries.

There are other fine topiary gardens in England ranging from Athelhampton and Parnham in Dorset to Packwood in Warwickshire as well as Beaumont's former gardens

The box parterre.

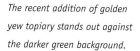

The recent addition of golden yew topiary stands out against the darker green background.

at Hampton Court. However Levens Hall is in a class of its own on account of its age, originality and maturity, together with a reassuring air of permanence and consistency in an ever-changing world. Appropriately in the year of its tercentenary Levens Hall was awarded the prestigious Christies / Historic Houses Association Garden of the Year Award. Guillaume Beaumont's high standards are undoubtedly being maintained. *P.B.*

Schönbrunn

VIENNA, AUSTRIA

The Dovecote in the eastern bosquet *garden.*

Trellis pavilion in the eastern Chamber Garden.

'With its gardens, site of the world's first zoo in 1751, Schönbrunn makes a remarkable baroque ensemble and a perfect example of Gesamtkunstwerk.*'*

UNESCO WORLD HERITAGE COMMITTEE REPORT, 1996.

Originally conceived in the 16th century as hunting grounds, Schönbrunn Park was first defined by a system of hunting paths. The gardens in the newly laid out 18th-century palace park were similarly divided by a geometric system of diagonal and radial avenues.

The area near the palace (constructed, 1696–1700) is characterised by a contrast between the open section of the main *parterres* and the flanking hedged sections, intersected by avenues. The main *parterre* with its 19th-century ornamental planting is located on the longitudinal axis of the palace. The conclusion of this overwhelming vista is formed by the Gloriette on Schönbrunn Mountain, a late-18th-century belvedere that provides a breathtaking view of Schönbrunn and Vienna.

Flanking the narrow sides of the palace to the west and east are the Chamber Gardens, which were not accessible to the public. These *giardini segreti* were enclosed by *berceaux* painted dark green, and had flower *parterres* at the centre. Adjacent to the eastern Chamber Garden [Kammergarten] is the 660-foot-long baroque Orangery (1754). It still contains the myrtle plant presented by the Grand Visier of Constantinople as a wedding gift to Empress Maria Theresa.

The bosquets flanking the main *parterres* contained geometrical mazes and 'chambers' in the interior. The intersections of the radial avenues were emphasised with fountains, and garden structures often stand as focal points at their ends. The geometrical pattern of the paths was continued up the slope of the Schönbrunn Mountain in the form of criss-crossing glades in the woods.

The soaring, up to 39-foot-high avenue walls are formed by precisely topiaried trees some of which are over 250 years old. Some avenues have vertically trimmed walls open at the top; others are covered by a tunnel-like roof of foliage. The resulting alternations of light and shade and the visual contacts with various pavilions, fountains and statues mitigate the occasional geometrical monotony of the long axes.

Contemporary view of the Roman Ruin, 1777.

1569 Emperor Maximilian II acquires the Katterburg, and lays out a hunting park.

1683 Hunting seat and park destroyed by the Turks during the Siege of Vienna.

1689 First ideal design for reconstruction of palace and park by Johann Fischer von Erlach for Emperor Leopold I.

1699 Layout of Orangery Garden.

1743–49 Reconstruction and extension of park by Empress Maria Theresa.

1749 Redesign of Chamber Gardens after plans by Louis Gervais and Jean Nicolas Jadot.

1750–55 Redesign of park, extension of *parterre*, addition of new star-shaped avenues.

1753 Creation of Botanical Garden.

1772 Construction of Gloriette based on plans by Johann Hetzendorf von Hohenberg.

1778 Opening of park to the public.

1801–02 Layout of Tyrolean Garden.

1869–86 Reworking of garden by Court Director of Gardens Adolf Vetter.

1896 Redesign of main parterre by Court Director of Gardens Anton Umlauft.

Bernado Berllotto, The Garden Side of the Imperial Palace, 1759.

Brief mention should be made of some of the key park structures around the *bosquet*. The visual conclusion of the avenue leading south-east from the palace is provided by the early neo-classical Obelisk Fountain (Johann Hetzendorf von Hohenberg, 1776). Consisting of an obelisk set on a grotto-like substructure, its cascades and fountains play beneath a terrace from which a view of the avenue and palace opens out. The Roman Ruin (1777) by Hetzendorf von Hohenberg, originally called the Ruins of Carthage, stands at the end point of another axis. Representing the upper part of ruins that have apparently sunk into the earth, its architectural fragments were taken from another building — the Neugebäude, an imposing Renaissance palace east of Vienna. This early example of the then fashionable romance of ruins was possibly influenced by Piranesi´s engravings and visions of phantasmagorical ruins. A circular, late-baroque menagerie (1751) forms the conclusion of the south-west diagonal axis. At the midpoint of the circle of animal cages stands an octagonal lookout pavilion. Unlike its model in Versailles, which is no longer extant, this menagerie is still in use, and is the oldest zoo in the world. To the west of the menagerie is the Botanical Garden, which originates from the baroque period. The 375-foot-long Palm House (1896) is a masterpiece of cast-iron architecture. *A.G.*

Castle Howard

YORKSHIRE
ENGLAND

Vanbrugh landscape seen from Henderskelf Lane: south lake, waterfall and Garrett's Bridge.

The Atlas fountain.

Curved, clipped hornbeam stilts beside the walled garden.

'Nobody had informed me that at one view I should see a palace, a town, a fortified city, temples on high places, woods worthy of being each a metropolis of the Druids, the noblest lawn in the world fenced by half the horizon and a mausoleum that would tempt one to be buried alive; in short, I have seen gigantic palaces before, but never a sublime one.'

HORACE WALPOLE

Castle Howard was the first building John Vanbrugh had ever designed and its successful realisation was thanks to the skills of architect, Nicholas Hawksmoor. The preliminary drawings and wood model produced in 1699 to replace the burnt out Henderskelf Castle inspired the Duke of Marlborough to approach them for Blenheim.

Very few private houses had been designed with such classical grandeur, boldness of outline and grouping to create 'movement'. Five miles of arrow-straight beech avenue lined the approach from York turning at the 100-foot-high Obelisk into double rows of lime leading to the house. Architectural features enhance the furthest reaches, starting with Hawksmoor's Carrmire Gate which straddles the road, Vanbrugh's military curtain wall and the fanfare Vanbrugh designed to greet arrivals — the Gatehouse. Away on the easterly reaches following the ancient track, Henderskelf Lane, which skirts Ray Wood, lie Vanbrugh's Temple of the Four Winds and Hawksmoor's Mausoleum and the Pyramid on St Anne's Hill. These furthest reaches mark the transition in English garden design from the Forest Style (radiating clipped avenues) to the Serpentine Style by the retention of the meandering ancient track. The Temple was inspired by Palladio's Villa Capra, based on mathematical proportions using the circle, the square and the principle of harmonic proportion: thus these buildings became part of the 'natural' world. Vanbrugh designed the South Lake and waterfalls down to the New River that flowed below the Temple. Hawksmoor's Mausoleum started the trend for great families to create appropriate last resting-places in their grounds rather than be buried at their parish churches.

George London advised on the layout of the gardens until his death in 1714; fortunately many of his Forest Style ideas were not implemented. His assistant, Stephen Switzer (1682–1745), created an 'incomparable Wood the highest pitch that Natural and Polite Gardening can possibley ever arrive to' by introducing a labyrinthine network of paths furnished with waterworks and statues in the ancient Ray Wood. Some 250 years later it became a living museum for the Sunningdale collection of rhododendrons including original plants collected by Sir Joseph Hooker from the Sikkim in 1852 as well as those of George Forrest, Frank Kingdon-Ward, Frank Ludlow and George Sherriff. The Great Lake to the north was not constructed until the 1790s although it had been proposed by Hawksmoor. In the 1850s W. A. Nesfield (1793–1881) was commissioned to design New Pleasure Grounds in the Italianate style for the grand south façade. The elaborate *parterres de broderie* were created in dwarf box with coloured gravels centred on the magnificent Atlas fountain which was exhibited at the Great Exhibition in 1851. All bar the outer hedges and fountain were swept away in the 1890s. The walled garden was part of George London's layout and was redesigned in 1976 into a series of rose gardens divided by curving clipped hornbeam. Their formality and serpentine form are a modern testament to the garden history that lies without the walls. *C.H.*

1699 3rd Earl of Carlisle commissions Vanbrugh and Hawksmoor and George London: house, gates, wall, Temple of the Four Winds (1726–28), Mausoleum (1728), Pyramid.
1718 Switzer redesigns Ray Wood.
1790 North lake created.
1850s Nesfield designs New Pleasure Gardens.
1968 James Russell introduces the Sunningdale collection into Ray Wood.
1976 Rose garden created in memory of Lady Cecilia Howard.

Vanbrugh's Temple of the Four Winds.

Blenheim Palace

WOODSTOCK, ENGLAND

'Having a very beautiful Situation (the West end looking down the Valley and River) may perhaps be thought proper for a distinct retired room of Pleasure — that kind of Detached Buildings have ever been extreamely valued where there has happened anything particularly fine for their Situation. And I believe there is not a finer Example than this.'

JOHN VANBRUGH
concerning the site of the greenhouse to Sarah Churchill, Duchess of Marlborough, 1709, quoted in Kerry Downes, *Vanbrugh — a Biography*, London: Sidgwick & Jackson, 1987.

The parterres de broderie.

12th–14th century: Woodstock, Royal Hunting Park with bower, water gardens and menagerie.
1705 Vanbrugh and Hawksmoor start work on Blenheim Palace, Henry Wise assists in *parterres*, tree avenues and walled garden.
1720s River Glyme canalised under bridge.
1763 'Capability' Brown arrives.
1896 and 1925 Achille Duchêne works on the garden.

The landscapes surrounding Blenheim Palace are acknowledged as the masterpiece of Lancelot 'Capability' Brown (1716–1783). The history and evolution of the park provided a sublime backdrop while the grand order created by Sir John Vanbrugh (1664–1726), Nicholas Hawksmoor (1661–1736) and Henry Wise (1653–1738) for the 1st Duke and Duchess of Marlborough was grassed into beautiful landscape.

Medieval Woodstock Palace included a Royal Hunting Park enclosed by an inner ditch and high stone wall. Here Henry II courted the Fair Rosamund and Rosamund's Well is the relic of her bower and water gardens inspired by Arab gardens in Sicily. In 1705 Queen Anne conferred 'Woodstock Manor-House, and all that ... ground called Woodstock Park' on John Churchill, 1st Duke of Marlborough. Such exalted status required buildings and grounds as impressive as Castle Howard so the architect Vanbrugh was engaged with Hawksmoor to design a sumptuous Palace named for the victory of Blenheim. Henry Wise helped to create gardens of military precision without a cohesive design leaving Vanbrugh's magnificent bridge soaring over the trickling River Glyme. Sarah, Duchess of Marlborough, opined: 'Tis a chaos, which only God Almighty could finish', and so it remained until after her death in 1744. 'Capability' Brown arrived in 1763, designing a naturalistic landscape for the Palace and its more than 2,470 acres using his hallmark features: the 'belt', an outer ring of trees that provided shelter and a backdrop through which visitors could circumnavigate the park while enjoying carefully orchestrated vistas; and the 'clump', groups of trees that were designed to seem random but displayed or concealed vistas to and from the Palace or the landscape.

Horace Walpole wrote that Vanbrugh's bridge 'begs for a drop of water', and Brown's consummate skill with water magnificently transformed Blenheim's landscape by creating the Great Lakes, a sinuous river and two cascades. His lakes covered 148 acres following the curving valley and giving purpose to the bridge; he calculated the correct height, adjusting it by constructing a downstream canal. An artificial river was created from the main lake and upper cascade to the River Evenlode which 'flows with a serpentine sweep through an expanded vale, embellished with scattered groups of flourishing young plantation.... Its style partakes rather of the beautiful than the sublime' (W. Mavor, *New Description of Blenheim*, 1789). The upper and lower cascades created picturesque drama in the course of the artificial river. During the 1770s and 1780s William Chambers (1723–1796) designed a New Bridge below the cascade and The Temple of Diana. By 1892 Brown's lawns next to the Palace had become overgrown shrubberies, and its imposing architecture needed a return to grand formality. The 9th Duke approached French landscape architect Achille Duchêne (1866–1947) who had restored the *parterres* at Vaux-le-Vicomte. The

Herm statuary surrounding a niche.

latter designed a *parterre de broderie* with tubbed orange trees and statues for the eastern side. He returned in 1925 to design a *parterre d'eau* modelled on Versailles, the low box hedging enclosing water channelled from Rosamund's Well and brought to life with fountains. The 9th Duke wrote to Duchêne: 'It is only by thought, constant thought and mature reflection, that artists have left their great works for the enjoyment of posterity'. Posterity does indeed enjoy Blenheim's great works which still provoke thought and reflection. *C.H.*

Vanbrugh's bridge over the River Glyme.

Governor's Palace

WILLIAMSBURG, VA, USA

An arbour in the Ballroom Garden.

'One hundred and fifty acres of beautiful ground finely broke planted with tulip trees, oaks and pines and watered by rivulets. I am told that the meadows are covered with white clover in Spring.'

GOVERNOR NORBERT BERKELEY, BARON DE BOUTECOURT
in 1768, shortly after arriving to succeed Governor Francis Fauquier. Cited in Peter Martin, *The Pleasure Gardens of Virginia,* Princeton NJ, 1991.

In 1695 the College of William and Mary was founded at Middle Plantation in the British colony of Virginia, and by 1698 it was decided that this location was ideal for creating a new, imposing capital. The formal and informal landscaping of the Governor's Palace was a crucial element within the civic design. In 1706 £3,000 was allocated to this task, however, by its completion in 1722, under Governor Alexander Spotswood, the elaborate building and its gardens had aroused considerable criticism.

The restoration and re-creation of Colonial Williamsburg in the 1920s can be attributed to to the vision of the Reverend W.A.R. Goodwin and the generosity of John D. Rockefeller who created a living (and in some cases contested) textbook of colonial American garden design. In restoring the Palace gardens, original wall foundations were excavated whose gate openings have determined the lines of garden walks. The 'Bodleian Plate', an engraved copper plate of c. 1740 held in the Ashmolean Museum at Oxford University, shows the Palace with oval beds in the forecourt and diamond-shaped beds in the *parterre* behind the Palace.

The grand central vista created by Spotswood on the north–south axis imbues the Governor's Palace with a sense of power and order. Palace Green is flanked by Palace Street, a double avenue of Catalpa trees spaced 100 feet apart meeting in a gracious oval at the Palace gates. The forecourt is walled, and entry is through an ornate gate decorated with royal heraldic beasts, simple oval beds providing the only planting. Geometric formal gardens frame the house on all sides.

Spotswood created terraces in the Dutch style to the west of the Palace descending

1706 Construction of Governor's Palace begins.
1710 Governor Alexander Spotswood initiates creation of gardens.
1751 Governor Robert Dinwiddie adds ballroom and supper room.
1926 Start of restoration.
1934 Colonial Williamsburg opens to the public.

William and Mary style is evidenced in these formal flowerbeds.

to a canal (or what he described as 'the Fish-Pond and Falling Gardens') and to the north-east a bowling-green. The orchard and kitchen gardens are walled and terraced formally for maximum yields; part of the orchards became a burial ground during the Revolution. In the Palace Governor Robert Dinwiddie added a ballroom and supper room, steps from which lead to the central axis of the Ballroom Garden, a *parterre* whose clipped diamonds of *Ilex vomitaria* and topiary seem to form a dance pattern. A cross-axis leads away to the bowling-green to the east and to orchards in the west. Two long, rectangular flowerbeds continue the main axis flanking a central flowerbed, a design which again recalls Dutch canal gardens. The transition is gently marked from the *parterre* to the park by ornate wrought ironwork — an echo of iron *repoussé* specialist Jean Tijou (fl. 1680s-1710s). The pavilions, classically topped with cupolas on each corner, were necessaries whose 'soil' was carefully collected and recycled in the gardens.

The holly maze is modelled on the one designed for Hampton Court Palace and the mount above the ice-house provides a vista into the maze and formal gardens as well as over the 63 acres of park surrounding the Palace. The Governor's Palace combines the architectural symmetry of the late 17th-/early 18th-century Dutch style echoed in the immediately surrounding gardens with the naturalistic informality of picturesque prospects into the park where cattle or deer grazed. The gardens have been furnished with details from the original inventories such as wooden settees, wrought-iron gates and lead finials and urns.

C.H.

The north–south vista to the house has a quiet formality.

Ilex vomitaria *in the Ballroom Garden.*

Peterhof

ST PETERSBURG, RUSSIA

'Gardens immense,
More glorious than the gardens of Armide.'

PUSHKIN

Work on Peterhof began during a period of war, and in 1714 the first drainage and reclamation work began. On 16 November 1715 Peter the Great wrote a memorandum and in 1717 an engraving was made of a small three-winged palace. Alongside the Tsar the architects Johann Friedrich Braunstein, Jean-Baptiste Alexandre Le Blond (1679–1719) and Niccolò Michetti (d. 1759) were responsible for the first building phase up to 1724. Later Michail Zemtov was involved followed by Bartolomeo Rastrelli (1700–71), who enlarged the palace extensively from 1745 and gave it the look of another Tsarskoe Selo.

A major feature of Peterhof is its upper and lower gardens whose design can be ascribed to Le Blond. In front of the palace large lawn *parterres* and ponds were installed, quietly mirroring the palace itself; while behind the palace, the dramatic descent to the Gulf of Finland offered the opportunity of installing a Grand Cascade and other water features. The palace occupies a central position between these two areas of garden, which afforded Peterhof great fame even during the lifetime of Peter the Great. The

Catherine House in Monplaisir Garden.

The six levels of the Grand Cascade.

Engraving by Niquet after a drawing by Louis Nicolas Lespinasse (1734–1808), c. 1784.

Across the dramatic descent of the Grand Cascade the palace affords views of the Gulf of Finland.

1709 Alexandre-Jean-Baptiste Le Blond, pupil of Le Nôtre, publishes designs in Dezallier d'Argenville's *La Théorie et la pratique du jardinage*.

1715 Le Blond begins work on Peterhof.

1745 Bartolomeo Rastrelli takes over work on Peterhof.

central feature is a six-level cascade at the foot of the palace whose fountain, driven by hydraulic machinery, reaches 25 feet. The central axis is decorated with 17 statues, 29 bas-reliefs and dozens of fountains and streams, ending in the figures of Samson and the Lion — a symbol of the ruler but also of the victorious battle in Poltava on St Samson's Day, 27 June 1709. Given the proximity of the sea all the statues have either a connection to water or to Peter's military victories, as he had captured this area from Swedish armies. Thus we find a Perseus fountain, and a Triton fountain created by Carlo Rastrelli (Bartolomeo's father) in 1726, river gods, warriors, and in the upper garden in the middle of the pool, as pendant to Samson, a Neptune fountain, a piece from Nuremberg of 1650–58 which was only installed in 1799.

There are also many amusing water features, such as the Umbrella Fountain, the seat which squirts water and a Little Oak Fountain, whose branches run with water, as well as Peter's own Pyramid Fountain, Basket Fountain and the Sun Fountain decorated with dolphins. On the middle axis of the Monplaisir Palace (1714–23) are the Roman Fountains, based on those in St Peter's Square in Rome (Karl Blank, 1739), and the Dragon Fountain; nearby is the Wheat Fountain which is surrounded by four streams called clocks. The Eve Fountain (Giovanni Bonatti, 1726) was derived from the Hermitage's Adam Fountain of 1718–21 by the same architect. The château of Marly (1719–23) inspired Peter's Golden Hill Cascade of 1721–23.

All these influences created a baroque garden which looked to western European stylistic elements but which Peter the Great transformed into a unique mixture. Thus he showed that even in climatically unpropitious and provincial regions of Europe great artistic achievements could be created. *M.K.*

Stowe

BUCKINGHAM, ENGLAND

'The whole space is divided into a number of scenes, each distinguished with taste and fancy; and the changes are so frequent, sudden and complete, the transitions so artfully conducted, that the same ideas are never continued or repeated to satiety.'

THOMAS WHATELY
Observations on Modern Gardening, 1770.

The interrelation of buildings in the landscape is an important feature.

c. 1680 Formal gardens laid out by Sir Richard Temple.
From 1715: Transformation to grand baroque layout by Viscount Cobham.
From 1735: Gradual naturalising of gardens.
From 1751: Further landscaping and naturalising by Earl Temple.
1848 Sale of contents of the house.
1922 Purchase of estate by Stowe School (opened 1923).
1990 Gardens formally conveyed to National Trust ownership.

Stowe was the most famous garden in Britain in the 18th century and also the most influential, its inspiration reaching through Europe to Russia. It had more visitors and was better known than any other garden of the time. It was a garden, though, that developed and changed through the century, and embodied different phases of style and approach. From an inherited simple, formal layout, Viscount Cobham (1675–1749) created the most magnificent and elaborate baroque garden imaginable, under the direction of the Royal Gardener, Charles Bridgeman (d. 1738). The house stood on the top of a great slope, leading down through *parterres* and a white poplar walk to an octagonal basin. Geometry dominated: straight *allées* crossed and connected in an area bounded by a bastioned ha-ha, and buildings were set at key visual points by Sir John Vanbrugh.

In the 1730s there was a dramatic change. Cobham employed William Kent (1685–1748) to redesign an area to the east which became known as the Elysian fields, with a naturalising of the landscape and a group of buildings which had a political meaning. Cobham had fallen out with the Whig government in 1733, and a Whig Opposition group (the 'Cobham Cubs') formed round him. Ancient medieval and Saxon virtues consonant with Whig Opposition ideology were championed through such buildings as the Gothic Temple (James Gibbs, 1741), while the Prime Minister, Sir Robert Walpole, was satirised as a headless statue beside a ruined rubble wall called the Temple of Modern Virtue. Kent and Gibbs also continued a theme announced earlier by Vanbrugh, of erotic love, and expressed further themes of friendship, valour and independence of thought through buildings such as the Temple of Friendship and the Temple of British Worthies.

'Capability' Brown (1716–83) worked at Stowe in the 1740s as head gardener. It is thought that he designed the curving grassed Grecian Valley, which is very much in the style he was to go on to employ so widely elsewhere. After Cobham's death, Earl Temple continued the process of landscaping the grounds and obliterating Bridgeman's geometry, but added some further buildings (and modified existing ones) to emphasise aspects of triumph and empire: thus the Grecian Temple became the Temple of Concord and Victory, and a monument to Captain Cook was erected. The First Marquis of Buckingham continued in the same vein to conclude what Earl Temple had started. The gardens were substantially complete by 1813, and the 19th century was a story of debts and disaster which left them virtually unaltered. Saved by the opening of Stowe School in 1923, the estate survived, but conservation was a struggle. Since 1990 the National Trust has worked on an ambitious programme of restoring not only the buildings but the appearance of the gardens in their late 18th-century maturity *M.S.*

The Gothic Temple.

The Temple of British Worthies.

The Palladian Bridge.

Villa Gamberaia

SETTIGNANO, ITALY

'It combines in an astonishingly small space, yet without the least sense of overcrowding almost every typical excellence of the old Italian garden: fine circulation of sunlight and air about the house; abundance of water; easy access to dense shade; sheltered walks with different points of view; variety of effect produced by skillful use of different levels; and finally breadth and simplicity of composition.'

EDITH WHARTON
Italian Villas and their Gardens, 1904.

1619 Villa Gamberaia becomes the property of Jacopo and Andrea Lappi.
1688 Gamberaia mortgaged to pay off debts on the death of Andra Lappi.
1717 The property is bought by the Capponi family, creators of Gamberaia's existing gardens.

The lemon garden.

Right: The south façade with topiary and pink azaleas on the parterre.

The secret garden with its white wisteria and terracotta vases.

For generations Gamberaia has been seen as one of the most perfect examples of garden architecture. The American novelist and travel writer, Edith Wharton's description of it still holds good today, despite the garden's virtual destruction during World War II. It is most fortunate that it was bought by Signor Marcello Marchi in its ruined state and perfectly restored.

Villa Gamberaia was built at the beginning of the 17th century for Zenobi Lappi. In 1619 it passed to his nephew, Andrea, said to have been a passionate builder of fountains. No trace remains of the Lappi family in the garden, for it was under the Capponi, who bought the villa in 1717, that the site assumed its present form.

The villa stands at the mid-point of a bowling-green. This stretch of impeccably smooth grass runs the length of the site. On one side it is flanked by buildings and on the other it is enclosed by the high retaining wall of the upper terraces. The wall is decorated with painted panels and topped by majestic urns. At its northern end the alley is closed by a mossy nymphaeum standing in the shadow of ancient cypress trees. To the south, a statue of Diana stands silhouetted against the magnificent view of the Arno valley.

Opposite the villa, elaborate wrought-iron gates lead to a secret garden. The retaining walls of the upper terraces enclose the garden on three sides. These walls are divided into panels by bands of rustic stonework. Smiling statues stand in niches. Four flights of balustraded steps link the secret garden to the lemon garden on one side and the *bosco*, or wood, on the other. The *bosco* is planted with ilex and cypress. This 'wild' area was a vital element of the Renaissance garden, and it creates a pleasing contrast to the manicured perfection of the bowling alley.

A pretty loggia on the first floor of the villa's south façade overlooks the water *parterre*. This area was once a traditional *parterre* garden planted with herbs and roses. When Princess Ghyka of Serbia bought Gamberaia at the end of the 19th century she replaced the flowerbeds with sheets of clear water. The effect of this transformation is magical. Narrow paths run between the clipped hedges that surround the pools and the composition is completed by a semicircular cypress arcade. The magnificent view is glimpsed through arches that pierce the cypress hedges of the arcade. A terrace runs along the western side of the villa. It is bounded by a wall on which charming statues of dogs stand. Beyond the dogs and the roses that entwine them, there is a glorious view of Florence on the plain below.

H.A.

Schwetzingen

NEAR HEIDELBERG
GERMANY

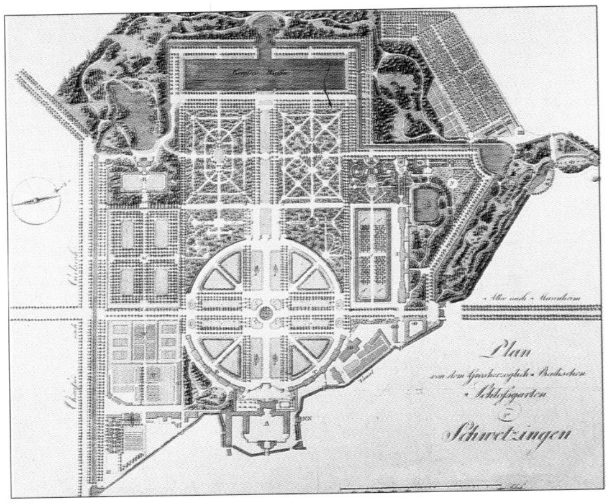

Plan of the gardens by Johann Michael Zeyher, 1809.

Pigage's Birdbath, c. 1762.

Pigage's Perspective, 1766–72.

'Before I die I want to carry out one more duty and enjoy one consolation: I want to see Schwetzingen again.'

VOLTAIRE.

Schwetzingen Palace park is one of the loveliest gardens created in the latter half of the 18th century; and it has survived almost unaltered to this day. Under the rule of Prince Elector Karl Theodor of the Palatinate, its contractor, the park went through two entirely different phases of development. The first was that of a geometrically arranged rococo garden. This was followed, only a few years later, by the design of an early English landscape park. It speaks for Karl Theodor´s pride in his accomplishment that the rococo garden was left unaltered when, bowing to the tastes of the day, he had it expanded to incorporate a landscape park.

Before undertaking the redesign, Karl Theodor took over hunting grounds with radial cuts through the woods, supplanting it by a stately rococo park. First a circular *parterre* was laid out in front of the palace, around which were grouped two circular structures with orangery, theatre and festival halls to the east, and two *berceaux* to the west. The main axis of the *parterre* is underscored by two rows of trees along the rectangular middle zones. Located at the point of intersection of main and transverse axes is the round Arion Fountain. Four square *parterres de broderie* flank the fountain, and two rectangular *parterres à l´anglaise* abut these to the east and west. To the west, beyond the *parterre* zone, are *bosquets* divided into two halves by the extension of the main avenue. This vista extends beyond the great pond to the rolling hills of the Palatinate Forest.

Located in the northern *bosquet* zone is the large orangery, the Parnassus with Temple of Apollo on an artificial hill, and, in front of these, the open-air theatre and the unusual, wave-shaped Birdbath. A high point in the garden is the early neo-classical Bath House group (1766–72). A latticework path leads from the Bath House to the Bird House, an oval-shaped *berceau* with bird cages and a central fountain, where sheet-copper birds perched on the upper edge of the lattice spew water (a motif borrowed from the labyrinth in Versailles). Interrupted by a wide open space, the dark, trellised tunnel leads to a grotto room with a view of a painted ideal landscape, representing 'The End of the World'. This is known as the 'Perspective', a masterpiece of *trompe-l'oeil* architecture.

Beyond, to the north and west, is the English Garden, laid out by the renowned landscape gardener Friedrich Ludwig von Sckell (1750–1823) in the 1770s. This is the site of the famous 'Arboretum Theodoricum' with the Temple of Forest Botany. The ruins of a mock Roman aqueduct (1776–79) form the culmination of this section of the garden to the north. Further artificial structures are a Chinese Bridge and the ruins of a Temple of Mercury (1784–87), which serves as a lookout tower. Across from it is the Turkish Garden with its famous Mosque (1780–85). The interior court is enclosed by a latticed walk embellished by sayings from the Koran which enjoin the visitor to practise tolerance and humility.

A.G.

Pigage's Mercury Temple, 1778.

1427 The Count Palatines of the Rhine acquire Schwetzingen Castle.

1720–24 Palace garden laid out under Karl Philipp, Prince Elector of the Palatinate.

1748–50 Building of the North Circular House as orangery, by Alessandro Galli da Bibiena and Guillaume d'Hauberat for Karl Theodor, Prince Elector of the Palatinate.

1752 Theatre annex to North Circular House by Nicolas de Pigage.

1753–54 Erection of South Circular House as festival hall, by Franz Wilhelm Rabaliatti.

1753–58 Prince Elector Karl Theodor entrusts architect de Pigage and Court Gardener Johann Ludwig Petri with redesign of palace garden.

1761 Extension of park by de Pigage.

1761–76 Open-air theatre with Temple of Apollo by de Pigage.

1762 Concert by seven-year-old Mozart in the Circle.

1776–79 Layout of Wiesental by von Sckell.

1802 Layout of Arboretum by Court Gardener Michael Zeyher for Grand Duke Karl von Baden.

1924 Palace garden opened to the public.

1970–75 Reconstruction of *parterres*.

Rousham

OXFORDSHIRE, ENGLAND

'The most engaging of all Kent's works.'

HORACE WALPOLE
On Modern Gardening, 1770

Rousham, between Oxford and Banbury, has preserved William Kent's landscaping of the late 1730s remarkably intact. Kent was brought in by General Dormer, who inherited Rousham on his brother's death in 1737, to alter an existing formal garden by Charles Bridgeman. While respecting the basic structure of Bridgeman's work and keeping some of the earlier features such as the straight Elm Walk, Kent effected a total transformation in terms of design, effect and meaning. He created a series of pictures or tableaux within the garden, which depend on being seen in the correct sequence, and at the same time provided contrasting views outside. The garden itself is classical — militaristically so on the upper level, with the figures of the Lion Attacking a Horse and the Dying Gladiator, and rurally in the lower part, with Pan and Faun in the Vale of Venus. The sculpture on the upper level is of stone and that on the lower level is of lead to emphasize the contrast. Horace Walpole described Rousham as Kent's most engaging work, saying it was fit for the retreat of a Roman emperor. There are therefore parallels with the retirement of General Dormer after a long and successful military career.

While the inward views of the garden are classical, those outside the garden were quite different. Over the River Cherwell (the boundary of the property), Kent added a Gothic porch to the mill, metamorphosing it into the Temple of the Mill. He also erected a Gothic eyecatcher, an arched screen in a distant field on the hill opposite. Thus the eye was drawn outside to reminders of a native medieval past, England's own heritage.

Rousham is, as landscape gardens go, comparatively small, and Kent's triumph was to create a number of surprises by concealing scenes before they were frontally visible. Thus, the upper walk passes on top of the Praeneste Arcade although the visitor does not know it at the time. The centrepiece, the Vale of Venus, is hidden from view until the visitor emerges from the Elm (now Lime) Walk. Kent's approach was that of an artist: he devised his set-piece scenes as major elements and linked them cleverly. His long sojourn in Italy had given him a taste for Italian gardens and plantings, and the cascades at Rousham owe something to the villa gardens such as Aldobrandini. Kent's drawings also suggested Italianate cypresses, though there were some innovations such as underplanting of flowering shrubs among the trees.

Kent's importance in the evolution of the landscape garden is considerable. Although he did not totally abolish straight lines, in Walpole's words he leapt the fence and saw that all nature was a garden. He handled wood, lawns and water in increasingly naturalistic ways, and he established the idea of the circuit, which was to play so crucial a part in the design of Stourhead and Painshill among others. His strong pictorial approach was also adopted by many designers later in the century, both in England and abroad.

M.S.

The sculpture Lion Attacking a Horse in the upper garden.

The Praeneste Arcade.

The rose-filled parterres.

1720s Bridgeman: formal geometrical layout.
from 1738: Kent transforms garden into series of pictures.

The statue of Pan in the Vale of Venus in the lower garden.

Painshill

COBHAM, ENGLAND

'The spot is laid out in an elegant garden taste [...] the space before the house is full of ornament; the ground is prettily varied; and several sorts of beautiful trees are disposed on the sides in little open plantations.'

THOMAS WHATELY
Observations on Modern Gardening, 1770

Above: The Gothic Temple.

Right: A perfectly framed distant view.

1738 Charles Hamilton moves in to Painshill.
1773 Hamilton retires to Bath; succeeded by Benjamin Bond Hopkins.
1948 Estate split up into lots.
1981 Painshill Park Trust set up to restore gardens.

Painshill, near Cobham in Surrey, was the achievement of one man, the owner, the Hon. Charles Hamilton, who between 1738 and 1773 created a masterly landscape garden from unpromising Surrey heathland. Although he may have inherited one or two formal elements from previous owners, the grounds as a whole (gardens plus park) show Hamilton pushing more and more in the direction of natural appearance while making the experience of going round an artistic one by means of ever-changing pictures and garden buildings which continually surprise by being seen at different distances and angles. Painshill is one of the great circuit gardens, where it is necessary to follow the series of visual experiences in the correct sequence. Buildings seen initially in the far distance are not approached directly, and have probably been forgotten when one comes upon them close up later in the circuit, while, conversely, buildings seen close at an early stage now appear distant themselves.

It has been calculated that there are 100 or more vistas, i.e. framed views, at Painshill, across the lake, between islands and so on. This makes the circuit endlessly productive of new sights and surprises: nor is it in any case a simple circuit, moving from lake level to a hill and a plateau looking down on the lake. Not only is the visual picture continually changing but the mood is skilfully varied, with buildings and their surrounding plantings combining to produce an effect. Thus the ruined Mausoleum (a Roman triumphal arch) is set in unkempt grass and surrounded by yews to give what was described at the time as a 'dreary effect', while in contrast the beautiful light classical Temple of Bacchus was set in a lawn of colourful shrubs to lift the spirits. Likewise, the rustic Hermitage, a retreat for meditation, was placed at the edge of a dark, gloomy wood of evergreens.

Painshill is a garden of illusion too. Part of the subtlety of Hamilton's design is that things are not always what they seem. The lake cannot be seen all at once and has

deceived many visitors into thinking it is larger than it is. It also appears to be a lake, canal or river when seen from different points. Similarly, the pine forest in the western part of the grounds seems extensive at ground level until you climb the Tower and are able to see how confined in area it is.

Hamilton was passionately interested in plantings, and many trees and shrubs were brought in especially from North America. These made for greater botanical interest but also enabled Hamilton to create his landscape with a wider palette than was available to earlier designers such as William Kent.

One of the most extraordinary creations at Painshill was Grotto Island. Tufa, a limestone rock, was used to dress a brick core for rocks, niches, an arch and a magnificent grotto. The grotto had a main chamber 36 feet across, decorated inside with crystals, spars and stalactites. The underside of the bridge and a long tunnel to the main chamber were similarly ornamented. The gardens have been restored by Painshill Park Trust Ltd.

M.S.

Architecture is glimpsed between the water and shrubs.

A tufa niche on Grotto Island.

Middleton Place CHARLESTON, SOUTH CAROLINA, USA

Schadow's Wood Nymph.

'The Property [...] is esteemed the most beautiful in this part of the country.'

FRANÇOIS, DUC DE LA ROCHEFOUCAULD-LIANCOURT
1769, *Travels through the United States,* London, 1799.

While the English colonies of the New World were still in their infancy, a grand formal garden was carved out of marshy land on what is now the coast of South Carolina. Conceived by the plantation owner Henry Middleton and designed by an unknown English landscape gardener, the grounds of Middleton Place are America's oldest extant gardens.

The gardens are a reflection of the architectural style of gardening popular in England and Europe in the 17th and early 18th century, superbly married to the natural and wild beauty of the Carolina Low Country. They were begun in 1741, the year that Henry Middleton built his Jacobean-style manor house on property acquired as dowry when he married his wife. The house, which was destroyed in 1865 during the height of the Civil War, was built on a bluff overlooking the Ashley River. As was typical of a manor house, an expansive greensward stretched from the estate's main gate to the house. To the south and east of the house the day-to-day business of Middleton's rice-growing enterprise took precedence. But to the north and west of the house, the formal gardens, designed both to please and to impress, stretched to the broad Ashley River. The gardens took ten years to complete, and relied on massive amounts of slave labour.

Laid out on a triangular grid, Middleton's formal gardens are based on the principles elucidated by André Le Nôtre at Versailles and Vaux-le-Vicomte. Precise geometries, grand gestures and elongated vistas predominate. A main axis runs the length of the estate. Starting at the entrance gate, the axis runs across the ruins of the house, through a *parterre* garden and a terraced grass lawn, across two butterfly-shaped lakes, and finally terminates in the gentle curve of the Ashley itself. Paths and *allées* divide the rest of the property into a series of small enclosed gardens, which afford a sense of privacy while providing views of the marsh and surrounding woodland. While there were once statues at most of the critical focal points, only one of the original statues survived the ravages of war and neglect that once nearly overwhelmed Middleton. That statue, the Wood Nymph (c. 1810) carved by Johann Rudolf Schadow, now rests at the end of the Azalea Pool.

The trees and plants of Middleton Place tell their own fascinating tale. One of the most loved trees of the American South is the live oak, and among the largest known oaks is the Middleton Oak. Believed to be nearly 1,000 years old, the tree was used by the Indians as a trail marker long before Europeans ever saw the Carolina shores. With a limb spread of 145 feet, the oak still presides over the gardens. Also of great horticultural interest are the camellias. The renowned French botanist André Michaux visited Middleton Place in 1786, and brought four *Camellia japonica*. These natives of Japan were planted in the front *parterre*, and are among the first camellias planted in American soil. One miraculously still survives and continues to bloom. *S.G.M.*

The House Museum.

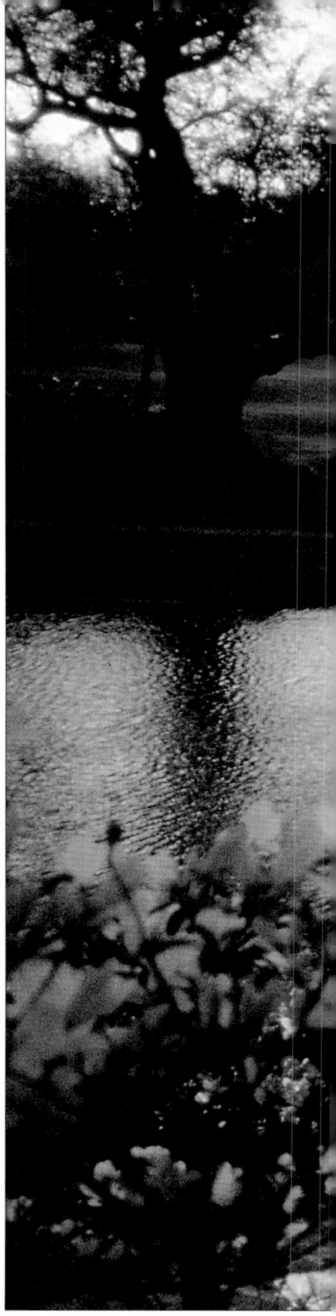

The terraced lawns.

The Azalea Hillside and Halfmoon Bridge.

1741 Henry Middleton begins work on the gardens.
1786 French botanist André Michaux visits Middleton bringing four camellias, which become among the first to be planted in the Americas.
1865 Union troops destroy the main dwelling at Middleton and desecrate the grounds during the Civil War.
c.1870 William Middleton plants some of the first *Azalea indicas* to be grown on American soil.
1925 Mr. J. J. Pringle Smith and his wife, Heningham Ellett Smith, inherit Middleton Place and begin work to restore the gardens.
1941 Garden Club of America awards Middleton Place the Bulkley Medal and proclaims Middleton to be 'the most interesting and important Garden in America'.
1974 Middleton Place Foundation is established.
1991 The International Committee on Monuments and Sites names Middleton Place one of the six United States gardens of international importance.

Stourhead

WILTSHIRE, ENGLAND

'One of the most picturesque scenes in the world.'

HORACE WALPOLE
on the view from the Temple of Apollo.

Stourhead, although much modified in respect of plantings, represents substantially the creation of its owner, Henry Hoare II, between 1744 and 1780. Some planting of firs may have taken place earlier, but work on the garden effectively began after the death of Hoare's wife in 1743. His initial concept, fuelled by a three-year Grand Tour spent mostly in Italy, was the composition of a classical landscape mediated via the paintings of Claude Lorrain and Gaspard Dughet. This entailed the damming of streams and small ponds to form the lake, around which one walked, with views across it changing continually. Buildings modelled on actual classical Roman originals were placed strategically round and above the lake, e.g. the Pantheon and the Temple of Apollo. Visually it would evoke an imagined classical scene (Hoare spoke of one view forming a 'charming Gaspard picture') but the visitor was brought back from pagan to Christian thoughts by the prominence of the church and the Bristol Cross erected in 1764.

It is possible to apply a Virgilian interpretation to the circuit. The first building, the Temple of Flora, has an inscription from Book VI of the *Aeneid*: 'Begone, you who are uninitiated'. This warning is itself the key, for the circuit mirrors Aeneas's journey to found Rome in that same book of Virgil's epic. The grotto represents the underworld, and Hoare even quoted Virgil to his daughter: 'Easy is the descent to hell, but to find your way back to the upper air, that is the hard task'. The slope down into the grotto is accordingly gradual while steep steps up are found at the far end. The River God points the way up the steps, the figure being taken from an engraving of the god of the River Tiber pointing the way to Aeneas. After the grotto the Pantheon is encountered, as if to indicate that Aeneas has reached Rome. The central statue in the Pantheon is that of Hercules, symbol of physical strength and moral courage, who often featured in gardens. A sub-theme may be the Choice of Hercules, a familiar Renaissance image (and one which appeared in Hoare's own collection of paintings), wherein Hercules has to choose between the steep path of virtue and the easy path to vice or pleasure. Further on in the circuit there is just such a choice, between the steep zig-zag path up to the Temple of Apollo and a gentle descent back to the lake.

In later years Hoare responded to garden fashion by incorporating other, non-classical, features. These included a Chinese Umbrello, a Turkish Tent, a rustic Hermitage and an enormous 'medieval' tower some way away from the circuit.

Stourhead was immensely inspirational in England and abroad, both for its stunning visual beauty and for its associationism. Many elements of Stourhead found their way into other gardens, for example Wörlitz. It was widely visited, and designers from the continent would often come to get ideas for development back home. *M.S.*

The Pantheon.

- 1744 Work on the gardens starts.
- 1785 Henry Hoare II dies; succeeded by Sir Richard Colt Hoare.
- 1838–94 Many new species of tree introduced.
- 1894–1938 Further plantings, especially azaleas and rhododendrons.
- 1946 The National Trust takes over.

The River God in the Grotto.

The Temple of Flora.

Sanssouci

POTSDAM, GERMANY

One of a pair of flanking pavilions which separates the palace from the so-called 'Lark Heathlands'.

1660 Friedrich Wilhelm makes Potsdam his second residence in addition to Berlin. During his reign, landscaping work in Potsdam begins.

1740 Friedrich II becomes King of Prussia.

1745–47 Sanssouci Palace and Park are built and laid out according to Friedrich II's ideas.

1785 Friedrich Wilhelm II, becomes Prussian King (to 1797). New Garden and Peacock Island are created.

1795 Friedrich Wilhelm III becomes King of Prussia.

1816 Peter Joseph Lenné comes to Potsdam.

1816 Commencement of work on the Glienicke landscape garden.

1826 Work begins on the Charlottenhof landscape garden for Crown Prince Friedrich Wilhelm.

1833 First plans for layout of Babelsberg Park, on the eastern bank of the River Havel. Peter Joseph Lenné´s plans for beautifying the Potsdam area.

1840 Friedrich Wilhelm IV becomes Prussian King. Further expansion of Potsdam Park until Lenné's death in 1866.

1990 Potsdam and Berlin Gardens included in World Cultural Heritage list.

'Quand je serai là, je serai sans souci!'

FRIEDRICH II OF PRUSSIA

Sanssouci is the most important legacy of garden design left to the world by Friedrich II of Prussia [Frederick the Great]. Now about 700 acres in area, the park is a unique ensemble of gardens, palace and garden buildings which was begun under the king´s supervision in the mid 18th century and expanded in the 19th by Friedrich Wilhelm IV.

When his work on the gardens commenced in 1744, Friedrich II was following in the footsteps of his forebears. Towards the middle of the previous century the Prince Elector of Brandenburg, Friedrich Wilhelm (1620–88) had already chosen Potsdam as his second seat of government, connected Potsdam Island by bridges with the surrounding areas, began to develop them, and erected several pleasure seats and laid-out gardens.

The focal point of the park is the palace rising above six sweeping vine terraces. Friedrich´s summer residence, Sanssouci, formed the nucleus of all subsequent park designs in Potsdam. As its name indicates, the monarch hoped to find relief there from the worries and concerns of government. In spring 1744 he began to acquire the 'wasteland hill' and areas to the south with an eye to laying out a garden with terraced vineyards. This idea was unprecedented in the history of garden design. The Frederician baroque garden that grew up around the terraces over the next three decades, in contrast, took up elements of the French and Dutch garden traditions. The northern conclusion of the park was formed by Ruins Hill, topped by Roman ruins and a great water basin. Although the question as to the garden's creator still remains to be answered, it is incontestible that, apart from Friedrich himself, his Court Architect Georg Wenzelslaus von Knobelsdorff (1699–1753) was responsible for the design.

The single-storey palace with its two elongated wings flanking a central, oval bay topped with a cupola, rises above a six-tiered vineyard of parabolic plan in whose glazed niches grapes and figs are cultivated. A sweeping staircase on the central axis leads down to the main formal beds at the foot of the slope, the central pleasure garden area, with its

Yew topiary divides the terraced vineyards.

circular fountain surrounded by marble statuary. Entry to the park is provided by the two main avenues that intersect here. The main east–west axis begins at an Egyptian Revival Obelisk and ends about one and a quarter miles away at a group of structures built in 1763–69, the New Palais and Communes, late-baroque household buildings belonging to the palace. Along this central axis, a succession of garden zones are arranged like pearls on a string: to the east, ornamental hedge gardens with rondels and basins, and to the west the central *parterre* of the Deer Park, which developed out of a former hunting reserve and was integrated in the overall conception between 1746 and 1750. Based on plans by Court Gardener Friedrich Zacharias Saltzmann, this section incorporated early elements of the sentimental landscape garden. Towards the middle of the 1770s, work on the Frederician garden was completed.

Shortly after the death of Friedrich II, parts of the formal areas of the garden were altered under Friedrich Wilhelm II (1744–97). Eyserbeck the Younger (1763–1801), a gardener from Wörlitz, was responsible for the changes. Between 1818 and 1825 Peter Joseph Lenné, who had been active in Potsdam since 1816, transformed the garden into a classical landscape garden in the English style, while retaining the east–west axis and striking terraces.

A.K.

Johann David Schleuen the Elder (1711–1771), View of Sanssouci at Potsdam, *1748, coloured engraving.*

One of the statues by Pigalle and Adam which encircle the fountain in the centre of the parterre.

Queluz

LISBON, PORTUGAL

'At night the pathways were illumined by Chinese lamps and the palace façade giving on to the garden glowed with pieces of parti-coloured glass and transparent pictures [...].'

PORTUGUESE NEWSPAPER REPORT, 1793.

Above left and right: Views of the Palácio showing fountains and a parterre de broderie.

Above centre: The azulejos.

The gardens of the Palácio de Queluz, on the road from Lisbon to Sintra, Estremadura in southern Portugal, are among the finest in the country. The complex was built between 1746 and 1776 for Don Pedro second son of King João V. It transformed a former hunting lodge situated near the fertile banks of the River Jamor into a palace which soon became a perennial royal retreat from court business in Lisbon. Its pretty and buoyant façade and irregular ground-plan offers a relaxed contrast with, for example, Mafra monastery (completed 1735).

Both the gardens and the (formerly polychrome) sculptures that line the avenues and decorative work on and around the rose-pink façade were designed by Jean-Baptiste Robillion (?–1782). The energetic figures in lead are by John Cheere (1709–87), a sculptor active at Stourhead and Easton Neston. Aquatic mythological personages make up a predictable majority, though the Fonte do Dragão (dragon fountain), some stone *singeries*, and a sphinx sporting a *fraise* ruff introduce a fantastic note. The richness of the swags, flower-baskets and other vegetable ornaments that unify house and garden may reflect Don Pedro's personal interests which are also evidenced by the exotic plants in the Botanical Garden.The Palace is linked to the park by a balustraded terrace set with box, yew and topiary and punctuated by urns. This inner formal space possesses a fountain dedicated to trident-wielding Neptune which gives it its name, Jardim de Neptuno, though it is now known as Jardim Pênsil. Flanking this larger garden is a further smaller formal one known as the Jardim de Malta, after the Order of Knights.

The elegantly swinging balustrade of the fine two-branched imperial staircase (the Escaderia Robillion) that connects terrace and lower garden is adorned with scrolls and lions. It gives onto the now dry Canal Grande whose sides are lined with yellow and blue rococo *azulejos* depicting scenes visible from punts passing on the narrow canal.

Among the famous visitors to Queluz, mention must be made of the garden enthusiast and orientalizing novelist *extraordinaire*, William Beckford, who arrived on

1644 A hunting lodge at Queluz is donated to the Infante Don Pedro (Don Pedro II).

1746–52 First and main phase of reconstruction starts under Mateus Vicente de Oliveira (1706–86), a military engineer by training.

1755 Work on the upper gardens by Dutchman Geraldo José Van den Kolk.

1755 First of John Cheere's lead garden statues are cast in London. Beginning of work on the Canal Grande.

1756 Jean-Baptiste Robillion who had trained as a silversmith commissioned for initial work on the garden and park.

1758–63 Jardim de Malta planted out.

1758–64 The Escaderia Robillion (or de Leões) staircase constructed.

1760 Marriage of Don Pedro to Dona Maria Francisca (the future Dona Maria I). Marble statues imported from Italy.

1762 Main lines of garden design completed by Robillion.

1765 *Parterres de broderie* added to the Jardim Pênsil.

1769 Botanical Garden founded.

1775-76 Manuel da Costa Rosado's Canal Grande completed with *azulejos*.

The Fonte do Dragão.

14 June 1794. After an inadequate reception, Beckford mournfully retired to apartments 'shabby enough [and as] bare as many an English country church and not much less dingy'. The visit brightened up shortly when he was permitted to walk the park and 'see the curious birds and flowers last sent from the Brazils. [...] Cascades and fountains were in full play; a thousand sportive *jets d'eau* were sprinkling the rich masses of bay and citron, and drawing forth all their odours, as well-taught water is certain to do upon all such occasions. Amongst the thickets, some of which received a tender light from tapers placed low on the ground under frosted glasses, [were] the Infanta's nymph-like attendants [near] an avenue formed of catalpas and orange trees'. For long a retreat from the dictatorial rule of First Minister the Marquês de Pombal, the palace was the royal residence from 1794 to 1807, at which time Napoleon's troops obliged the reigning family to repair to Brazil. The palace was abandoned and remained hardly used after the monarchs returned to Lusitania in 1821.

D.R.

'New' Summer Palace

BEIJING, CHINA

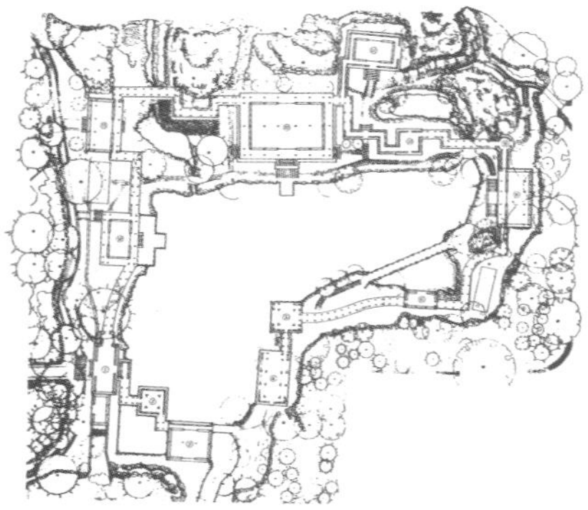

The Garden of Harmonious Interest, viewed from the east, is a small garden within the 'New' Summer Palace.

The gardens are punctuated with buildings whose features frame and create views of the landscape for the visitor.

'Where in all Yan-shan is the mind so free?
Peerless sight, the wind and moon over Lake Kunming.'

EMPEROR QIAN LONG
mid-18th century

Yi He Yuan [Garden of the Preservation of Harmony] covers an area of 716 acres to the north-west of Beijing. The majority of the garden consists of the extensive Kunming Hu [Vast Bright Lake], while on the northern shore rises Wan Shou Shan [Longevity Hill]. The major period of garden design and construction started in 1749 and lasted for fifteen years. It took place under the auspices of the Emperor Qian Long, who was a keen admirer of gardens, and he called his creation Qing Yi Yuan, [Garden of Clear Ripples]. The garden was to survive until 1860, when it was ransacked and burnt by British and French troops. Fortunately the Dowager Empress Ci Xi preferred to spend her summers close to the Forbidden City and had part of the imperial garden rebuilt and renamed Yi He Yuan. It is alleged that the rebuilding of the garden was funded with money that had been intended for the Chinese Navy. This process was repeated when the garden was again damaged during the Boxer Rebellion of 1900.

Ci Xi stayed at Yi He Yuan from the flowering of the magnolias to the withering of the chrysanthemums, and the garden contained features which would provide entertainment for the imperial court and a pleasant escape from the summer heat. Dragon-prowed boats took parties out on the lake, as they still do today, providing views of the impressive 17-arch bridge which spans the water from the eastern shore to the Island of the Dragon King. Longevity Hill was covered with flowering trees and offered smaller more intimate gardens. The Garden of Harmonious Interest was built in 1811 on the site of an earlier garden designed for the Emperor Qian Long, and consists of a central pool surrounded by a covered corridor and crossed by the 'fish-knowing bridge' which, like so many of the features in the gardens, recalls a literary reference.

The areas of entertainment included a feature entitled Suzhou Creek, where the Emperor Qian Long and his court could play shopkeepers in a replica of a Suzhou canalside market. One of the most well-known features is the Painted Corridor which stretches for 4.5 miles along the north shore of Kunming. Originally built in 1750, the corridor's crossbeams feature paintings from Chinese classical literature and some folk stories. At the west end of the corridor is the famous 'Marble Boat' (1893), sited on the edge of the lake as if about to set out on a crossing. The original Chinese-style boat was destroyed and rebuilt by Ci Xi in 1893, when the boat took on the western appearance of a paddle-steamer. The imagery of boats in not unique to this garden and is an allusion to the stability and power of the owner. Despite the war and the pressures caused by the large numbers of visitors, the garden is still a masterpiece. *J.R.*

A view across the Kunming Lake from Longevity Hill.

1153 Creation by one of the Jin emperors of a temporary residence on the site.
1368–1644 Imperial residence built and the area is called the Garden of Wonderful Hills.
1749 The Emperor Qian Long begins enlarging the lake, renamed Kunming Hu, and the surrounding hills are built-up. Jar Hill is renamed Longevity Hill [Wan Shou Shan].
1750 Painted Corridor constructed.
1764 The Emperor's major building programme is completed.
1860 Pavilions and other buildings destroyed by British and French troops.
1888 Ci Xi rebuilds the imperial garden now called Yi He Yuan.
1900 Second destruction of the garden.
1902 Ci Xi rebuilds the imperial garden again.
1908 The Emperor Guangxu dies at Yi He Yuan, followed the next day by Ci Xi.
1911 Yi He Yuan opened to the public.
1924 Yi He Yuan declared a public park.
1949 Park undergoes restoration after years of neglect.
1998 Yi He Yuan added to the UNESCO World Heritage List.

Master of the Nets Garden

SUZHOU, CHINA

'He who plants a garden plants happiness. If you want to be happy for a lifetime, plant a garden.'

CHINESE PROVERB.

A filigree screen around a window frames the garden beyond.

Above centre: The Moon Door provides a view into the next courtyard.

Above right: A covered corridor links the various buildings and garden courtyards.

Suzhou has long been known for the beauty of the small literati gardens which have survived there. These were often created by court officials who had fallen from favour and wished to be seen living the life of a cultured hermit. The Master of the Nets Garden [Wang Shi Yuan] covers less than 2.5 acres, but contains more that ten small enclosed gardens. The property has been through a number of cycles of neglect, restoration and redesign reflecting the fortunes of its various owners.

The garden lies to the west of the main residence and is entered from the rear of the property via an alleyway of white-washed walls whose most ornamental feature is the decorative pebble paving. A characteristic feature of this, and other Chinese gardens, is that surfaces consist of stone and ornamental flooring in pebbles and tile shards, the latter in stylised patterns or pictures. From the entrance corridor the visitor passes through a series of buildings, corridors and their associated courtyard gardens.

The residential buildings are inextricably linked with views of the garden which are framed by screen-work around the openings of windows and doorways. One of the first courtyard gardens is viewed through the strong vertical lines produced by a row of pivoting windows. The scene includes the major features typical of such a garden with rocks (highly valued for their unique shapes) intricate pebble- and tile-paving in the design of plum blossom, and limited planting to contrast with, but not distract from, the other components. The plant use in the garden is representative of the Chinese gardening tradition: despite a huge range of native plants the palette is restricted, and plants are chosen for their symbolic references to the seasons, literature or other cultural associations. For example, bamboo represents unyielding integrity since it bends but does not break in the wind.

1140 Original garden, Yu Yin [Fish Shade], created by Shi Zhengzhi.

1760 The garden undergoes redesigning by Song Zenghuan, and is renamed Wang Shi [Master of the Nets].

c. 1940 Restored by the Wang family.

c. 1950 Some additional buildings added.

1958 Property is taken over by the city of Suzhou.

1980 The Late Spring Studio is used as the model for the Astor Court garden in the Metropolitan Museum of Art, New York.

1982 The site is listed by the Chinese Government as a cultural relic of national importance.

1990 The start of night-time tours of the garden for visitors.

The pavilion 'The Moon Sinks and the Wind Gets Up' with its upturned eaves.

The play of shadows on walls adds another dimension to the Chinese garden.

The central part of the garden is dominated by a pond surrounded by buildings including a six-sided pavilion with sharply upturned eaves called 'The Moon Sinks and the Wind Gets Up'. The name of the pavilion and inclusion of a 'goose-neck' rail to lean against encourages the visitor to consider the possibility of sitting there at night to admire the moon's reflection and the breeze on the pond's surface. A covered corridor connects the pavilion with other buildings (essential in Suzhou's wet climate) and has a whitewashed wall pierced with windows allowing views to the adjacent courtyard. The use of views from windows and doorways often into small landscaped spaces between buildings allows the designer to create an intricate and interesting garden that gives the viewer the experience of a being in a site much larger than is the reality.

In the Wang Shi residence and garden the gradual journey from the busy street to the heart of the garden allows the visitor to be transported away from the city just beyond the garden walls, into a representation of nature and literary allusions, an escape made by the owners of such gardens from the storms of court politics. *J.R.*

Royal Botanic Gardens, Kew

LONDON, ENGLAND

Top: The Palm House.

Above left: The Nosegay Garden in the Queen's Garden.

Above right: The Pagoda.

'The gardens at Kew are not very large. Nor is their situation by any means advantageous [...] but princely magnificence, guided by a director equally skilled in cultivating the earth, and in the politer arts, overcame all difficulties. What was once a Desert is now an Eden.'

WILLIAM CHAMBERS

The Garden and Buildings at Kew in Surry, London: J. Haberkorn, 1763.

The site of the Royal Botanic Gardens, Kew was gardened by William Turner (known as 'the father of English botany') for Henry VIII's sister, a Tudor link expressed in its sunken Nosegay Garden. Kew's evolution from palace gardens to botanical centre of world importance has involved a panoply of royalty, plant hunters and botanical illustrators who forged the shape of Kew while its designers amalgated its needs.

In 1759 Princess Augusta (mother of George III) created a nine-acre botanical garden and then commissioned Sir William Chambers (1723–96) to design the ten-storey octagonal Pagoda as well as numerous temples and other structures. When George III inherited the adjoining property he formed Kew Gardens, appointing Joseph Banks (1743–1820) as the first Director. Lancelot 'Capability' Brown (1716–83) organised the Staffordshire militia to excavate the Rhododendron Dell and Bamboo Garden. The botanic beds were and still are laid out systematically within the informality of the Landscape style surrounding the botanic structures. In 1836 the Aroid House, modified by Jeffry Wyatville, moved to Kew from Buckingham Palace and the Great Stove was built (now the wisteria arbour).

In 1841 Kew Gardens, a total of 200 acres (rising to 300 by 1846), with 11 acres opened to the public, were handed over to the state. Decimus Burton and Richard Turner(c. 1798–1881) designed and constructed the curvilinear Palm House (completely restored in 1984–89) set in Italianate style rose gardens and *parterres* designed by William Andrews Nesfield (1793–1881). Burton also designed the Pleasure Garden, gates, Economic Botany Museum (the first in the world to display the practical application of plants), the Herbarium, Library and rebuilt the Temple of Aeolus. His other dominant structure was the Temperate House started in 1860 and built in stages until 1899 (restored 1978–82) and Turner designed the Waterlily House (1852, restored and reopened 1992). In 1876 Sir Joseph Hooker (1817–1911) founded the Jodrell Laboratory (rebuilt 1965, substantially extended 1993) and in 1882 created the Rock Garden (iconic in

View of the Lake, the Orangery and the Temple of Aeolus at Kew, *unsigned engraving from* Plans et Jardins, *c. 1774.*

Sir William Chambers's Temple of Aeolus.

1728 Queen Caroline acquires the Dutch House (Kew Palace).
1759 Princess Augusta sets aside nine acres for a botanic garden.
1761–62 Chambers creates the Pagoda, Temple of Aeolus, The Orangery, Temple of Bellona, King William's Temple, and Ruined Arch.
1772 George III inherits the adjoining property and forms Kew Gardens; he appoints Joseph Banks as unpaid Director
1841 11 acres opened to public: 9,000 visitors. Sir William Jackson Hooker (1785–1865) appointed Director.
1844–48 Construction of Palm House.
1865 Appointment of Sir Joseph Dalton Hooker as Director; he commissions Jodrell Laboratory and Rock Garden; and prevents Kew becoming a pleasure park, retaining its scientific and educational status.
1963 Wakehurst bequeathed to National Trust, then leased to Royal Botanic Gardens, Kew.
1987 Kew: Princess of Wales Conservatory built.
August 1995–October 1996 Kew: Japanese Landscape created around Chokushi Mon Gate.
1996 Kew: Evolution House built.

realism, scale and planting) and reorganised the Arboretum. Queen Charlotte's Cottage and its grounds offered a fine example of an Arts and Crafts wild garden with reputedly one of the finest bluebell woods in the country. The Japanese Gateway, Chokushi Mon, was transferred to Kew after the 1910 Anglo-Japanese Exhibition, and during 1995–96 a 'lake and island' Japanese landscape was created.

The 1980s and 1990s witnessed the opening of the Alpine House, the spectacular Princess of Wales Conservatory with ten climatic zones, and the Evolution House. Chambers's Orangery is now a restaurant.

In 1903 Gerald Loder bought Wakehurst Place in Sussex (originally owned by the Culpeper family) and developed the gardens to nurture and display plant collections from East Asia, South America and New Zealand. Today plant collections are arranged according to their geographical origins. A 2-mile walk around the grounds encompasses traditional walled and water gardens, a Himalayan Glade or native Wealden Woods, the Tony Schilling Asian Heath Garden, wetlands and meadows.

The beauty of the gardens at Kew and Wakehurst Place is more than skin deep; they are a showcase for the largest and most diverse living collection in the world of more than 40,000 different kinds of plant. *C.H.*

Wörlitz

NEAR DESSAU, SAXONY-ANHALT, GERMANY

'Wanderer, achte Natur und Kunst und schone ihrer Werke [Wanderer, venerate nature and art and honour their works].'

INSCRIPTION IN THE SCHOCH GARDEN.

The Rousseau Island.

Prince Franz von Anhalt´s park in Wörlitz was among the earliest landscape gardens in Germany. Upon his return from journeys to Italy and England in 1763–64, Prince Franz, inspired by the latest developments in England, decided to lay out a landscape garden in Wörlitz. The old hunting seat was replaced by an early neo-classical villa which served the prince as a summer house. The design was based on the principles of the new garden art advanced by Alexander Pope: contrast, surprise and the concealment of the garden´s borders. Italy provided a second key source of inspiration for Wörlitz.

The park comprises five different areas, the first three of which were laid out almost simultaneously. These sections are grouped around a lake, which extends at each end into two main arms and is connected with smaller ponds by canals. This permits nearly the entire park to be viewed from a boat: the park was open to the public from the outset, and no gates or walls were foreseen.

The section known as The Garden This Side of the Lake comprises the gardens grouped around the palace. It contains the only remaining symmetrical elements, including rows of trees which frame the palace on two sides. Instead of being centrally located typical of the baroque, the palace is at the edge of the park, directly adjacent to the village of Wörlitz. However, a belvedere on the roof provides a view of almost all of the key areas of the park.

The Neumark Garden (1772), north-west of the palace, consists of several sections. On a canal lies the Eisenhart, a terrace paved with iron ore on which two pavilions are located. These house a library of garden literature and a museum with items collected by the Forsters, natural scientists who accompanied Captain Cook on his voyages in the South Pacific. A belt walk encompasses the island and leads to various other attractions: a large coppice, a labyrinth, and the Elysium, an oval clearing planted with exotic

The Gothic House, 1773.

Views, from left to right, of the Synagogue, the Church Tower and the Altar.

Contemporary rendering of the eruption of Vesuvius on the Stone.

vegetation that forms the end point of the labyrinth. Rousseau Island (1782), intended to recall the philosopher´s grave in Ermenonville, is located in the northernmost corner of the park.

The Schoch garden (1773) extends along the large lake and is criss-crossed by canals. At its centre stands the Gothic House (1773–74), erected as private quarters for the prince and serving to house his collections of medieval art. This is the earliest specimen of neo-Gothic architecture in Germany. A Nymphaeum, the Temple of Venus (1793–97), and other architectural features accentuate this section of the park.

The Garden on the Weidenheger (1781) and the New Gardens (1787), were later additions in which fields and meadows were brought together as a 'designed landscape'. A Pantheon with an Egyptian grotto (1795–96) and the Stone (1799–94) opposite the Grotto of Egyra are high points of this section. The Stone, a miniature version of Mount Vesuvius, and the Villa Hamilton, a replica of the original in Naples, were conceived as reminiscences of the prince´s sojourn in Italy. At that period, audiences in an amphitheatre were treated to mock volcanic eruptions in which shards of glass represented the lava and smoke and fire spewed from a hidden combustion chamber. Italian pyramid poplars rounded off the picture of a Neapolitan landscape. *A.G.*

1764 First garden layout in the vicinity of the old Wörlitz hunting seat, designed for Prince Franz by Court Gardener Johann Friedrich Eyserbeck.

1765–67 Prince Franz and architect Friedrich Wilhelm Freiherr von Erdmannsdorf make grand tour to Italy, France and England

1769–73 Reconstruction of neo-classical palace based on von Erdmannsdorf´s plans.

1770–71 Garden destroyed by Elbe River flood.

1772–1817 New layout of gardens by J.F. Eyserbeck and J.G. Schoch

1785 Prince Franz´s third journey to England.

1785 Prince Franz´s last journey to England.

1788 Goethe visits Wörlitz.

1791 Iron Bridge.

1797 Temple of Flora.

Ermenonville

OISE, FRANCE

'Take what nature offers, know how to do without what it refuses, become especially attached to the simplicity of its accomplishment.'

LOUIS-RENÉ, MARQUIS DE GIRARDIN.

Mayer's sepulchre, Temple of Philosophers, Rousseau Island.

Le jeu d'arc.

Louis-René, Marquis de Girardin (1735–1808) was widely travelled with a knowledgeable appreciation of William Kent and the English Landscape Movement as well as the paintings of Boucher and Watteau. From 1766 to 1776 he employed a Scottish master gardener with 200 English gardeners to create a bucolic paradise. He was inspired by Jean-Jacques Rousseau's dream garden in *La Nouvelle Heloïse* (1761), the antithesis of Versailles and other French formal gardens. Ermenonville was initially to be jolly rather than contemplative, a sentimental landscape to enhance the lives of the marquis's villagers, with farmland seamlessly incorporated into a *jardin paysager*.

The architect, J.-M. Morel was commissioned to turn the park into Arcadie, a *jardin anglais* elaborated with *fabriques*, seats and walks, while the adjoining Désert (now belonging to the Abbaye de Chaalis) was more anglo-chinois and was left as a wilderness where the visitor could experience nature in the raw. The picturesque River Launette babbles across the park between and around the lakes; paths lead to rustic bridges at several points allowing people to move freely in the landscape. The Beech Circle was a popular meeting place for the youth of Ermenonville, and music and dancing took place in this Arcadian grove. Girardin also created a *bocage* with the Lover's Fountain, a grotto and a temple dedicated to Pleasure and the Muses. Archery could be enjoyed nearby in the specially constructed target ground with an adjacent bowling-green. The *fabriques* were destroyed in the French Revolution and the beech in a storm in 1818.

The visitor could climb into the woodland to the deliberately unfinished classical Temple of Philosophers dedicated to Montaigne. Each supporting column recalls a great man: Descartes, Newton, Penn, Montesquieu, Voltaire, Rousseau. The remainder, according to Girardin, 'that lie here will stay for several centuries; for it is far easier to achieve a place at the Academy than merit a column at Ermenonville'. Below, by the brook, is the small self-explanatory Altar to Dreams, originally with a moss-covered bench (moss, like the Désert, was inspired by the Chinese reverence for undisturbed nature).

Rousseau arrived on 20 May 1778 to herborise and, enchanted by what he found, stayed until his unexpected death on 2 July. Ermenonville, the realisation of a philosopher's dream, became his shrine, and his island tomb, framed by poplars whether viewed across the lake or from the Temple of the Philosophers, recalls the ancient meadows and waters of eternal oblivion.

New contemplative *fabriques* were created by Girardin after Rousseau's death. Rousseau exalted maternal love (his mother had died shortly after his birth) and this is embodied in La Table and Le Banc des Mères. Georges-Frédéric Mayer lived and painted at Ermenonville from 1777 until his death in 1779, drawing Rousseau at Ermenonville. His sepulchre was erected on the edge of the Prairie Arcadienne within view of Rousseau's tomb. Le Banc de la Reine records Marie Antoinette's visit here and to nearby Chantilly where a *hameau* had just been created — bucolic echoes which would reverberate at Versailles.

C.H.

1762 René-Louis Girardin inherits the 2,100-acre estate of Ermenonville.

1766 Girardin starts sweeping away the formal gardens and incorporating the countryside.

1777 Girardin publishes *De la composition des paysages sur le terrain ou du moyen d'embellir la nature autour des habitations en joignant l'agréable à l'utile*.

1778 Rousseau visits, stays and dies at Ermenonville.

1780 14 June: Louis XVI and Marie Antoinette visit to pay homage to Rousseau.

1793 Girardin and his family imprisoned under the Terror; the *fabriques* are vandalised.

1874 Ermenonville bought and restored by Prince Constantine Radziwill who discovered the prehistoric cave.

1938 Ermenonville placed under the protection of The Touring Club of France.

1984 Acquired by the Conseil General de l'Oise.

Rousseau's tomb encircled with poplars.

Monticello

VIRGINIA, USA

'Planting is one of my great amusements, and even of those things which can only be for posterity, for a Septuagenary has no right to count on any thing but annuals.'

THOMAS JEFFERSON
Letters & Garden Book.

Like the man himself, the gardens and landscapes conceived by Thomas Jefferson (1743–1826) at Monticello were revolutionary for their time and place. Along with his voluminous correspondence regarding all matter of garden-related subjects, Jefferson's *Garden Book*, a diary account of gardening activities kept for nearly 60 years, reveals the complexity of his ideas and the scope of his knowledge and interest in the topic. He began to make his mark on the Monticello landscape as early as 1771, when he laid out elaborate plans for the grounds to include thinning the forests, constructing elaborate road systems and planting shrubberies. In a letter to William Hamilton written in 1806, Jefferson wrote that, for the British, the 'canvas is of open ground, variegated with clumps of trees distributed with taste.... But under the beaming, constant and almost vertical sun of Virginia, shade is our Elysium'. Thus, Jefferson's grove retained the trees of 'loftiest stature', which were then trimmed up to give the appearance of open ground. Within this setting, thickets of evergreens and flowering shrubs were added, and sitting stones and stumps were retained.

Jefferson directed many projects through letters and memoranda to his daughter, Martha, his granddaughters and overseers. In 1807, in preparation for his retirement from the office of president, he began to lay out the final design for his flower gardens at Monticello, starting with 20 round and oval beds to be situated in the angles or corners of the house on both the east and west fronts. He soon determined that these beds — which contained a curious mixture of bulbs, perennials and native wild flowers — were insufficient to accommodate the many varieties of plants he wished to cultivate. The ornamental gardens were enlarged to include the entire levelled west lawn with a winding walk bordered on each side by narrow flowerbeds. In 1812, with a view toward greater accuracy and ease of record keeping, Jefferson divided the beds into ten-foot compartments in which a single variety would be planted.

Jefferson's massive vegetable garden was carved out of the south-eastern slope of the mountain, levelled and terraced into three gradually descending platforms. The garden's entire 1,000-foot length was supported by a stone wall that reaches 12 feet in height and on which stands, at the garden's mid-point, a cubic temple or pavilion. This garden — with dozens of cabbage, pea, lettuce, bean, squash and melon varieties — would occupy Jefferson's attentions almost exclusively in his later years. Yet Jefferson's eye for beauty of design can be seen even in the Kitchen Garden's layout, where he combined rows of alternating white and purple eggplants, green and purple sprouting broccoli, and an entire square of tomatoes surrounded by okra. An arbour for flowering beans of various colours was constructed along the garden's outer edge primarily for beauty and shade. Although Jefferson's ten-foot high paling fence surrounding the Kitchen Garden was built for practical reasons, a step through its gate revealed a seemingly endless panorama across the vegetable beds, fruit trees, vineyards, berry squares, and beyond to the rolling Virginia Piedmont — one of the most sublime prospects in America.

P.C.

Jefferson's large Kitchen Garden (seen right foreground).

A mixture of bulbs and perennials in the front flowerbeds.

1764 Jefferson inherits a Piedmont Virginia property from his father.
1769 First mention of the name 'Monticello' in Jefferson's diaries.
1771 First plans for the garden.

Exterior view of Monticello, watercolour. Blérancourt, Musée de la coopération Franco-Américaine.

Arkadia

NEAR WARSAW, POLAND

Sphinx on the terrace of the Temple of Diana.

from 1778: Created by Zug and Ittar.
1821 Death of Helena Radziwill, followed by decay of estate.
1945 Open to the public as part of the National Museum of Warsaw
from 1991: Restoration of park.

The Temple of Diana.

The 'Roman' aqueduct.

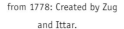

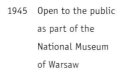

'J'ai fait l'Arcadie et j'y repose.'

Inscription on the tomb of Princess Helena Radziwill on Topolowa Island.

Arkadia, 50 miles west of Warsaw, was designed for Princess Helena Radziwill (1753–1821) by Szymon Zug (1733–1807) over a period of 20 years from 1778, the work then being continued by Henryk Ittar (1773–1850) in the early 19th century. There is no record that Zug had actually visited England, but he was an ardent proponent of the English landscape style, with buildings, a lake and other features in a natural-looking park setting. But what was created was no mere copy of the kind of templescape that could be seen in many an English estate: it was an intensely personal vision of Helena Radziwill, an expression of feelings, particularly melancholy, which a tour of the garden was calculated to inspire. The circuit was artfully composed to play upon different feelings or emotions in turn, the key being the inscription 'Et in Arcadia ego', equally sad or wistful in either of its interpretations: 'I too was once in Arcadia' or 'Even in Arcadia, I (Death) am present'. The entrance, between the cottages of Philemon and Baucis, suggested welcome and hospitality, with an appropriate inscription on the fountain: 'One only enjoys what one shares'. Helena Radziwill's own guide book of 1800 describes the circuit and its intended effects. Next came the Island of Offerings or Feelings, where altars stood dedicated to Love, Friendship, Hope, Gratitude and Remembrance. The tour then took in the Sybil's Grotto, the Gothic house ('sanctuary of adversity and melancholy'), a classical arcade, a 'Greek' arch representing victory over Time, the Margrave's House and the central feature, the Temple of Diana, which had three different appearances according to which side it was seen from. The inscription over the portico to the temple facing the lake reads 'Where I find peace from all my troubles'. The interior of the temple was furnished and painted to represent classical scenes and decoration, with elements of Freemasonry (the Princess belonged to an order which admitted women).

The tour continued with a bridge disguised as a ruined classical aqueduct, the now vanished Knight's Tent, a shrine to Pan, the House of the High Priest (with another inscription, 'Hope feeds delusion and life slips away'), and the Isle of Poplars. This was based on Rousseau's tomb on the Isle of Poplars at Ermenonville, a copy of which was also at Wörlitz and of which Zug knew. On the isle was the tomb that the Princess intended for herself, with the 'Et in Arcadia' inscription on one side and on the other, 'I created Arcadia, and I rest there'. The way out was through a classical Circus.

Helena Radziwill applied a fashionable sensibility to the creation of her garden, a Romantic taste for feelings, reflections and the sadness of passing time. It is true that most visitors admired the garden only for its appearance and beauty, but it represented the elegiac dream of its creator, and each feature contributed to that dream. Restoration of the landscape and to the buildings has been ongoing in recent years. *M.S.*

Margrave's House and the 'Greek' arch.

Haga

SOLNA, SWEDEN

'In the interior of the grotto...water trickles like a gentle rain from the strainers concealed in the vaults of the niches, and all this water finally runs down irregular little falls and cascades into the nearby artificial lake, from which the sunbeams are reflected.'

FREDRIK PIPER, garden designer to Gustavus III on Painshill, 1770s, cited in May Woods, *Visions of Arcadia*, London: Aurum, 1996.

The Turkish Tent.

The royal park of Haga, situated to the south of Stockholm, is the first real Swedish example of English landscape gardening. The main structure of the park was made up of a small wooden building with flanking wings. Attached to this was an insignificant pleasure garden and kitchen garden. However it was not this that fascinated King Gustavus III, but the picturesque position of the park by the Brunnsviken lake. The English park that Gustavus III first designed and had constructed during the summer of 1772, consisted of only one gazebo, and a few promenades on the three islets, situated in the vicinity of the main building. Nothing more was done until 1781, when the architect Fredrik Magnus Piper (1746–1824), who had recently returned home to Sweden, worked out a suggestion for a new English park. Piper was familiar with developments in the art of landscape gardening after a three-year stay in England where he worked with Sir William Chambers (1723–96) among others. This made Piper the most competent Swedish architect in the area at that time, but he was anything but willing to compromise. In his suggestions he erased the French garden completely and replaced the *parterres* with oval lawns. Possibly his most radical move was on the lakeside where one of these lawns was allowed to join directly to the main building without anything in between, not even a gravelled path. Nothing like this had ever been created in Sweden before.

1771 King Gustavus III acquires the estate at Haga.

c. 1785 F.M. Piper completes work on gardens.

1786–87 Large lawn.

1786–88 Turkish pavilion.

1787–89 Tempelman's royal pavilion.

1787–90 Desprez's copper tents.

Piper wanted to change everything that seemed artificial and astonishingly the king gave him *carte blanche*. During the early years the work was concentrated on the three islets where the lakeside promenade and the man-made canal was given a more natural course. Then there was extensive ground preparation work and new planting. A new road was laid parallel to the new promenades. The *allée*, originally straight as an arrow, now took on the character of a meandering line. Everything ended in a large lawn (now called

Haga palace seen from the lake.

J. F. Martin, The Royal Palace of Haga.

Vasaslätten) in front of the main building. According to Piper's intentions this oval grass surface was to be edged with clumps, all framed by a promenade, which on one side came to a halt where the ground began to widen, while its mirror image curved parallel to the road.

For Piper roads and paths represented not only the nervous system to the park, but were also a way of illustrating the topography and the way the vegetation was spread out. The same can be said about the park buildings, which marked the highest points in the grounds. The only gazebo designed by Piper that would be constructed, was the Turkish pavilion. At this time the aim of the work in the park changed; this was not only related to the expansion of the area of the grounds, but also to Piper's role. From having both managed the work, and being the architect, he had to be content with artistic leadership. Piper designed the large lawn as well as the archipelago in the north and south, but in reality he had been out-manoeuvred. Instead Gustavus III's own wishes now dominated. The king was first assisted by Olof Tempelman, who designed the royal pavilion and later by Jean-Louis Desprez (1743–1804), who was responsible among other things for the palace that was never completed as well as the so called Koppartälten [copper tents]. By marginalizing Piper's contribution the proportions between buildings and the grounds were lost. More radical changes such as the lowering of the surface of the lake at Brunnsviken in 1863 and, more recently, the building of the motorway along the park's west boundary has drastically damaged the park. In spite of this Haga is nevertheless one of the best examples of English landscape gardening in Sweden. *M.O.*

Piper's general plan of Haga.

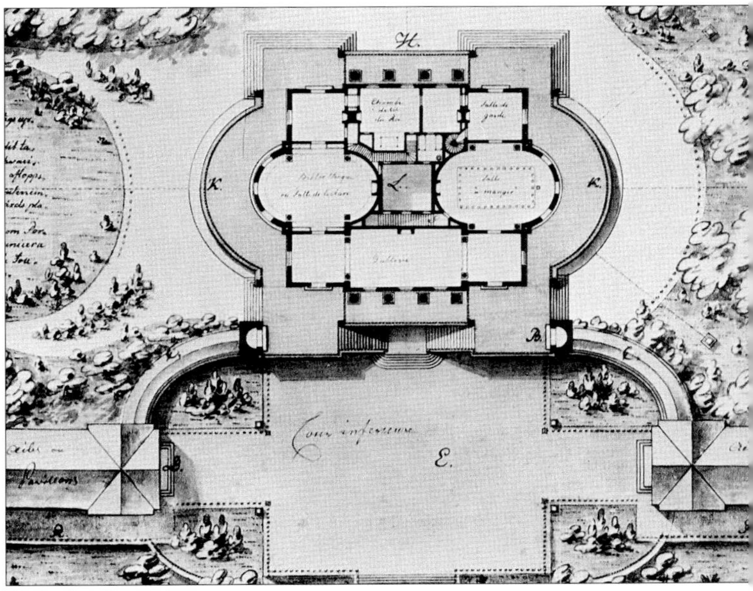

Heligan

CORNWALL, ENGLAND

'The whole of its grounds are rendered delightful by their natural unevenness, deep valleys where the rays of sun scarcely ever penetrate, watered by pooling brooks, enlivened by cascades, are happily contrasted by conical mountains the surfaces of which are covered with lively plantations and adorned with temples. The walks wind over shady precipices and afford agreeable resting places at convenient distances.'

GILBERT, 1824, quoted in Tim Smit, *The Lost Gardens of Heligan*, London: Gollancz, 1997.

19th-century wall and rockery.

Apple trees trained to form a decorative border in the vegetable garden.

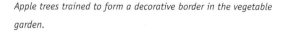

A chance encounter in 1990 between new owner, John Willis, and Dutch-born former pop music arranger and composer Tim Smit, led to the renaissance of a great 19th-century English garden which had almost disappeared due to neglect.

In its heyday, the garden at Heligan, situated at the head of a valley overlooking the small Cornish fishing village of Mevagissey, was a Victorian showpiece owned by the wealthy Tremayne family. This was the era of intrepid professional plant hunters, such as Sir Joseph Hooker (1817–1911), George Forrest (1873–1922) and Ernest 'Chinese' Wilson (1876–1930), who risked their lives in the Himalayas in order to bring back rhododendrons and other exotic new specimens to Britain. Hooker sent back seeds to Heligan which flourished in the mild West Country climate.

With the outbreak of World War I in 1914 the gardeners of Heligan departed to France to fight for King and country; many never returned. The Tremaynes lost heart and left Heligan. Gradually the gardens decayed, were choked with brambles and covered in ivy and fallen trees, while rampant laurels formed impenetrable barriers and glasshouses and other garden buildings fell derelict. Finally the storms of 1990 brought further havoc, felling more than 700 trees. Heligan had become a lost garden, cocooned in a time warp which Tim Smit and his companions were determined to revive.

Beneath this wilderness miraculously much of the original planting had survived, including Hooker's rhododendrons and early japonica camellias. A decade later it had once again become one of the nation's most romantic gardens due to expert advice from people such as Philip McMillan Browse, former director of the Royal Horticultural Society Garden at Wisley, and a huge amount of hard labour, much of it voluntary, under the direction of John Nelson, Tim Smit's co-partner.

In the Northern Garden, the Cornish Red is reputedly the largest rhododendron in the world. The vegetable garden is restored to its original two and a half acres, producing fruit and vegetables in the Victorian manner. The glasshouses together with their vines, peaches and citrus fruit, the Melon Yard, Pineapple Pit and Bee Bole Wall (vaulted cells housing bees) are all back in working order. There is a one-hundred-foot-long herbaceous border, while the area known as 'New Zealand' contains huge tree ferns. Further down the valley lies the 'Jungle', complete with pools, bamboos and newly planted banana plantation, while the Lost Valley, containing a large lake and water meadows, was opened to the public in the spring of 1997. Heligan has been the largest garden restoration project in Europe, a unique living museum of 19th-century horticulture, covering approximately 100 acres. Tim Smit's vision and fund raising has been vital, yet he is not a man to rest on his laurels. He has gone on to mastermind the Eden Project, commissioning leading architect Nicholas Grimshaw to create the largest glasshouse in the world on a former china clay pit at nearby St Austell. *P.B.*

c. 1800 Henry Hawkins Tremayne engaged Thomas Gray to draw up a plan for the garden at Heligan.

c. 1850 Sir Joseph Hooker sends seeds to Heligan from the Himalayas.

c. 1875 John Hearle Tremayne establishes his 'Jungle'.

1914 Outbreak of World War I: most of gardening staff join the army.

1916 The house is seconded to the War Department.

1943 American servicemen billeted at Heligan.

1970 The house is sold for development.

1990 Tim Smit first visits Heligan.

1991 Restoration work begins.

1992 The gardens open to the public.

1994 Original design of the 'Jungle' revealed and garden restored.

1997 The Lost Valley opens to the public.

On the edge of the 'Jungle'.

Giant ferns.

Sezincote

GLOUCESTERSHIRE
ENGLAND

'But if from the best models of Indian structures such parts only be selected as cannot be compared with any known style of English buildings, even those whom novelty cannot delight will have little cause to regret the introduction of new beauties.'

THE LANDSCAPE GARDENING AND LANDSCAPE ARCHITECTURE OF HUMPHRY REPTON
ed. J.C. Loudon, London, 1840 (new ed.).

Right: 'Stone' bulls and a serpent decorate Cockerell's bridge.

Far right: The Indian pavilion.

The conservatory at Sezincote inspired the Royal Pavilion at Brighton.

At Sezincote Humphry Repton (1752–1818) was brought in by Sir Charles Cockerell to design gardens. These were to complement the Indian-style house by Thomas Daniell, who was responsible for a collection of plates called *Oriental Scenery* (1795 onwards), which illustrate Hindu and Muslim architecture. The house itself was to inspire the Prince Regent to construct the Indian fantasy of the Royal Pavilion at Brighton for which Repton produced the original designs (both house and gardens), although the commission eventually went to John Nash. Repton created a garden from c. 1803 which combined lawn and woodland planting with Indian artefacts and motifs, mostly taken from Daniell's drawings. One area was known as the Thornery, which contained varieties of thorn-bush: Repton planted another at Woburn Abbey.

Cockerell himself took a keen personal interest in the design. There is a bridge with small Brahmin bulls on the balustrade, a serpent entwined round an upright pole, a mushroom-shaped fountain and a temple which houses a figure of the god Souriya. To this was added, as a kind of garden building, the Indian conservatory which extends in a curve from the house. The park and lake are likely to be by Repton.

Although some of Repton's work remains, along with the Indian adornments, there have been many changes in planting during the 20th century. The areas to each side of the descending stream have been planted up as rock and flower gardens, and at Graham Stuart Thomas's suggestion a small canal was formed in front of the conservatory, from a Mogul design. Overlooking this is a small Indian-style pavilion designed by Sir Cyril Kleinwort (1961), near a grotto contemporary with the house.

Elements of philosophy and symbolism are conveyed by the garden. In the original Repton/Daniell scheme, Souriya was the sun-god who was said to stimulate the intellect of the worshipper, while the bulls represent Nandi, the 'happy one'. The South Garden, dating from the 1960s, is modelled on the gardens of Paradise, with the canal and paths dividing the garden in quarters representing the rivers of life. The octagonal shape of the fountain and the pavilion in this garden brings together square and circle, symbolising respectively life's physicality and eternity. *M.S.*

c. 1803 Humphry Repton creates garden for Cockerell family.

1884 Estate bought by James Dugdale.

1944 Estate bought by Sir Cyril Kleinwort; house and gardens restored and extended.

The South Garden.

Munstead Wood

SURREY, ENGLAND

'Where [in the woodland] the sun catches the edges of the nearer trunks it lights them in a sharp line leaving the rest warmly dark; but where the trees stand in shade, the trunks are of a cool grey that is almost blue, borrowing their colour, through the opening of the track behind me, from the hard blue cloudless sky.'

GERTRUDE JEKYLL
Home and Garden, 1900.

1877 Jekyll's widowed mother buys Munstead House near Godalming. Jekyll lives there with her and lays out the garden.
1883 Jekyll buys the Munstead Wood property across the road from the House, and begins the garden layout.
1889 Edwin Lutyens is introduced to Jekyll by his client, Harry Mangles.
1892–94 Lutyens designs the gardener's cottage and The Hut, his first works at Munstead Wood. The Hut serves as a temporary home for Jekyll until the main house is built (1896).
1900 Jekyll writes her account of the creation of Munstead Wood in her book *Home and Garden*.
1932 Jekyll dies at Munstead Wood.
1940 Jekyll's personal papers relating to Munstead Wood and her other garden designs are acquired by the American garden designer Beatrix Farrand; they are later transferred to the University of California.

Above: Pergola at the end of the main flower borders.

Above right: Door from the Summer Garden.

Above far right: The Primula Garden.

Gertrude Jekyll (1843–1932) conceived her house and garden at Munstead Wood conforming to an Arts and Crafts ideal, heavily influenced by John Ruskin and William Morris, which applied a simplifying, disciplined aesthetic to all matters of daily life.

Jekyll had a deep love for this pocket of England, having been brought up in nearby Bramley and then in Wargrave only a few miles away in Berkshire. She took up gardening in the 1870s, turning from the intricate watercolours and decorative work to which she had devoted herself in her youth because of failing eyesight. After 1883, when she bought the land at Munstead, her first priority was to create a garden rather than to build a house. Munstead became not only her home, but also the centre of an increasingly successful commercial operation — both a factory and a shop front — as she became the most celebrated garden designer of her day.

Jekyll made a virtue of the site's poor sandy soil by retaining the character of the former heath, taking as her cue the self-sown mixed woodland which occupied much of the property. Everything was carefully designed to give the impression of a modest dwelling in a natural setting: there was no carriage-drive up to the front door of the house, while the formal and cutting gardens were limited to the northern tip of the irregular triangular plot. The layout was determined by the varying possibilities offered by soil and position, and by the need to have some kind of display throughout the growing season. The showpiece was the south-east-facing herbaceous border, 200 feet long, designed to be in continuous bloom from July to October. To the south, radiating rhododendron-fringed walks through the wood gave oblique, partial views of the main front of the house.

1947–48 Munstead Wood is sold and its contents dispersed.
Since 1986: An extensive programme of restoration, including a survey by the Royal Commission on the Historic Monuments of England, is carried out on the main part of the garden at Munstead Wood and continues until the present day.

The creation of Munstead Wood provided the basis for a working relationship between Jekyll and the young architect Edwin Lutyens, which endured until almost the end of the former's life and which provided the latter with an ideal to which henceforth he consistently aspired. However, because Lutyens's house was planned after the garden had been started, the overall scheme had an ad-hoc quality unlike those they devised later for other clients. The only part of the garden on which Lutyens advised was the formal area adjoining the half-timbered court to the rear of the house. Here short flights of steps descend around a tank, originally surrounded by ferns and lilies. Further on, a path leads to a silver birch shading a wooden, tomb-like bench, christened the 'Cenotaph of Sigismunda' by one of Jekyll's friends. This spot for contemplation and repose, though not designed by Lutyens, was the conceptual origin of the Cenotaph Lutyens designed for Whitehall in 1919 to honour the dead of World War I.

Although the land owned by Gertrude Jekyll has been split into different plots, the main part of her garden now looks better than it has ever done since her death, owing to a splendid restoration programme carried out since the 1980s. *D.C.*

Aster borders.

Naumkeag

STOCKBRIDGE
MASSACHUSETTS, USA

'I want all my places to seem the homes of children and lovers. I want them to be comfortable and if possible slightly mysterious by day, and vistas and compositions appealing to the painter. I want them to be delirious in the moonlight.'

FLETCHER STEELE.

The tree peony and terrace garden.

Alcázar de Sevilla, Madrid, 1943

1884 Joseph Choate purchases property in Stockbridge for a summer home.

1885–86 The 26-room, Norman-style home designed by Stanford White is built.

1886 The gardens are designed by Nathan Barrett.

1917 Joseph Choate dies; his daughter Mabel remains at Naumkeag with her mother.

1926 Fletcher Steele, working closely with Mabel Choate, begins work at Naumkeag.

1937 The Chinese House is built to house Miss Choate's oriental treasures collection.

1938 Steele begins work on the Blue Steps.

1958 Miss Choate dies. She bequeaths Naumkeag to The Trustees of Reservations, who open the house and garden to the public.

Nestled in the steep and hilly Berkshires, the Naumkeag gardens were an inviting canvas for the brilliant young landscape architect Fletcher Steele (1885–1971) when he first encountered them in 1926. The gardens and the rambling home to which they were attached had been the summer residence of New York lawyer Joseph H. Choate and his family since the mid-1880s. The gardens, designed by Boston garden designer Nathan Barrett in 1886, were dominated by steep lawns and ample Victorian borders that had been faithfully bedded out with annuals every year for over forty years. For Steele, the gardens and their surrounding mountain would provide the inspiration to experiment with novel interpretations of old garden formulae.

Steele had graduated from the Harvard School of Landscape Architecture in 1909, where he had been steeped in the Beaux-Arts tradition. But his extensive European travels after graduation left him greatly influenced by the Modern movement in architecture and garden design. Contemporary French designers, particularly André Vera (fl. 1919–50), inspired Steele with their manipulation of levels and their innovative use of perspective.

When Steele met Miss Mable Choate, the daughter of Joseph Choate and inheritor of Naumkeag, in 1926, it marked the beginning of a thirty-year friendship. Miss Choate was intelligent, widely traveled, and keenly interested in gardening. She had been impressed by the 'garden rooms' she had seen in California, and wanted a garden room of her own

The Moon Gate.

to enjoy on summer afternoons. The result was the Steele-designed Afternoon Garden, a whimsical interpretation of a Renaissance garden. In addition to pools, fountains, and boxwood *parterres*, the garden features oak pilings carved and painted to resemble Venetian gondola posts. In a testament to both the client's and the designer's eclectic tastes and willingness to toss aside tradition, a classical sculpture by noted artist Frederick MacMonnies stands next to Roman 'thrones' made of pink concrete.

Following the success of the Afternoon Garden, Steele embarked on an ambitious transformation of the Naumkeag property, albeit with a measured appreciation of its heritage. Steele admired Barrett's basic design, yet he saw possibilities that Barrett — working in an earlier era — had not been able to exploit. Steele frequently spoke of himself as a landscape sculptor, and nowhere is this more evident than on Naumkeag's South Lawn. Under Steele's direction, the former steep hill was transfigured into a curving, sloping land mass modelled on the mountain range beyond it.

Steele's most famous feature at Naumkeag, and the one which most clearly illustrates his imaginative manipulation of levels and perspective, is the Blue Steps. Functionally no more than a way to traverse a steep hill without slipping and falling, the steps are an artistic feat rarely equalled in garden design. Reminiscent of Italian water staircases, the Blue Steps nevertheless celebrate modern lines and abstract forms. Descending in curving sweeps down which water gurgles into cavernous basins, the blue-painted steps are planted within a grove of native birch, whose vertical trunks resonant perfectly with the railing's risers.

S.G.M.

The Birch Walk and Blue Steps.

'The Perugino View', sketch by Fletcher Steele, November 1931.

Giverny

EURE, FRANCE

'For me, a landscape does not exist in its own right, since its appearance changes at every moment; but the surrounding atmosphere brings it to life — the light and the air which vary continually. For me, it is only the surrounding atmosphere which gives subjects their true value.'

CLAUDE MONET.

View to house with pink roses, purple sage and sweet william.

Double iron arches straddling the Grande Allée.

At Giverny, Claude Monet (1840–1926) used his wealth to create a horticultural paradise of design and plantsmanship. The gardens are in two distinct sections: the first, the Flower Garden, is laid out on a rectilinear grid softened by the abundance of planting; the second, the Water Garden, Monet bought in 1893 in order to create something 'for the pleasure of the eye and also for motifs to paint'. The house, studios and other buildings line the northern border with the symmetrical Flower Garden drawing the eye south down the Grande Allée and network of side paths. Monet did not train plants up the house's façade but took 'the pictorial composition into the sky' by training climbers over an extensive network of iron frames. The Grande Allée is designed to evolve into an exuberant tunnel. The wide gravel path is lined with carp's back flower beds, i.e. the soil is built up centrally, and the double iron arches straddle from 'backbone' to 'backbone', clad in festoons of climbing and rambling roses. Seasonal flowers in the beds cascade down with nasturtiums trailing across the gravel gradually closing the circle by autumn. Long, paintbox flowerbeds run parallel to the Grande Allée, their mixture of climbing, perennial and annual plants giving an impressionistic effect, focused by spikes of colour and sentinel standard roses. Giverny was a family home so there are three lawns for sitting, playing and picnicking bordered by flower beds under fruit trees with narrow single entrances turning each into secret gardens. The clumps of narcissi in the grass were a novelty popularised by English contemporary William Robinson (1838–1935) who, like Monet, encouraged Joseph Bory Latour-Marliac's waterlily hybridisation.

In 1893, inspired by the landscapes of Hokusai and other Japanese printmakers, Monet bought the meadowland that lay across the railway line opposite the Flower Garden. Monet diverted the River Ru to create the Water Garden, not as an architectural feature or naturalistic landscape, but as a plant environment with constantly changing colour and light. Like the gardeners of 'beautiful' 18th-century landscapes, Monet designed naturalistic pools whose banks appeared to merge into the water, the latter mirroring the waterlilies. All this was tended by a gardener whose sole task was to maintain their compositional order, with the willows, the sky, the sun and the celebrated Japanese Bridge aligned to the Grande Allée. As well as the Japanese Bridge there are five other bridges, three crossing the Ru, the sluice gate and one to a rose arbour. Each provides a platform to view the sparkle of light on water through a veil of greenery. The prettiest is undoubtedly the rose arbour from which Monet took his boat to paint. Interestingly, no other artist painted Giverny until after Monet's death.

Giverny is a painterly garden where Monet developed his artistic style without the distraction of a horizon. Its rigorous symmetrical design frames massed plantings whose colour and shapes offer vibrancy, balanced by an asymmetrical green oasis where weeping willows, wisteria and the ever-changing sky join the waterlilies in green reflections.

C.H.

The rose arbour bridge.

1883 Monet rents the house and land at Giverny.
1890 He buys Giverny and devotes himself to the garden.
1893 He buys the lower meadowland.
1901 An overhead arch is added to Japanese Bridge and extended water garden.
1911 Water Garden is extended again.
1923 Operation to remove Monet's cataracts restores his sight.
1926 Monet dies.

Front façade with pink tulips and myostosis.

Biltmore

ASHEVILLE
N. CAROLINA, USA

'The first point to be kept in mind then is the preservation and maintenance as exactly as is possible of the natural scenery; the restriction, that is to say, within the narrowest limits consistent with the necessary accommodation of visitors, of all artificial constructions and the prevention of all constructions markedly inharmonious with the scenery or which would unnecessarily obscure, distort or detract from the dignity of the scenery.'

FREDERICK LAW OLMSTED
Yosemite and the Mariposa Grove: A Preliminary Report, 1865; reprinted in 1995 by the Yosemite Association

The pergola in the Walled Garden which bisects a formal parterre.

Biltmore is a huge landscaped estate with many fine trees and productive forests.

1888 Olmsted hired by G.W. Vanderbilt to work on the Biltmore estate,

1891 Work starts on the garden design.

1895 Work completed on the gardens.

The gardens of the Biltmore Estate near Asheville in North Carolina are one of the most ambitious creations of Frederick Law Olmsted, America's premier landscape architect and creator of New York's Central Park. The estate belongs to the Vanderbilt family and surrounds a chateau conceived in the French style commissioned by George Washington Vanderbilt and opened in 1895.

Access to this vast 8,000-acre estate is strictly by car along a three mile approach designed by Olmsted, a great supporter of sustainable, extractive forestry practices. A short walk through scented pines brings the visitor to the front vista of the house and its formal lawns. To the south side of the house a formal terrace, densely shaded by large wisterias and trumpet creepers protects from summer heat and affords spectacular views of Mount Pisgah and the Blue Ridge Mountains. To the south-east is a long, narrow Italianate water garden with three pools. South of this the mood changes to the informal with a shrub garden built on a slope with magnolias, azaleas, dogwoods, redbuds and Japanese maples, mostly at their best in spring.

The formal gardens below this are enclosed by a wall and comprise four acres in all. Bizarrely, the visitor is forced to cross the exit roadway through the estate which traverses two sides of the Walled Garden. Planting here is of subtropical bedding within a formal *parterre* including magnificent cannas, annuals and tender perennials. A pergola leads through to the lower half of the garden which features rose varieties contemporary with the house and the current All-America Rose Selections. Stairs descend to a small semi-circular herb garden which forms the frontage to an iron conservatory range with a stone and brick façade. The central Palm House houses pot grown specimens of some size and is flanked by other houses displaying orchids and a variety of exotics which would once have served the house for pot and cut flower display. The entire range was restored in the 1990s.

The gardens below the walled garden descend further into a mass of azaleas, hard to be beaten outside Europe or Japan, and lead on into an area of walking trails surrounding the delightfully informal Bass Pond. To the east of the walled garden is a similarly informal area of paths called the Spring Garden which ascends to the end of the Italian Garden.

The gardens are best seen in the context of this extraordinary imitation of an aristocratic French lifestyle by a pioneer American industrialist and were unique in the America of the 1890s in scale and opulence. In Britain a similar experience can be obtained by visiting the French château-style estate of the Rothschilds at Waddesdon.

The rest of Biltmore is a working operation with forests, vineyards with a winery and deer herds among which wind the Swannanoa and French Broad rivers. The visitor sees most of this by car — which makes it a particularly American experience — but is the only way the scale of this estate can be appreciated. *S.M.*

Spring bedding displays in the Walled Garden south-east of the château.

Hestercombe SOMERSET, ENGLAND

*'A very enchanting [...] building called the Witch's Cave, composed of Stocks and Roots of trees twisted into the most fantastic shapes. In the division of the octagon is the figure of an old witch with her beard, high crowned hat and broom, and in another nick [*sic. = *niche] is painted an owl and another a cat.'*

HENRY HAWKINS
owner of Heligan.

The Rotunda.

The Orangery.

The Great Plat with the pergola in the distance.

1750–86 Coplestone Warre Bampfylde creates Landscape garden.
1761 Witch House, Mausoleum, Gothick Seat created.
1762 Great Cascade built.
c. 1775 Temple Arbour.
1904–09 Lutyens and Jekyll rework gardens.
1942 Viscount Portman dies, and the house is leased by Somerset County Council for the headquarters of the County Fire Service.
1973 Discovery of Jekyll's original garden plans initiates their restoration.
1997 Restoration of Bampfylde's Landscape gardens.

Hestercombe stands on the southerly slopes of the Quantocks with extensive views over Taunton to the Blackdown Hills and offers jointly and separately two decisive periods in English garden design. The gardens behind the house were created in the Landscape style, while those to the south are a magnificent example of a collaboration between Sir Edwin Lutyens (1869–1944) and Gertrude Jekyll (1843–1932).

The Landscape Garden covering some 35 acres was designed and built between 1750 and 1786 by Coplestone Warre Bampfylde, a watercolourist whose sketches provide an invaluable record of his creation. The wooded hillside with natural springs provided the perfect setting for a series of classical and rustic buildings from which to enjoy the prospects. Meandering walks through the woods, alongside the culvert and over the rivulets reveal the naturalistic design, and at one point England's only surviving *capriccio*.

The Box Pond at the top of the hill feeds the babbling brook that runs down to the beautiful Pear Pond, originally impounded in 1698, and supplies, by means of a brick-lined culvert (still intact), the Great Cascade whose tumbling waters were captured by Bampfylde in pencil and watercolour. (Henry Hoare commissioned Bampfylde to design the Cascade at Stourhead in 1766.)

Classical buildings include the Temple Arbour which provides a regular reference point for the visitor and a pleasing prospect down to the Pear Pond; and to the 1786 Pope's Urn from which the Cascade and Witch House can be seen. The latter two were both constructed in 1761, providing a striking contrast between filial respect and the occult. The seats (now lost) were testaments to the contemporary influence of the Chinese and the 'Gothick' (both

View across Pear Pond to the temple.

recorded in 1761) and also saw the addition of an Alcove (recorded 1771).

The visitor descends from this Georgian landscape into the 20th century via the Chinese Gate or Lutyens's daisy steps. When Clive Aslet wrote: 'The harmony between formal planning and informal planting in a Lutyens–Jekyll or Harold Peto garden represents an ideal synthesis, in which the country-house garden was possibly more successful than the country house', Hestercombe has to be the supreme example.

In 1904 the Hon. E. W. B. Portman commissioned Lutyens to design a new garden with Gertrude Jekyll. Terracing from the house exaggerates the slope and enhances the theatricality; the top terrace provides an overview, and the Grey Walk between was planted to achieve Jekyll's 'effect [of] grey-green and silver grey with flowers of white, pastel pink and blues' leading down to the Great Plat.

The Plat has a *parterre* design centred on a saltire of grass edged in stone whose shape is reminiscent equally of Scottish and Islamic gardens. Any trace of the rigid formality associated with *parterres* is softened by the use of a flight of rounded steps at the southern corners and the pergola of climber-swathed alternating round and square piers which frames the countryside beyond. The design consists of four large beds edged in generous-leaved Bergenia and filled with flowers and grasses; the cracks, crevices and pockets in the walls burgeon with plants. The lateral terrace walks, with a wych-elm arbour to the west and ornate font to the east, have central, Islamic-inspired rills but with stone-edged circles for arum lilies, which Jekyll described as being in 'the manner of the gathered ribbon strapwork of ancient needlework'. *C.H.*

Old Westbury Gardens

LONG ISLAND, NY, USA

'The human hand works in concert with nature here — exactly as it should be in the garden.'

DR. ELLEN HENKE
Flower and Garden Magazine, April–May 1992.

The wrought-iron entrance gates.

As one of the pre-eminent English-style gardens in America, Old Westbury is a testament not only to the good tastes of the early 20th-century monied set, but to plain old-fashioned nostalgia. John S. Phipps built the Georgian style home and gardens on the north shore of Long Island to delight his English wife, Margarita Grace Phipps. Designed by the famed British architect George Crawley in 1905, the house and gardens reflect a love of all things English.

The monumental wrought-iron entrance gates, *allées* of little-leaf lindens and beech and wide sweeps of green lawn declare the grandeur of Old Westbury. Yet, like other great estates of the era, Old Westbury encompasses a series of formal, intimate gardens within its expansive, pastoral landscape. These smaller gardens overflow with colour and lush greenery, epitomising grace and elegance while quietly inviting plant lovers to explore.

The most remarkable formal garden is the Walled Garden, which was designed by Crawley in an architectural style meant to complement the house. As an English interpretation of an Italian Renaissance garden, the Walled Garden is based on the orderly, symmetrical division of space. Geometric shapes and structural elements, such as the domed pergola and the 8-foot wall surrounding the garden, predominate. Vistas and cross-axes — fundamental features of Italian gardens — are in evidence in bisecting paths and in the formal *parterres* that converge on an ornate fountain. Whereas the garden originally had few flowers, Mrs. Phipps, in her quintessentially English fashion, enlivened the borders with a profusion of flowering plants over the years.

Equally beautiful is the Boxwood Garden. Created in 1928, this garden reflects formal 18th-century design principles. Boxwoods, already over 100 years old when they were transplanted from Virginia, surround a reflecting pool graced with waterlilies. At the far end of the Boxwood Garden, European weeping beech trees anchor a Grecian colonnade that shelters a statue of Diana, the Huntress.

A fascinating aspect of the Old Westbury gardens is that despite their grand scale they gracefully bear witness to the personality of their original owners. One of the most charming features of the gardens is the Ghost Walk, a tunnel of hemlock that resembles the yew walk that Mrs. Phipps enjoyed at Battle Abbey in Sussex, where she grew up. Equally engaging is the Children's Garden, reached by way of the Primrose Path. The garden features a miniature thatched cottage given to the Phipps's daughter, Peggie, on her tenth birthday. The Children's Garden itself is a lush English-style cottage garden replete with roses, foxglove, climbing clematis and other colourful flowers tucked behind a picket fence. During World War II, the 30 children who were sheltered at Old Westbury loved to play in the cottage garden. Their grateful families presented the Phipps family with a pair of eagle statues, which now flank the Lilac Walk. *S.G.M.*

1905–06 Westbury House built for John S. Phipps and his wife Margarita Grace Phipps.
1928 Boxwood Garden designed. One-hundred-year-old boxwoods are brought from Virginia.
1940s Two eagle statues are presented to the Phipps family by the families of 30 English children who were sheltered at Westbury during World War II.
1958 John Phipps dies; Westbury house and gardens endowed by the J.S. Phipps Foundation.
1959 Old Westbury opened to the public.
1960s Herbaceous borders reworked. Demonstration gardens and Woodland Walk added.

The domed pergola.

The Walled Garden is structured by intersecting gravel paths.

The Children's Garden.

Villandry INDRE-ET-LOIRE, FRANCE

'Peace...If one word can capture Villandry, this is the one. The reigning order, the serenity emanating from a perfect peace, the silence which even the murmur of water in the pools fails to disturb, the landscape imbued with infinite softness — everything here conspires to convey peace and pleasure in living.'

MAURICE FLEURENT
Villandry — Le Jardin du bonheur, Paris: Sous le Vent, 1989.

The jardin potager.

One of the potager squares.

1533–45 Jean Lebreton builds château in new Italian (Renaissance) style.
1906 Joachim and Ann (Colman) Carvallo buy Villandry, restoring château to 16th-century appearance and researching contemporary garden designs.
1910 Joachim Carvallo converts to Catholicism.
1914 Jardin d'Ornement completed.
1914–18 Creation of Jardin Potager.

Right: The jardin d'ornement *with French crosses seen beyond 'tender love'.*

In 1906 Joachim Carvallo and his American wife, Ann, bought the delapidated château and gardens of Villandry. After careful research Carvallo removed later extraneous masonry from the Renaissance château and decided that the indifferent *jardin anglais* denigrated the architectural whole. The garden designs were inspired partly by traditional modest Loire gardens recorded in Jacques Androuet Du Cerceau's (c. 1515/20–c. 1584) *Les plus excellent bâtiments de France*, an incomparable record of 16th-century French palace and château gardens, especially in the Loire area, and the *Monasticon gallicanum* records of Benedictine Abbey gardens. The implementation of Carvallo's researches was fuelled by his conversion to Catholicism, and his search for spiritually uplifting nature.

The château and its three established axes required a balanced layout, so the *jardin anglais* was reformed into four tiers representing different hierarchical levels that conformed to Carvallo's understanding of cultural and aesthetic order. On the western boundary an earlier bastion creates a belvedere from which a lateral axis forms the transition from the lower terraces to the upper water *parterre*, the central channel from this *pièce d'eau* providing the third axis. The appearance is of elegant squares; the reality is cleverly honed trapeziums.

An Arab-Andalusian influenced *jardin d'ornement* adjoins the château, symbolising four stages of love in clipped box *compartiments*. The first, tender love, is a balanced composition of four hearts each licked by two flames and topped with masks; the second shows whirling hearts in a dance; the third, fickle or adulterous love, is cornered by fans, separated by horns of lust with the central motif of a torn-up letter; the fourth, tragic love, is a discordant arrangement of four swords, four daggers and a broken heart.

Box *compartiment* beds flank a secondary lateral axis, beyond which lie the three crosses of France worked in clipped box, topiary yew and bedding plants. The east wing of the château overlooks the lower *jardin potager*, an array of vegetables designed with classical flavour but redolent of modern tastes. This is nine, seemingly square, quadripartite gardens each designed to display vegetables and random plantings of standard roses which represent monks constantly tending their plots. Each square is framed with trellis fencing, goblet-trained pears and a *plate-bande* filled with bright bedding plants. The design is inward looking, held by 16 arbours arranged in fours around quatrefoil pools on each corner of the central garden. Four flights of steps aligned to the broad Loire sandwalks lead to a vine-covered tunnel arbour from which three *parterres de compartiment* form a colourful and seemingly musical pattern. The alignment of the two viewing balconies on the fourth terrace are subtly altered and approached by sweeping Italian-style slopes. The *pièce d'eau* feeds the moats and water features. The creation of Villandry worked on Humanist principles but its iconic vision was Carvallo's, a legacy embellished by his descendents: during his granddaughter-in-law's tenancy the *potager* became voluptuous, but it has now returned to its original masculine order. *C.H.*

Hidcote Manor

GLOUCESTERSHIRE, ENGLAND

Top: The Bathing Pool Garden.

Above: The Pillar Garden.

The Old Garden with the overhanging Cedar.

'What I should like to impress upon the reader is the luxuriance everywhere; a kind of haphazard luxuriance which of course comes neither by hap nor hazard at all....'

VITA SACKVILLE-WEST
Hidcote Manor Garden, [1949], London: National Trust, 1952.

Some of the finest English 20th-century gardens evolved in the hands of well-travelled cosmopolitan owner–designers such as American-born Lawrence Johnston (1871–1958) at Hidcote Manor. Johnston took 40 years over his work but left no plans, no diaries, no notes. He drew his inspiration from Italy, France, his friends and neighbouring cottage gardens to which he added consummate plantsmanship. There is no obvious relationship between the house and gardens, in which yew, beech and grass set the architectural tone while topiary and plants, rather than statues or urns, are the key players.

The gardens evolved in three stages: the first was influenced by the Arts and Crafts movement with brick paths linking geometrically arranged box-edged beds whose formality and topiary birds contained abundantly informal planting. The second architectural linear style was cool and classical, typified by the vast Theatre Lawn which terminates in a raised, encircled beech. Running parallel to this the Stilt Hedge framed the vista from the venerable Cedar into the countryside to the west. The third and continuing phase evolved alongside Johnston's Mediterranean home, La Serre de la Madone: knowledgeable plantsmanship and time created a daring and complex structure of garden rooms and vistas.

At Hidcote, there is effectively no main axis but the dramatic sweeps of the Theatre Lawn to the west and the Long Walk to the south are the lungs — deep inhalations between the many garden rooms. The visitor steps from the Theatre Lawn into the Circle encompassed by a 'tapestry' hedge bejewelled with sparkling *Tropaeolum speciosum*. The eye is drawn west through the celebrated red borders of foliage, bark and flowers, up a flight of steps whose treads are softened by horizontal planting flanked by brick gazebos, and onwards through the nave of the Stilt Garden into the countryside beyond. To the east are the cottagey comforts of the Old Garden, then the Cedar, before entering the White and Maple Gardens.

The circles repeat southwards through the Fuchsia Garden into the Bathing Pool Garden which seems to brim to the very edges of its yew hedging, before becoming a further quiet circle of green. Classical water is replaced by streams and the planting of trees, shrubs and bog plants that meander onto and away from the Long Walk. The western Stream Garden leads up to the Rock Bank, naturalistic but with specialist plants, and into the Pillar Garden balanced on the other side by Mrs. Winthrop's Garden. These gardens are inspired by the Mediterranean: the former is terraced with pillar-clipped yews whose backdrop walls carry the Stilt Garden above; the latter is paved, restrained and very sheltered.

The green expanse of the adjacent Theatre Lawn invites a return to the house and northern gardens. The Camellia Corner and Pine Garden are separated by a formal pool while a broad path draws the visitor into the rose borders. *C.H.*

Exuberant herbaceous plantings using perennials and annuals.

1907 Lawrence Johnston's mother, Mrs. Gertrude Winthrop, buys Hidcote Manor with 300 acres; first gardens created near house.

1914–20 Stilt Garden, gazebos, Mrs. Winthrop's Garden.

1920–30 Long Walk, Stream Gardens.

1924 Lawrence Johnston buys La Serre de la Madone, Menton, France.

1927 Plant hunting in South Africa (Drakensburg Mountains) with Captain Collingwood (Cherry) Ingram and George Taylor.

1931 Plant hunting with George Forrest.

1948 Hidcote Manor donated to National Trust.

Villa Ephrussi

CAP FERRAT
FRANCE

Sentinel exotic agaves in the French garden.

'Here I have achieved my purpose of defying the laws of Nature and common sense.'

BÉATRICE DE ROTHSCHILD, BARONESS EPHRUSSI
cited in Miriam Rothschild, *The Rothschild Gardens*, London: Gaia, 1996.

The gentle winter climate of the Riviera drew an international, cosmopolitan *élite* during the Belle Epoque. The breathtaking views from the isthmus of Cap Ferrat, combined with its proximity to Nice and Monte Carlo, attracted royalty such as King Leopold II of Belgium, from under whose nose Madame Maurice Ephrussi acquired an adjoining rocky terrain for her sumptuous palazzino (initially named Villa Ile-de-France).

The climate and the clientele telescoped history and travel into garden designs which were inspired by international styles and themed by culture and collections. The 17 acres spread over a rocky outcrop were levelled, and decent top soil and water were introduced to create a *jardin-vaisseau*. The topography was sculpted to resemble the decks of a smart cruise liner rising to its captain's palazzino. The house's name and its style were inspired by Mme Ephrussi's cruise on the liner Ile-de-France and her favourite colour — pink.

Born Baroness Béatrice de Rothschild, Madame Ephrussi (1864–1934) was an outstanding collector. Those who come to view the treasures within the villa look south over a formal French garden in Creole style with its sentinel palm trees and agaves terminating in a copy of the Trianon's Temple d'Amour. A *grand cour* with a grotto fronts the villa, and a tour of the 'decks' offers more earthly treasures. The westerly itinerary starts with a sunken perfumed 'Spanish' garden: the rill and arches echo its Moorish heritage and that of Rome in the pink marble columns supporting the cryptoporticus, above which the villa can be glimpsed. A horseshoe staircase provides a delightful grotto as well as giving the option to ascend or continue. The Florentine terrace is a series of gentle steps lined with cypress and stone balustrades with spectacular views over the Mediterranean.

The next three gardens typify contemporary fashion: the lapidary garden contains all the architectural salvage and statuary that could not be used, arranged perhaps to illustrate chaos; the Japanese Garden boasts a ceramic pagoda; and a *jardin exotique* contains steep winding paths around impressive cacti.

The 'ancient' rosary is laid out in formal beds terraced in a fan from a hexagonal pavilion, climbers scramble over columns and faience pots of santolina give a Persian air. The garden's extremity disappears into a wilderness of gnarled olives and aloes that evoke an untouched landscape — the final theme. The *jardin provençal* falls away to the easterly seaboard while sinuous paths wind through the pine wooded area of the *jardin anglais*, a naturalistic area in the spirit of the Landscape style with a small shady temple.

Through the pines, the curvaceous Venus within the Temple d'Amour marks the return to civilisation and a dramatically staged view across to the villa. Water cascades down steps to the formal canal and pool which mirrors the imposing pink Italian confection. The broad, white gravel paths that outline the symmetrical *parterre* contrast with its verdancy — a floral ballroom for first class passengers designed by Le Nôtre revivalist Achille Duchêne (1866–1947).

C.H.

1905 Mme Ephrussi de Rothschild acquires 17 acres on Cap Ferrat.

1912 House and gardens completed (during which at least 11 architects are dismissed).

1916 Death of Maurice Ephrussi. Mme Ephrussi never lives here again.

1917, 1926,1956 and 1985 Frosts destroy exotic plants.

1934 Villa bequeathed to the Institut de France.

Westerly vista over the parterre à l'angloisse from the palazzino.

The palazzino mirrored in the French garden canal.

Top: Stone is a major landscape element.
Above left: Clipped evergreen shrubbery delineates areas within the formal gardens.
Above right: The 17th-century travertine fountain.
Opposite: The parterres de broderie.

1912 James Deering purchases property on Biscayne Bay for a winter retreat; Deering and Paul Chalfin, the newly hired artistic director for Vizcaya, travel through Europe purchasing antiquities and statuary for the estate.

1914 Diego Suarez is hired as the landscape architect of the gardens; construction on the estate begins.

1916 Deering moves into his winter residence.

1921 Gardens completed following an interruption in construction caused by World War I.

1925 Deering dies; Vizcaya remains neglected for nearly 30 years.

1952 Vizcaya opens to the public as a museum.

1994 Vizcaya is designated a National Historic Landmark.

Villa Vizcaya

MIAMI
FLORIDA, USA

'Suarez had looked with an artist's eye past the noonday glare of Vizcaya down the long allées *of history to the time of Xenophon and the beginnings of garden art in the West.'*

JAMES T. MAHER
The Twilight of Splendor: Chronicles in the Age of American Palaces, 1975.

In 1911 James Deering, a quiet and intensely private middle-aged bachelor, was seeking a refuge from cold Michigan winters. As one of the heirs of the International Harvester Company, he had plenty of money with which to indulge his tropical dreams. In a propitious move, he hired Paul Chalfin, a flamboyant former curator at the Boston Museum of Fine Arts, to build and decorate a house at the edge of Biscayne Bay. Chalfin's overriding zeal and his vision of an Italian-style villa was to leave its imprint on every aspect of Vizcaya. It was Chalfin who whisked Deering to Europe to soak in the ambiance of Italian villas, as well as to purchase an astronomical number of antiquities. Five years later — thanks to Deering's money and Chalfin's impeccable taste — there arose out of the Florida wilderness an incredible Italianate palazzo housing one of the most remarkable collections of 15th–19th century antiquities and decorative arts in America.

Deering moved into his winter residence in December 1916, with the gardens still in shambles. Five years later the baroque gardens emerged from the construction dust. But the long-suffering Deering, who had waited through numerous construction delays, was to enjoy the gardens for only four seasons before he died in 1925.

The gardens, which lay neglected for nearly 30 years before being opened to the public in 1952, are a brilliant interpretation of a 16th-century Italian garden. Designed by Diego Suarez, a landscape architect who trained in Italy, the gardens are highly structured. They depend not on colour or flora for their appeal, but on controlled views, manipulative geometry and neatly sheared shrubbery. Enlivened by exquisite statuary and splashing fountains, the gardens become magical.

Using the principles articulated by Andrea Palladio (1508–80), who believed that a landscape should be intimately related to its associated building, Suarez designed a garden whose main axis is a continuation of the main axis of the house. From the villa's south terrace, the land was sculpted to give a sweeping view over an elevated reflecting pool edged by an *allée* of live oaks. Beyond a grotto-flanked water stairway, the focal point is a Sicilian *casino*.

On either side of the main axis the garden is carpeted with intricate *parterres*. Frankly imitative of the *broderie* patterns at the La Reggia gardens outside of Naples, the *parterres* tacitly acknowledge the sub-tropical climate of south Florida, being edged in wild jasmine rather than the more traditional boxwood. Two long walkways fan out at angles to the left and right, flanked by statuary *allées* of mythological gods and goddess. Beyond these are a series of smaller Renaissance-style gardens — a maze garden, a *giardino segreto*, a theatre garden reminiscent of the Villa la Pietra in Florence, and a rose garden centred on a monumental 17th-century fountain that once served as the village fountain of Bassano di Sutri outside Rome.

S.G.M.

View along the main axis to the dome of Viceroy's House.

1911 Transfer of the Government of India to Delhi announced.

1912 Lutyens is appointed to the Delhi Planning Commission.

1913 Lutyens and Herbert Baker appointed to design government buildings in the new city, Lutyens responsible for Viceroy's House and garden.

1917 Lutyens designs Viceroy's Garden.

1928–29 Planting in the garden is carried out in with the help of William Robertson Mustoe of the Punjab Horticultural Department.

1931 New Delhi is finished. Viceroy's House and its garden are handed over to the Viceroy, Lord Irwin. Lutyens, already knighted, is made Knight Commander of the Indian Empire for his work there.

1938 Lutyens makes his last trip to India, during which he supervises the restoration of the garden following alterations carried out against his intentions.

Stone screen and steps between parterre *and tennis courts.*

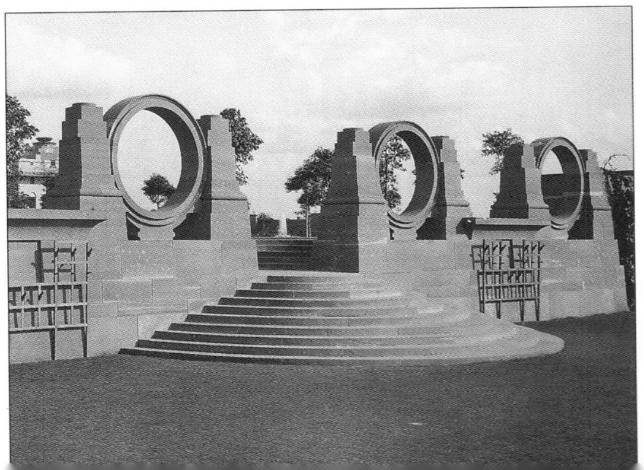

Viceroy's Garden

NEW DELHI, INDIA

'A paradise of which the enjoyment never waned.'

(VICEROY) EDWARD FREDERICK LINDLEY WOOD, FIRST EARL OF HALIFAX
Fullness of Days, London: Collins, 1957.

Viceroy's Garden in New Delhi is Sir Edwin Landseer Lutyens's (1869–1944) grandest garden design. A fusion of Eastern and Western gardening traditions, it was intended to express the power of the British Raj.

Lutyens's gardens always had strong formal elements, a trait which became more pronounced from c.1905, when he moved away from the vernacular style of his early buildings towards monumental classicism. His long involvement with the new capital of India provided a crucible in which he honed his skills in classical design. Nevertheless, although the vast garden Lutyens created for Viceroy's House is a far cry from the cottage style of Munstead Wood, it also includes personal touches which hark back to the early tuition in gardening taste he had received from Gertrude Jekyll.

Following Lutyens's appointment in 1912 to the Delhi Planning Commission, which decided on the site and planning of the new city, he gained sole responsibility for Viceroy's House, the single most important building, and its garden. The overall city plan was based partly on principles derived from the Beaux-Arts tradition and partly on the ideals of the English garden city movement (Lutyens contributed to the design of Hampstead Garden Suburb from 1906). On Lutyens's insistence, Viceroy's House was predominantly Western and classical in style, although it incorporates Buddhist, Hindu and Mogul features.

In contrast, the Viceroy's Garden, designed in 1917, embodies a more equal balance of European and Oriental ideas. Lutyens was asked to make a design inspired by the gardens laid out for the Mogul emperors in the 16th and 17th centuries at the Taj Mahal and in Srinigar, Lahore and the Red Forts of Delhi and Agra. Like its Indo-Persian models, Lutyens's huge main *parterre* (440 feet square) has a quadripartite plan, divided by canals and studded with fountains. However, where the centre of a Mogul layout would be occupied by a water tank, there is a square lawn for Viceregal tea parties. Although Lutyens's use of water draws on Mogul models, this was already a notable element in many of his English gardens, for example Deanery Garden, Berkshire (1899) and Hestercombe, Somerset (1906).

The cleverest aspect of the design is its integration with the palace it serves and the layout of the city beyond. The garden is raised on ramparts of rhubarb sandstone which are a continuation of the sub-basement of Viceroy's House. Its plan corresponds to the axial grid of the house, and its central line is that of the main ceremonial axis of the city, stretching from the King George V Memorial at India Gate over two miles away. After passing through the *parterre* and a long walled garden, whose central section is shaded by a monumental pergola, this axis terminates in a circular sunken garden arranged around a pool. Lutyens had this part of the garden filled with plants attractive to butterflies — a touch of whimsy quite in accord with the paradisiacal theme implied in the adoption of Indian garden traditions.

D.C.

View of the parterre *showing canals and fountains.*

Dumbarton Oaks

WASHINGTON, DC, USA

View to the Hornbeam Ellipse.

'On an early summer evening the sound of falling water and the song of the wood thrush bring the peace of Innisfree that comes "dropping slow" even to the most restless mind.'

BEATRIX FARRAND
Dumbarton Oaks Garden, New York, n.d.

In 1922 Robert and Mildred Bliss commissioned Beatrix Farrand (1872–1959) and in the following 26 years they created one of the finest gardens in the United States. Dumbarton Oaks exudes the genius of Farrand: her architectural and gardening talents combined the skills of Lutyens and Jekyll, and swirls with the additional flourishes of colleagues and disciples. The pace is set by the Georgian manor house with formal upper terraces descending asymmetrically through separately conceived walled terraces, glimpsing the possibility of following meandering brick walks through orchards and trees into a naturalistic park. Farrand perfected asymmetrical design: she deliberately did not extend a main axis from the North Vista so that just as the visitor begins to sense a symmetrical pattern a sinuous meander leads away to half-hidden delights.

Stone, brick and elaborate pebble-work combine with sculpted basins, fonts, pools and rocky streams to create the rhythms and refrains that run through the gardens. Farrand collected antique statuary and designed new sculpture which was executed by Frederick Coles. She eschewed traditional holly, boxwood and yew but in any case the Washington climatic extremes proved too much for box. The replacement ideas such as the stone walls overhung with wisteria lining the North Vista, Ruth Havey's clipped ivy in the Box Terrace and Alden Hopkins's Hornbeam Ellipse improve rather than devalue the original concepts. The North Vista, Green and Zodiac terraces by the house are grassed with one or two specimen trees, a green oasis from which to glimpse a swathe of pink cherry blossom in spring, the formal swimming pool or stone *parterre* (originally the tennis court).

The climate prevented Farrand from replicating Jekyll's colour schemes but she could create seasonal highs. She designed the autumnal herbaceous borders with yellow and red plants drifting downhill, interspersed with clipped yew, to a yellow pool of leaves; the eye is then carried up into the canopy of *Acer platanoides*. The 'ballroom' of her garden layout is the Rose Garden: the roses were only part of the scheme, its layout within stone and brick walls, and its accent box and low hedging being of equal importance. Initial box hedging was replaced with candytuft, and today the accent box and roses remain.

Double steps lead down into the Fountain Garden, a delightful staging post. The visitors then descends three semi-circular steps into the Arbor Terrace or follows the sinuous brick path through the trees to the theatrical Lover's Lane pool. Ruth Havey introduced curvaceous detail into sculpted stone in several parts of the garden including the Box Terrace, resplendent with central ornate pebblework outlined in clipped ivy. In 1961 the Tennis Court was converted into the Pebble Garden, a magnificent re-interpretation of *parterres de broderie* and *parterres d'eau*, branching and flourishing in sculpted stone, coloured by Mexican pebbles. Framed by a colonnade clad in wisteria, the pattern and effect are enhanced by outer planted 'speech marks', a spouting curvaceous pool and the merest sheet of water giving sparkle to the central pebbles. *C.H.*

1922 Robert and Mildred Bliss commission Beatrix Farrand.
1935 Ernest Clegg produces topographical watercolour of gardens.
1941 The Blisses donate Dumbarton Oaks to Harvard University and Beatrix Farrand writes the Plant Book for Dumbarton Oaks. 26 acres donated to National Park Service.
1959 Alden Hopkins's replacement Hornbeam Ellipse.
1961 Conversion of tennis court into Pebble Garden.
1968 The Museum Courtyard created incorporating c. 500 AD octagonal mosaic pool.

The Pebble Garden.

White wisteria on the North Vista.

View through the arbour, just outside the Rose Garden, onto the Arbor Terrace.

Sissinghurst

KENT, ENGLAND

The pink border.

1930 7 May: Harold Nicolson and Vita Sackville-West buy Sissinghurst. They create a lake on the southern perimeter, discover moat wall, and clear the Nuttery.

1931 Central arch in entrance opened. Stone paths in Cottage Garden, grass paths in Orchard, turfed Moat Walk and Tower Lawn created.

1932 Poplar avenue and Lime Walk planted, yew for Yew Walk and the Rondel planted, courtyard paving completed as well as other paths and steps.

1933 Erectheum, or pergola on fragments of classical columns, built in corner of White Garden.

1934 Fastigiate yews planted and dwarf box hedging.

1935 Delos dug, semi-circular wall in Rose Garden completed, construction on house.

1936 Path through Lime Walk, more hedges.

1937 Vegetable garden converted into Rose Garden, Orchard planted as wild garden.

1938 Herb Garden created.

1962 Vita Sackville-West dies.

1967 Sissinghurst handed over to National Trust in lieu of death duties.

1968 Harold Nicolson dies.

1971 Iron framed arbour replaces almond trees in White Garden.

'Beauty, and use, and beauty once again
Link up my scattered heart, and shape a scheme
Commensurate with a frustrated dream.'

VITA SACKVILLE-WEST
Sissinghurst, Dedicated 'To V.W', printed by hand by Leonard and Virginia Woolf and published at the Hogarth Press, London, 1931.

In 1930 Vita Sackville-West discovered that one of her ancestor's homes, Elizabethan Sissinghurst Castle, was for sale — a ruin of Sleeping Beauty proportions swathed in brambles. Sackville-West and her husband, Harold Nicolson, had lived in Persia, travelled throughout Europe and created their first garden at Long Barn near Sevenoaks in Kent. Inspired by castles such as Stokesay and the gardens at Avebury and Hidcote Manors, Harold Nicolson designed an architectural framework for the flat 6.9-acre gardens using the ruins; formal hedges and vistas which he created between 1930 and 1932 have never been altered.

An avenue of poplars leads to the Castle which opens onto a walled green courtyard dominated by the Tower. There Sackville-West had her study with magnificent views over the entire gardens, and in many respects it forms the garden entrance. Straight ahead a vista sweeps across the Yew Walk to the Orchard and moat, terminating in a statue of Dionysus. Stepping across the Tower Lawn a lateral vista offers the White Garden through the Bishop's Gate to the north, and to the south along the yew-clipped Rondel Garden to the statue of a Baccante topping the Lime Walk. Three subsidiary vistas are formed by the Lime Walk and the Moat Walk leading up and down between the garden rooms, and the lateral Yew Walk below Tower Lawn. The design uses these axes to link formal, straight-pathed gardens centred on a pot or urn enclosed by Elizabethan or clipped, living walls radiating from the Tower as well as the wild garden under the Orchard above the Moat. The Lime Walk (also known as The Spring Garden) is mathematically planned, the 30 lime trees spaced exactly, 15 on each side, immaculately pleached and standing in squares planted, according to Anne Scott James 'as though a Botticelli goddess had passed that way flinging flowers as she went'. Large Tuscan planted pots adorn the spaces and the axis is continued through the wilder effusion of The Nuttery. After the War Sackville-West continued her Jekyllesque colour schemes for borders into the renowned White Garden. Dwarf box-hedged beds frame massed white plantings centred on a Ming pot canopied by an iron framed arbour draped in the white flowering *Rosa longicuspis* (originally four almond trees). The beds in the Rose and Rondel Garden display roses gently trained and in abundant harmony with a rich selection of herbaceous plants and shrubs giving year-round interest. The Herb Garden is approached across a 'Persian carpet' of creeping thymes, at the furthest point in the garden, where the herb beds billow over the paths. It is a sensual garden for sight, scent and sound that can be appreciated from Edward the Confessor's seat created out of old masonry with a camomile cushion. The irregularity of the Moat Walk is disguised by a bank of azaleas that lead back towards the castle via South Cottage, fronted by four fastigiate yews and a mass of cottage plantings. One final small garden, Delos, named for the island birthplace of Apollo and Diana, reminds us that in sunshine and by moonlight Sissinghurst evokes the mythical garden paradise. *C.H.*

Shallow pots provide a focus for the paths radiating between the flowerbeds.

Main entrance to the Castle.

The topiaried yews echo the cylindrical Tower of the castle itself.

Ninfa

NINFA, ITALY

'Any visit is like trespassing in Sleeping Beauty's palace, in which gates, arches, towers, walls, churches and houses are spangled with flowers — wisteria, honeysuckle, clematis, passion flowers and, above all, roses — which soar heavenwards only to cascade down again.'

ROY STRONG, *Garden Party*, London: Frances Lincoln, 2000.

Gunnera manicata *growing on the banks of the river.*

Ninfa is a garden built among the rambling streets and ruined buildings of what was once a thriving medieval town. Its unique beauty has earned it an international reputation and it has become a place of pilgrimage for garden lovers.

Built on the main route between Rome and Naples, the town enjoyed many years of prosperity before it was razed to the ground during a civil war at the end of the 14th century. Any survivors soon fell victim to malaria and for 500 years Ninfa lay abandoned. Its transformation into a beautiful garden was the work of three women over a period of about ninety years. All of them were married or born into the Caetani, the family that owned Ninfa for 700 years.

Ada Wilbraham Caetani, the English wife of Duke Onorato Caetani, used to bring her six children to Ninfa for picnics. During these visits she planted rose cuttings against the crumbling walls. Her roses can still be recognised by the massive girth of their stems. Ada's successor was Marguerite Chapin Caetani, the Anglo-American wife of Duke Roffredo Caetani, and founder of two literary magazines. She began to work on the garden in 1932 and continued to be passionately involved with it until her death in 1958. She loved old-fashioned roses and in 1949 alone she ordered 128 different species from Hilliers, a famous English nursery. Today there are over 200 different species of rose in the garden, many of them unidentified.

The last of the Caetani was Marguerite's daughter, Lelia, a gifted painter who added another layer to the accumulated depth and intensity of the planting. She and her husband Hubert Howard devoted themselves to safeguarding the garden's future. In the knowledge that they would have no children, the couple set up the Caetani foundation to manage Ninfa after their deaths. After a considerable battle, they also established a conservation area around the garden to ensure that the river would never be polluted.

1297 Ninfa given to Pietro Caetani by the Pope.

1382 Town razed to the ground during a civil war.

1922 Ada Wilbraham Caetani begins to plant roses among the ruins.

1932 Marguerite Chapin Caetani takes over from Ada.

1958 Lelia Caetani takes on the garden at Ninfa after her mother's death.

1977 Lelia, the last of the Caetani, dies.

1986 Lelia's husband, Hubert Howard, dies, and the garden is taken over by a trust.

*The smoke tree (*cotinus coggygria*) with its flowers reflected in the river.*

Despite a torrent of visitors from all over the world, Ninfa has retained a profoundly peaceful atmosphere. In early spring it is filled by a sea of translucent cherry blossom. Later on, the crumbling walls that once enclosed houses, churches and workshops are smothered with cascades of roses, clematis, wisteria and powerfully scented summer jasmine.

The sound of water penetrates all but the farthest reaches of the garden. Ice-cold and miraculously clear, the river rushes through the site, its course punctuated by the massive stands of gunnera and brilliant yellow flag irises. The huge flowers of *wisteria floribunda* 'Macrobotrys' hang from an ancient wooden bridge, trailing their tips in the water. The garden is threaded with numerous, powerful little streams — shining ribbons of water, often running flush with the mown grass. In places the water is channelled to create a tiny waterfall, in others it crosses over itself in a minute aqueduct. In late spring the perfect, waxy flowers of arum lilies pack the banks. *H.A.*

Wisteria floribunda *'Macrobotrys' trailing from a medieval bridge.*

Arum lilies thrive on the banks of a stream.

Fallingwater

BEAR RUN
PENNSYLVANIA, USA

'My money has brought me a great many fine things in life, but none of them have brought me greater joy than that house you built for me on Bear Run.'

EDGAR J. KAUFMANN SPEAKING TO FRANK LLOYD WRIGHT
Letters to Clients: Frank Lloyd Wright, (ed. Bruce Brooks Pfeiffer), London: Architectural Press, 1987.

The design for the house grew out of the ground and developed organically.

1935 Frank Lloyd Wright designs house.
1937 House finished.

Fallingwater, designed by the architect Frank Lloyd Wright (1867–1959), is generally considered his finest house. In the early part of the 20th century Wright had influenced modernism in Europe, initially in the Netherlands and later in other countries. However when the 1932 International Style exhibition in New York was held his architecture was considered as a preamble to modern architecture rather than being exemplary of it. His architecture differed in that it was not universal, but was connected to the earth, with regional identity, and grounded in the specifics of each site.

Trading on his reputation he set up the Taliesin Fellowship in 1932, based on other contemporary utopian communities, where architectural apprentices would pay Wright for the privilege of experience in the drawing office. One of these apprentices was Edgar Kaufmann Jr., a young art student who would later become a well-known art historian. His father, Edgar J. Kaufmann, was the owner of the Kaufmann Department Store in Pittsburg. During a visit to their son the Kaufmanns commissioned a country house on Bear Run, an Appalachian mountain stream in north-west Pennsylvania. Wright visited the site, yet nine months later there were no sketches, despite a number of reminders. One Sunday in September 1935 Kaufmann rang, enquiring as to the state of the design, and Wright responded with the legendary: 'We're ready for you', causing great consternation with the apprentices in the office. However within the next few hours Wright had produced the necessary designs.

The site consisted of steep woodland with a stream running through the middle of it, and a large waterfall forming the centrepiece. Kaufmann had expected a house with views of the waterfall, however Wright positioned the house directly above it. Kaufmann's imagined location would have resulted in a house with a north-facing aspect, whereas Wright's proposal exploits the dynamism of the waterfall and a south-facing aspect. The house was conceived as a series of concrete terraces floating above the waterfall, which were cantilevered into rough stone walls that mimic the local rocks. It was built around existing rocks, which were left *in situ*, even where they penetrate through the floors of the house. As a result the interior resembles a furnished cave. The flagstones used in the house reflect the colour of stone in the stream below, which is visible through a glass hatch in the floor. A stairway goes from here down to the stream, strengthening the connection with nature. There are no views of waterfall itself, which is felt and heard as if one is part of it. In all it provides the dichotomy of being simultaneously inside and outside.

The house is arranged at a slight angle to the stream so as to provide the best views from the various rooms of the house. It is approached from above and is first experienced half-obscured by apparently untouched woodland vegetation. A hidden entrance provides access to an asymmetrical building, the design of which grew out of the ground and developed organically. Hence the character of the site is the beginning of the building.

J.W.

The house was conceived as a series of concrete terraces floating above a waterfall.

The waterfall cannot be seen from within the house but can be felt and heard, as if one is part of it.

Villa Mairea

NOORMARKKU
FINLAND

'The plants and other "inconsistent" elements combine to create a new, multivalent world: in the villa, as in many a Modernist painting, the national and the international, the contemporary and the ancient, the local and the exotic, coexist in a provocative symbiosis.'

RICHARD WESTON, 'Between Nature and Culture: Reflections on the Villa Mairea' in W. Nerdinger (ed.), *Alvar Aalto: Toward a Human Modernism.*

Villa Mairea seen through surrounding pine woodland, with main entrance, far right.

1937-38 Villa Mairea designed by Alvar Aalto and his wife Aino.
1938-39 Villa Mairea constructed.
1939 Paul Olsson, landscape architect, advises on layout; follows up with annual visits; continued afterwards by his assistant Erik Sommerschieldt.
c.1957 Maj-Lis Rosenbröijer, garden architect and former assistant to Olsson, continues annual advice and development of the garden.

Villa Mairea was designed by Hugo Alvar Henrik Aalto (1898–1976) and contributed to establishing his international reputation as an architect. While historians have considered the villa's close relationship with the outside, the outdoor space is not generally discussed separately.

The villa was designed for a progressive young couple Harry and Maire Gullichsen. Alvar Aalto had first worked for the Gullichsens on a socially utopian residential scheme at the Sunila Sulphate Cellulose Factory, which he also designed (1935–39), and they had become friends. He was therefore the natural choice as a designer for their own home at Noormarkku in the west of Finland. The villa was proposed near the first mills of the Ahlström company, on the family estate adjoining Maire's grandfather's and her father's residences. Throughout the process Maire participated in the design of both building and garden. Architectural critics have aptly described the building as a collage of personal inventions and vernacular tradition, with inspiration from Japan in its use of natural materials and the design principles of Frank Lloyd Wright's Fallingwater. In all its modernity of treatment of materials and spaces it is rooted in national traditions and the building has subsequently become an icon of Finnish modernism.

The sauna, left, and outdoor living room arranged around the informal courtyard.

The villa has been carefully located in an area of natural pine woodland, retaining a maximum number of trees while creating a small open space. This provides immediate maturity for the setting and is inspired by the concept of living in a forest clearing. The villa and its additional buildings are arranged around an informal courtyard, derived from traditional Finnish farmyards. Two interlinked L-shaped buildings create a U, with the two-storey villa forming one side and the open-air sitting room and sauna building the other. The sophisticated spatial arrangement of the main building has been organised as continuous living space. This principle extends to the outside space with the living room being separated from the courtyard only by a glass screen, thus blurring conventional

The sauna and steps to the pool.

distinctions between inside and outside. The kidney-shaped swimming pool on the far side becomes an integral part of the courtyard composition, but its free form also is a clear reference to the transition with nature. The adjoining sauna with its turf roof and balustrade of slender fir poles fades into the surrounding woodland. The stone wall that delineates the outdoor sitting area echoes old churchyard walls, and the wooden fence around the courtyard is reminiscent of traditional farm fences. By contrast the pillars and screens, both in and outside the villa do not use the raw natural materials, yet they still resemble tree trunks of the surrounding forest. The sophistication appears to reach a peak at the roof garden of the villa, which is surrounded by a white painted balustrade resembling the handrails of an ocean liner, a paradigm of the modern movement. Yet all is not as it seems: the balustrade forms a wave-shaped outline and does not consistently follow the edge of the roof, thus moving away from the purely functional and providing a personal artistic touch. Thus Aalto's design is a dichotomy of nature and tradition, of sophistication and modern art, which above all provides a democratic domestic environment, related to the specificity of the site. *J.W.*

El Novillero

SONOMA
CALIFORNIA, USA

'It is important that the garden be built around a dominant idea. Do one thing well and let all others be subordinate in scale to this idea. [...] Peace and ease are the dominant characteristics of the new garden — peace and beauty for the eye and ease of maintenance for the owner. Fewer and simpler lines are being used in the garden, and fewer and simpler materials. All is calculated to give complete restfulness to the eye.'

THOMAS D. CHURCH.
Gardens are for People, Berkeley: University of California Press, 1995 [1955].

Above left: The swimming pool has become an icon of the free-form style.

Above right: The house is situated at the end of a winding driveway.

1941 Dewey Donnell acquires Lakeville Ranch Property (2,500 acres).
1943 Property extended with acquisition of some further 1,450 acres.
1947–48 Pool built according to Thomas Church design. Pool buildings finished, designed by Church associate George Rockrise.
1950 Lanai built, designed by Rockrise.
1949–50 House designed by Austin Pierpont.
1953 Church designs herb garden.

El Novillero has been referred to as one of the 'most significant', and 'one of the most famous' of 20th-century gardens. Its layout and specifically its swimming pool with sculpture by Adeline Kent has become an icon of the free-form style, and an emblem of Western living (the California Style). With an emphasis on outdoor living, gardens formed an integral part of this concept. Thomas Dolliver Church (1902–78), whose office produced the landscape plan for El Novillero, had followed a conventional Beaux-Arts training, but a visit to Europe in 1937 had a significant impact on his approach to design. The Finnish architect and designer Alvar Aalto (1898–1976) inspired him to work directly with the site and local conditions, rather than moulding it according to some preconceived idea. Church also took out a franchise of Aalto's wave-like glassware and his furniture on his return.

One of his most significant opportunities to apply the new design approach derived from a cattle-ranching estate in the southernmost part of the Sonoma valley, not far from the San Francisco metropolitan area. Dewey Donnell, the son of a wealthy family (Marathon Oil of Ohio), acquired the 4000-acre estate known as Lakeville Ranch Property, in parts in 1941 and 1943. The area consisted of low rolling hills, forming grazing land studded with rocky outcrops and California live oaks. From the hills there are long views southward onto marshes with winding creeks, and the northern part of San Pablo Bay. In 1942 Dewey converted an old boarding house for himself and renamed it El Novillero. Later that year he married and soon started a family.

Any ambitions for a new family home were halted due to a wartime restriction on materials and a shortage of water, but nevertheless in 1947 Church was asked to advice on the location of a new house and garden. While the ideas must have been agreed

shortly after, there does not appear to be any record of an original masterplan. The building of garden and house took place in stages with the first proposal for a swimming pool and pool buildings. These were thinly disguised as a reservoir (required before any building was put up) and farm buildings in order to obtain planning permission. This was extended with a lanai (a modernist living room) after building restrictions were lifted in 1950. At the same time a new house was built in an area below the pond. Both in the pool area and near the house existing live oaks were carefully preserved and provided a sense of immediate maturity to the setting.

A long sinuous drive gradually winds through the hills and ends at the house, which is situated in a dip under the well-wooded knoll, and contains the swimming pool. The house acts as a screen for what lies beyond. Views across salt marshes towards San Pablo Bay open up after entering the house, but the full extent of this dramatic view is not exposed until one reaches the top of the knoll with the swimming pool. The pool area has been carefully sculpted around the existing contours and vegetation, and gives the impression of being on top of the world with long distance views. Its free-form shape reflects the creeks in the landscape beyond, but may also have been inspired by Aalto's pool for Villa Mairea. The setting has been paved seemingly around existing features serving as a large outdoor terrace, which has been extended with decking, stretching over a small clump of live oaks. *J.W.*

The pool area, shaded by retained live oaks, gives the impression of being on top of the world with dramatic long-distance views.

J. Irwin Miller Garden

COLUMBUS, INDIANA, USA

'Kiley's impact upon world landscape is substantial and memorable, and will continue into the predictable future....In his quiet way he is a true leader.'

GARRET ECKBO

The allée *of honey locusts seen from the* tapis vert.

1953 Daniel Urban Kiley first visits the Miller house site; the house is under construction.
1954 The Miller garden is largely completed.
1973 The arborvitae hedge is replaced with a taxus hedge; this is one of the few changes made to the garden since its inception.
1980s The Millers, who had long jealously protected the privacy of their home and garden, allow photographs of their garden to appear in print.
1994 The Pritzker Prize dinner is held in the honey-locust *allée*.

The house's glass walls break down boundaries between inside and outside.

The echoing shapes of porch and trees bring the garden into the house.

One might reasonably assume that the garden widely hailed as the icon of modernism in America would be found in California, or perhaps even New York. Such an assumption would be far off the mark. Instead, the garden is in Columbus, Indiana.

It belongs to J. Irwin Miller, a conservative mid-Westerner who has a keen appreciation of modernism. When Miller decided to build a house in the early 1950s, he hired prominent modernist architect Eero Saarinen for the design. Saarinen strove for transparency — the modernist ideal which aims at erasing the boundaries between architecture and landscape. The result was a glass-walled, low-roofed structure that resembled a pavilion, with no single façade being more dominant than another.

For the landscape, Saarinen called upon Daniel Urban Kiley (1912–). Kiley had studied at Harvard University's Graduate School of Design, where he and fellow students Garrett Eckbo and James Rose had famously spoken out against the faculty's reliance on the Beaux-Arts tradition. In his own practice, Kiley had illuminated his ideas in a number of well-known public spaces. (One of America's pre-eminent landscape architects, Kiley is well known for such large-scale projects as the US Air Force Academy, the John F. Kennedy Library, and Lincoln Center.) At the Miller house, he was presented with a 10-acre rectangular parcel of land gently sloping down to the Flatrock River. With few if any physical constraints, the property was a landscape architect's dream, a ground-zero base on which to build freely a modernist geometry of articulated spaces. In keeping with the house's emphasis on functionality and transparency, Kiley created a truly modern landscape that was both respectful of the Indiana countryside yet universal in its appeal.

For twenty-five years after its completion, the garden was virtually unknown to the public. The Millers protected their privacy by rejecting any form of publicity. In the early 1980s, however, the Millers began to allow photographs of the garden to be printed in books and periodicals. The fully mature and meticulously maintained garden emerged — not as a dated period piece but as a timeless and serene masterpiece. Through photographs alone, it rocketed into the consciousness of contemporary landscape designers, and was immediately hailed as a stunning symbol of modernism.

The garden unfolds from the house, rejecting any notions of dualism between inside and outside. Beds of ivy next to the house's podium make the floor of the house seem to extend into the landscape, while magnolias and weeping beeches give the house a sense of groundedness. Reaching out from the house, linear hedges enclose functionally arranged outdoor rooms as well as dramatic *bosquets*. To the west of the house, an *allée* of honey locusts serves not merely as an axis, but also, in a remarkably innovative way, as a loggia. The locusts' trunks echo the columns of a porch, and, in a magical manipulation of perspective, the view across the long sweep of grass is enhanced by being seen through the tree trunks.

S.G.M

Little Sparta

STONYPATH
LANARKSHIRE, SCOTLAND

Temple Pool and the Temple of Apollo, with the inscription 'To Apollo: His Music, His Missiles, His Muses'.

1967 Stonypath garden begun.
c. 1980 Stonypath renamed Little Sparta.

'Superior gardens are composed of Glooms and Solitudes, not of plants and trees.'

IAN HAMILTON FINLAY
from 'Unconnected Sentences on Gardening', in Yves Abrioux, *Ian Hamilton Finlay; A Visual Primer*, London: Reaktion Books, 1985.

The international reputation of Ian Hamilton Finlay (b. 1925) as an innovative artist–gardener is centred on the four-acre, neo-classical garden around his home at Little Sparta in the Pentland Hills of southern Scotland. This former upland croft has been transformed from unvegetated desolation into an embowered haven, whose numerous glades and pools have been designed as settings for inscribed sculpture. Little Sparta continues to burgeon despite its seasonally embattled situation over three hundred metres above sea level. Although begun in 1967, and originally known as Stonypath, the 'garden' had been evolving since 1964.

By 1961 Finlay was an established figure in Scottish avant-garde literary circles. In 1963 he published his first collection of 'concrete' poems and, the following year, began to envisage concrete poetry that was integral to gardens. During 1964–66, he began to implement these ideas through the printed poem–gardens and the garden poem–sculptures at Ardgay and Coaltown of Callange, before moving to Stonypath. It is the programme of neo-classicising, which began during the 1970s and led to the redesignation of Stonypath as Little Sparta, that has shaped the place as it is today. As Finlay familiarised himself with the history of garden design, he became aware that the terse economy of text favoured by concrete poetry was evident in the classical genre of the inscription. Thus he came to appreciate that the classical inscription had the possibility, through the resonances invoked by association, of transforming a site through the poetics of metaphor. While the traditional gardenist conjunction of nature and culture is affirmed by the variety of inscribed sculptures, such as tree-plaques, benches, obelisks, planters, headstones, bridges and tree-column bases, Finlay's use of the inscription resists an exclusive focus on the sculptural object. Instead, the associations of the text complement the idea of each work by drawing attention to the sights, scents and sounds which amplify enjoyment of the sensuousness of 'place'. Animated by the weather, the garden becomes an Aeolian harp, whose cadence is played by wind soughing through trees and shrubs.

In the Woodland Garden: stone planter inscribed with the initials of the German philosopher, G.W.F. Hegel, with the Column of Fortitude beyond.

The aqueduct linking the upper and middle pools in the Woodland Garden.

In the Front Garden: headstone inscribed Achtung Minen [Beware Mines].

Little Sparta burgeons within and beyond the pre-existing, but tumbledown, framework of the farmstead garden, now known as the Front Garden. The farmyard midden has become the Temple Pool and is flanked by buildings converted into temples dedicated to Apollo and to Philemon and Baucis. The Woodland Garden is a labyrinth of hermetic glades. Here the sylvan dell of the Middle and Upper Pools embowers an aqueduct, a rill, a pantheon and a grotto. The Wild Garden encompasses plantation, moorland and lochan. During the 1990s the principle improvement has been the extensive Parkland, which offers a contrast to the intimate and secluded recesses that had characterised the garden.

Finlay's achievements are manifold. Not only has he reconciled the concrete with the neo-classical, modernism with post-modernism, but he has also invoked the tradition of the garden as a site of poetic, philosophical and political discourses. In this context, he has emulated the domestic scale of the Georgian poets, Alexander Pope and William Shenstone, whose gardens were designed as antidotes to the surrounding culture. P.E.

Views outwards from the central water basin.

1902 Barragán born 9 March in Guadalajara, Mexico.

1919–24 Enrols at the Escuela Libre de Ingeniera de Guadalajara, graduating with a degree in engineering, and then travels to Europe.

1924–35 Works as an architect in Guadalajara.

1935–40 Moves to Mexico City and has a productive period in architecture and building.

1940–45 Retires from architecture and concentrates on becoming a garden and landscape designer.

1945–52 Develops El Pedregal de San Angel, Mexico City.

1952–55 Trips to Europe and North Africa. Designs the Capuchin convent.

1955–66 Residential developments, civic sculpture and landscape design, including Satellite City Towers and Los Clubes.

1966–68 San Cristóbal.

1969–80 Various projects and consultancies.

1980 Awarded the Pritzker Prize for Architecture, where he delivers his seminal acceptance speech. Retires due to ill health shortly afterwards.

1985–87 Awarded Premio Jalisco in 1985 and the first exhibition of his work is held in Mexico City. In 1987 wins Premio América.

1988 Dies in Mexico City and is buried in Guadalajara.

San Cristóbal Stables

MEXICO CITY, MEXICO

'All that a well-built garden must contain is nothing less than the whole universe.'

FERDINAND BAC.

It has been over thirty years since San Cristóbal was completed, but it still remains the most complex of Luis Barragán's works. Its architectural simplicity and minimal landscaping are combined with a sensory and symbolic richness that defy preconceptions of soulless modernism. San Cristóbal was the first house and garden complex to fully encompass the design philosophy which Barragán eloquently described in his Pritzker Architecture Prize acceptance speech in 1980. He was alarmed that architecture, and hence landscape architecture, had banished the words 'Beauty, Inspiration, Magic, Spellbound, Enchantment as well as the concepts of Serenity, Silence, Intimacy and Amazement'. It was here that he was able to combine his passions for Mexico, gardens and horses, while entering his most mature and developed phase as a designer.

Situated in a harsh landscape in a northern suburb of Mexico City, San Cristóbal was not an easy site. Barragán developed a secluded area using dense boundary plantings, and that gave him the opportunity to focus the garden inwards towards the water basin in a manner reminiscent of a Moorish courtyard. Horses and equestrianism were also central, as the barn and stables form two sides of the courtyard, with the house and a wall completing the rectangle. Following the theories of the painter and landscape architect Ferdinand Bac, Barragán made the garden a magical environment. The interplay of old and new, space and colour, water and light are some of the devices used. Pure planes of wall and water define spaces with a restrained formality. The colour and texture of the walls add fun and are helped by the sights and sounds of the water-wall. The white-painted house is a hacienda, whose split-level planes exude pure modernism. The stables feel vernacular and rustic, but their clean lines and the portico bring them effortlessly into the modern. The waterspout creates a magical interplay between sunlight and water, and holes punched into walls frame romantic pictures of horse and rider. At San Cristóbal Barragán re-interpreted the serenity and beauty of his childhood surroundings through a modern functionality.

Barragán's training as an engineer made him pragmatic and practical. Self-taught as an architect and garden designer he was freed from orthodoxy and dogma. His trips to Europe introduced him to influences that would shape his philosophy and design ideas: the Moorish architecture of Southern Spain, the domestic architecture of the Mediterranean, the gardens of Ferdinand Bac, the theories of Austro-American designer Friedrich Kiesler and the writings and theories of Le Corbusier. Mexico, her culture and people were in his heart, as was his Roman Catholicism. This complex mix produced one of the most influential designers of this century. As he said in his Pritzker Prize speech: 'It will seem obvious then, that a garden must combine the poetic and mysterious with serenity and joy.' San Cristóbal stands as a testament to this assertion. *A.B.*

The waterspout.

The rill.

The use of framing arbours indicates Jellicoe's artistic influences.

Shute House

SHAFTESBURY
ENGLAND

'There was never any doubt that it was the thought, presence, act and sound of water that was holding together the competing ideas that had been introduced into the woodlands — ideas remotely associated with Islam, Greece, the Middle Ages, the primaeval and other times and cultures.'

GEOFFREY JELLICOE
'Jung and the Art of Landscape' in S. Wrende and W. H. Adams (eds.) *Landscape and Culture in the Twentieth Century*, New York: Museum of Modern Art, 1991.

The gardens at Shute House, on the Dorset / Wiltshire border, resulted from a close collaboration between the former owners, Michael and Anne Tree and Sir Geoffrey Jellicoe (1900–96), the eminent 20th-century landscape designer. Jellicoe produced the overall plan and engineered the water features which remain such a key element at Shute, while Lady Anne provided the planting — a partnership reminiscent of that famed Edwardian pair, Sir Edwin Lutyens and Gertrude Jekyll.

Jellicoe had created classical gardens at Ditchley Park in Oxfordshire for Ronald and Nancy Tree, so when their son Michael and his wife acquired the early 18th-century Shute House in 1968, they turned to Jellicoe for assistance in developing their garden. He was attracted to Shute's potential, recognizing the rare opportunity of being able to work uninterrupted on a single site which could become a test-bed for his ideas over a long period of time, and crown a lifelong experience in landscape design. Shute was to involve Jellicoe for almost two decades; reputedly he regarded it as his finest achievement.

Jellicoe was an intellectual, a man of impeccable taste, with a profound sense of the history of garden design and fully aware of the philosophical considerations governing the appreciation of landscape. Jellicoe had absorbed the writing of the ancient Greek philosophers and appreciated the landscape paintings of Nicolas Poussin and Claude Lorrain, so influential for English garden designers in the 18th century. Shute was to be a skillful fusion of these diverse influences and became Jellicoe's masterpiece.

Jellicoe was fascinated by water and its significance to landscape design. The garden at Shute lies on a sloping site facing south towards the distant downs. At the top of the slope is an ancient spring which is the source of the River Nadder. His successful exploitation of this vital asset was crucial in the creation of this much-admired garden.

Jellicoe utilised water at Shute in a dazzling variety of forms. He remodelled the canal, a long rectangular pool closely surrounded by a tall hedge, placing at the far end busts of Ovid, Virgil and Lucretius, his favourite Roman poets (recently replaced by 17th-century busts of Zeus, Neptune and Diana). There are shady pools in quiet groves, rhododendrons reflected in their calm surface together with classical statuary such as a lifesize recumbent Pan and Leda with the Swan. However, Jellicoe's showpiece at Shute is his rill, a narrow water-course descending via a series of musical sounding cascades, bubbling fountains and placid pools, to a strategically placed classical sculpture.

Rills, originally deriving from Middle Eastern irrigation channels, feature in other excellent 20th-century gardens, such as Lutyens' Hestercombe and Harold Peto's Buscot. However, Jellicoe's rill at Shute with copious planting at the upper level giving way to smooth lawn lower down, surpasses them all, making it one of the nation's outstanding contemporary gardens, still privately owned and beautifully presented. *P.B.*

1900 Jellicoe born in London.
1923 Graduates from the Architectural Association, London.
1935 Garden design of Ditchley Park, Oxfordshire.
1939 Becomes Principal of Architectural Association, London.
1939/47 Garden design, Sandringham, Norfolk.
1948 Founder President of the International Federation of Landscape Architects.
1964 Kennedy Memorial, Runnymede, Berkshire.
1969–88 Garden design at Shute House.
1973 Pool design at Royal Horticultural Society, Wisley.
1979 Jellicoe is knighted.
1980 Garden design at Sutton Place, Guildford.
1992 Historical Gardens at Atlanta, USA.
1996 17 July: Jellicoe dies.

Classical sculpture punctuates Jellicoe's use of water.

Rhododendrons and lilies reflected in the pool.

Parc André Citroën

PARIS, FRANCE

'You need a piece of the earth and eternity to make a garden.'

GILLES CLÉMENT.

The Parc André Citroën is part of a redevelopment area of approximately 99 acres in the 15th arrondissement of Paris, beside the River Seine, which used to be occupied by the Citroën automobile factory. The 35-acre park is the result of a design competition organised in 1985 by the city of Paris. Two teams were selected as winners and were asked to collaborate to produce a final design. The two multidisciplinary design teams were composed of a landscape architect associated with an architectural practice: Gilles Clément and Patrick Berger formed one of the teams and the other consisted of Alain Provost with Jean Paul Viguier and Jean François Jodry.

The two landscape architects adopted radically different theoretical approaches to design: Gilles Clément chose an ecological, horticultural and philosophical approach in the 'Garden in Motion' and the 'Serial Gardens'; Alain Provost relied on a geometrically controlled architectural design where hard landscape elements dominate. The tension between these two design approaches, epitomised in the White (Clément) and Black (Provost) gardens, create variety and excitement and the park has proved such a success that the same designers were asked to create two other new urban parks in the La Défense area of Paris.

The coherence of the Parc André Citroën is achieved through a large esplanade with two monumental greenhouses and rhythmic fountains at the highest point. This central, open space is classical in concept and may be compared to similar spaces along the River Seine such as the Champs de Mars or the Esplanade des Invalides, which have a monumental axis and *tapis vert* in the tradition of the 17th-century formal garden. The space is in proportion with the scale of the city and is able to accommodate large numbers of people.

By contrast, there are smaller gardens, especially Clément's six 'Serial Gardens', which offer intimate, precious spaces rarely seen in a public park. Iconography has been used throughout landscape design history but rarely in modern public parks. Here each

Top: Cut Magnolia grandiflora, *part of Provost's design.*

Above: One of the Serial Gardens.

1915–70s Site of the Citroën automobile production plant.

1985 Competition organised by the City of Paris, for the design of a new park of 35 acres, part of the ZAC (Zone d'Aménagement Concerté) Citroën-Cévennes.

1992–93 Construction of the combination of the two winning schemes designed by Jean Paul Viguier, Jean François Jodry and Alain Provost; and Patrick Berger and Gilles Clément.

garden is symbolically associated with a colour, a metal, a sense, a planet, a day, an atomic number and a form of water element; for example the Silver Garden evokes silver, sight, the moon, Monday, number 47 and a river. The other novelty in these gardens is the use of rare plants to illustrate the themes. They are not just there to fill up space but constitute one of the main attractions, with the planting plans for each garden engraved on a plaque displayed permanently on site. Furthermore these gardens offer Parisians who live in a densely built environment the atmosphere of private gardens where they can relax with a degree of privacy.

An elaborate concrete path through the Serial Gardens.

The *jardin en mouvement* or 'Garden in Motion', which forms the north-east corner of the park is probably its most complex part, even if its conception appears minimalist. It follows a philosophy developed by Gilles Clément in his own garden at La Creuse. Here the designer selected a number of plants as the starting point of an evolution, and over time the visitor is invited to observe the changes occurring to the vegetation. Human intervention is to be kept to a minimum leaving the plants to evolve, disappear and re-emerge. This space offers the experience of nature in the city, and is particularly well appreciated by Parisians.

L.P.

The Esplanade.

Glossary

'Landscape gardening is probably the most ambiguous, difficult and elusive art of all.'

Roger Caillois
Pierres réfléchies

Alcazaba (from Arabic) Large Moorish fortress, especially in southern Spain (> Alhambra).

Alhambra The famous garden in Grenada that spawned many imitations in the Moorish style which were known by the same name (> Alhambra, Kew).

allée (or allee; Fr. 'avenue, walk') A straight generally tree-lined walk laid with gravel, sand or turf, but not as broad as an avenue (> Middleton Place, Schönbrunn, Schwetzingen, Veitshöchheim, Vaux-le-Vicomte, Versailles).

alley A walk in a garden; also a bowling-alley.

amphitheatre Either a large curved band of turf cut into a stepped terrace; or an open-air theatre of the Roman shape for theatrical or operatic performances (> Hellbrunn, Wörlitz).

anglo-chinois (Fr. 'Anglo-Chinese') French term for the English landscape garden with added 'Chinese' or rustic elements; *jardin anglo-chinois* : garden in this style (> Ermenonville, Versailles).

arboretum A (perhaps scientifically devised) collection of growing trees (> Kew, Schwetzingen).

arbour Arch-shaped bower or shelter with foliage or climbing plants (> Giverny, Hestercombe, Kew, Villandry).

automata Mechanically-powered birds, animals or human figures (> Villa d'Este).

azulejo (Sp., prob. from Arabic) Often glazed tile of Islamic origin used to line pieces of garden architecture in Spain from the 12th century, the use of which lingered on in Portugal until the 19th century (> Queluz).

baroque 17th-century and 18th-century cultural tendency based on nobility and sumptuousness; and in art, on complexity, elaborateness, a balance between symmetry and asymmetry (see **rococo**) and a dynamic relationship between the curve and the classical line. Many gardens are in this dramatic style (esp. in northern Italy and east of the Rhine). In France, an attenuated form surfaces in some 'classical' gardens. Urns, vistas, and architectural grandeur are some characteristics of baroque gardens.

belvedere (It. 'beautiful to look at/from') An often tiered and Classically inspired structure raised above the landscape to provide an enjoyable view of the surrounds (> Veitshöchheim, Villandry, Wörlitz).

belt-walk Long, serpentine perimeter drive in an English-style garden (> Wörlitz).

berceau (Fr.) Trelliswork arch-shaped arbour with climbing plants (>Schönbrunn).

Bergenia Medium-sized perennial plant with heart-shaped leaves (> Hestercombe).

bocage (Fr.) Coppice; also, enclosed land generally, with hedges and copses (> Ermenonville).

bosco (It.) Grove (> Villa Lante).

bosquet (Fr.) Planted shrubbery (sometimes including trees) (> J. Irwin Miller Garden, Schönbrunn, Schwetzingen).

boulingrin > bowling-green.

bower A recess in a garden, especially one covered in plants or flowers without an excess of architectural elements (> Blenheim).

bowling-green A green, sometimes sunken, for the playing of bowls or one of its ancestors; in fact, many of the greens are of the French *boulingrin* type, and have no function as a games' area (> Governor's Palace).

box An evergreen shrub of the genus *Boxus* used for hedges, topiary and mazes especially in formal and Renaissance gardens; hence, boxwood (*passim*).

broadwalk, broad walk A broad path or ride (> Middleton Place).

candytuft Undershrubs of the genus *Iberia* used as cover (> Dumbarton Oaks).

carp's-back flowerbeds In which the soil is built up into a central rib (> Giverny).

cascade A natural or artificial fall of water enhanced with architectural or grotto-like elements to form a perhaps multi-tiered ornamental composition (> Blenheim, Chatsworth, Hestercombe, Het Loo, Peterhof, Schönbrunn, Shute, Veitshöchheim, Villa Aldobrandini).

casino (It.; also *casina*) An ornamental pavilion in 16th- to 18th-century Italian gardens (> Hellbrunn, Villas Farnese, Lante and Vizcaya); the word is also applied to the 18th-century English versions.

catena d'acqua (It. 'water chain') Gradually sloping artificial cascade of water conveyed in edged channels in a series of almost flat 'steps', like a narrow water staircase (> Villas Caprarola and Lante).

chahar bagh (Persian) This 'quartered garden' was inspired by the Koran that constantly refers to the garden as a symbol for Paradise which is crossed by four rivers running with water, wine, milk and honey (> Taj Mahal).

circus Roofless area, circular or oval in form for performances or equestrian events (>Arkadia, Veitshöchheim).

conceit An extended and intellectually complex metaphor in Renaissance and baroque rhetoric. In garden design, a kind of clever trick in e.g. perspective, arrangement, architecture or planting (> Introduction).

conservatory A wood or metal and glass construction, sometimes of large size, for protecting plants sensitive to naturally occurring climatic conditions. In the 19th and 20th centuries it refers to a construction attached to a house for plants as well as for taking the air in inclement weather (> Shute).

corbel Often ornamented (stone) projection beneath an arch or other element thrusting downward;

corbelled possessing such features in stone or else in brick as an elaborate cantilevered overhanging course (> Sigiriya).

cryptoporticus Enclosed gallery, often underground or sunken (> Villa Ephrussi).

culvert Channel beneath a built structure, such as a thoroughfare, for the passage of water (> Hestercombe).

cupola Dome roof on a circular base (> Governor's Palace).

curtain wall A non-load-bearing exterior wall, often erected to fill a space between columns (> Castle Howard).

Dutch style Formal style popular in the Netherlands on a smaller scale than the French with topiary, low-lying box and statuary dominant (> Governor's Palace, Levens Hall).

embroider or **embroidered *parterre*** > *parterre de broderie.*

English park A stretch of parkland in the > English style (> Haga, Schwetzingen).

English style Informal garden layout in the English landscaped style, as distinguished from the French formal design (> Ermenonville, Haga, Villa Ephrussi).

esplanade Large stretch of ground for promenading, characteristic of French-style gardens (> Parc André Citröen).

eyecatcher Feature placed on a distant hill outside the main grounds so as to attract the eye to the view (> Rousham).

fabrique Often rustic or pseudo-rustic 18th/19th-century garden structure, occasionally in a mock state of disrepair; sometimes in an exotic (e.g. Chinese) taste (> Ermenonville, Versailles).

finial Often elaborate ornament topping a spire, pinnacle or railing-head (> Governor's Palace).

folly Architecture feature characterized by its deliberate eccentricity (> Sacro Bosco).

formal gardening That according to the strict, essentially geometrical, principles of the French School.

gazebo ('Anglo-Latin', jocularly from 'gaze' with the Latin 1st person future suffix) A small sometimes storeyed pavilion which gives onto a vista (> Hidcote Manor).

giardino segreto A 'secret' enclosed area within a garden (> Villa Vizcaya, Hellbrunn).

giochi d'acqua (It. 'water games') Water conveyed through concealed pipes and spouted through jets or > automata designed to surprise or drench the unsuspecting visitor (> Villas Aldobrandini, d'Este, Lante; Hellbrunn, Schwetzingen).

Gloriette A decorative summerhouse offering a view; in the 19th century often in iron and glass. In France, also an arbour (> Schwetzingen).

Gothic Describes the typical mid-medieval style with pointed arches and crenellations ('battlements'), etc. Revived in 18th-century England ('Gothick') and thence exported to Europe (> Stowe, Arkadia).

Grand Tour A sometimes lengthy voyage through Europe and especially to Italy undertaken by the aristocracy in the 17th–19th centuries as part of their cultural education. Important as a source of written and visual material concerning foreign gardens.

greensward A stretch of green turf (> Middleton Place).

grotto A natural or more often artificial recess decorated to resemble an elaborate cave with figures and/or shellwork or mirrors (> Arkadia, Boboli, Hellbrunn, Little Sparta, Vaux-le-Vicomte, and Villas Aldobrandini, d'Este, Ephrussi, Lante, Vizcaya, Wörlitz). The classicizing architectural version is known as a > nymphaeum.

ha-ha A sunken ditch leading to parkland which protects the inner garden from cattle yet allows an unobstructed view beyond. It is only visible from close to and the term comes from the cry of 'ah-ha' uttered by the surprised visitor. Of French origin, it was popularized in 18th-century England.

hameau (Fr. 'hamlet') A (late 18th-century) collection of 'rustic' buildings designed into a kind of mock-village that provided the 'delights of the countryside' without any of its squalid drawbacks (> Ermenonville, Versailles).

herbarium Scientific collection of dried or pressed plants (> Kew).

herbaceous border Low bed bordering a length of lawn and along a wall (or hedge), set with flowers or non-woody plants (> Heligan, Munstead Wood).

herber (Medieval) herb-garden (> Introduction).

herm A head (originally of Hermes) placed on an often trapezoid pedestal. In Italy such works were widespread (> Palazzo Farnese); in England, they are mainly characteristic of the Classical taste.

hortus conclusus (Lat. 'enclosed, closed garden') The medieval walled garden often containing (medicinal) plants and flowers rather than trees. In the lyric of *fin'amors* or Courtly Love and in manuscripts, it often served as an image of the purity of the Virgin and, by extension, of the lady (> Introduction).

Humanism An art historical term denoting the 'human centered' rediscovery of the Classical world in the esp. Central Italian Renaissance. Crucially influential on the uptake of the Classical aesthetic in garden design in the 16th century (> Introduction).

ice-house A brick- or stone-lined shaft or free-standing construction in which (salted) ice (mainly for the preservation of victuals and not for cooling drinks) was stored for the summer months (> Governor's Palace).

jardin anglais (Fr. 'English garden') Informal garden in the English landscaped style, as distinguished from the French formal layout (> Ermenonville, Villa Ephrussi, Villandry).

jardin d'ornement (Fr.) Small-scale, ornamental and often highly stylized garden (> Villandry).

jardin paysager (Fr.) Landscape, or landscaped, 18th-century garden of picturesque style (> Ermenonville).

jardin potager > *potager.*

jardin-vaisseau (Fr. 'garden-vessel') Garden in the rough shape of a ship (nonce term) (> Villa Ephrussi).

kare-sansui (Jap.) Dry landscape garden, in which, however, water elements may be evoked by rocks and gravel (> Byodo-in).

Kammergarten (Ger.) Enclosed private garden of a palace or Schloss (> Schönbrunn).

labyrinth Large complex maze, often incorporating structures or multiple garden spaces (> Alhambra, Schwetzingen, Wörlitz).

lochan (Scots.) Miniature loch or lake (> Little Sparta).

loggia An open, roofed arcade or porch running along one side of a building; a free-standing structure in that form, often with an upper storey (> Villas Farnese, Gamberaia and Piccolomini).

Lustpark (Ger., Swedish) Pleasure garden; for promenading and the enjoyment of plants and garden features (> Haga, Hellbrunn).

Lusthaus (Ger.), ***Lusthus*** (Swedish) 'Pleasure-house', pavilion.

Mannerism (It. *maniera* = style) The main (pre-Baroque) tendency of art (esp. in Italy) in the mid- to late 16th century and even beyond. Characterized by the 'decadence' of the 'pure' Renaissance aesthetic that exaggerates forms (i.e. in serpentine lines, involved curves, and compartimentalised fantasies). In garden design, grottoes, pools, elaborate and often sensual statuary are typical (> Introduction).

Medina (fr. Arabic) The town seen as a market-place, with shops, workshops and houses, as in the case of the > Alhambra that served the Alcazaba and Palacios.

menagerie A collection of (most often confined) wild animals and fowl. The menagerie might be restricted to a single room and was not devised according to the scientific principles of the zoological garden, space often being found for the exotic or outlandish (> Blenheim, Schönbrunn).

mirador Belvedere or look-out tower (> Alhambra).

necessary(-house) An often architecturally elaborate convenience (> Governor's Palace).

nymphaeum An artificial and often architecturally elaborate > grotto with water features dedicated to the nymphs; sometimes containing statuary (> Villas Farnese and Gamberaia, Wörlitz).

obelisk A tall (usually orthogonal) stone pillar tapering to a pyramidal end serving perhaps to commemorate an event and/or enhance a vista (> Castle Howard, Isola Bella, Little Sparta) or decorate a water feature (> Schönbrunn).

orangery A (sometimes rather grand) free-standing building or conservatory ostensibly for the growing of climate-sensitive orange-trees (> Blenheim, Kew, Schönbrunn, Villa Medici).

pagoda Multi-storied Oriental-style tower, characteristic of 18th-century Chinese-style gardens all over Europe, sometimes as an eyecatcher (> Kew, Villa Ephrussi).

paintbox flowerbeds Beds of very varied colours, divided often in square sections (> Giverny).

palacio (Sp.) Palace.

palazzino (It.) An independent small 'palace' (i.e. elaborate building) in a garden (>Villa Ephrussi).

palissade A neatly clipped high hedge.

Palladian bridge Elaborate bridge ostensibly based on designs by Palladio, often with colonnaded superstructure (> Stowe).

parquet An ornate wooden floor; by extension, similar patterns of hedge or box in Renaissance or early formal gardens.

parterre (Fr. now, 'flower-bed') Flat, basically oblong terrace near the house laid out with flower beds in a regular, ornamental shape (> Biltmore, Castle Howard, Chatsworth, Governor's Palace, Haga, Hestercombe, Levens Hall, Old Westbury, Peterhof, Taj Mahal, Schönbrunn, Schwetzingen, Vaux-le-Vicomte, Versailles, Viceroy's Garden and Villas Ephrussi, Farnese, Gamberaia, Medici, Piccolomini and Vizcaya). The more flowing designs (from late 17th century) bordered with box or turf are called ***parterres de broderie*** and are sometimes known as 'embroider[ed] work' in English treatises (> Blenheim, Castle Howard, Dumbarton Oaks, Isola Bella, Schwetzingen, Vaux-le-Vicomte, Villa Garzoni). ***Parterres de compartiment*** are wholly symmetrical ***parterres de broderie*** (> Villandry). ***Parterres à l'anglaise*** (individual compartments known as > plats) are similar designs simply cut out of turf (>Schwetzingen, Vaux-le-Vicomte). ***Parterres d'eau* [water *parterres*]** are shaped by water channels (> Blenheim, Dumbarton Oaks, Hellbrunn, Versailles, Villa Lante, Villandry).

patio Often paved courtyard in ancient Moorish and Spanish buildings for growing plants and for recreation (> Alhambra).

pavilion A lightly constructed, free-standing garden building of medium size. Often in the 'Turkish' or 'Chinese' styles (> Haga, Hellbrunn, Schönbrunn, Veitshöchheim).

pelouse (Fr. 'lawn') A stretch of lawn in a landscaped garden.

pergola (It.) Vaulted open structure commonly of metal or wood that supports climbing plants and under which one can pass or walk. Some examples are still more elaborate with seats, tiles or architectural elements within (> Biltmore, Hestercombe, Old Westbury, Viceroy's Garden).

peristyle A free-standing colonnade or one surrounding or flanking a building; a columnated courtyard (> Introduction).

picturesque The Picturesque is an aesthetic stressing the less tamed aspects of nature first in painting and then in garden design that arose in England in the middle to the end of the 18th century. It opposed both French formality and 'Capability' Brown's easeful manner. Controversy raged around its status as a concept and its correct use; its supporters saw it as a justified third alternative to and as on an equal footing to the 'civilised' notion of Beauty (i.e. formality and ease) and the awesome sentiment of the natural Sublime (e.g. of mountains and storms) (> Blenheim). Picturesque is also used less helpfully to mean 'pretty', almost 'homely'.

pièce d'eau (Fr. 'stretch of water') A medium-sized mostly stone-lined pond in a formal garden (> Villandry).

pinetum Arboretum or collection of growing trees composed of conifers (> Chatsworth).

planter Large decorative plant-pot or urn.

plat Flat, relatively unadorned, area of lawn in a formal garden (> Hampton Court Palace, Hestercombe).

plate-bande Formal border to a parterre, often of a strip of sand and grass, or else of low box (> Het Loo, Villandry).

pleaching Intertwining and binding the branches of a line of trees to make a single barrier or hedge (> Sissinghurst).

portico A porch with columns; also a free-standing roofed structure with columns (> Arkadia).

potager (Fr.) Vegetable garden (sometimes including fruit trees) (> Versailles, Villandry).

promenade (Fr. 'walk') Path or esplanade for pleasure walking (> Haga).

'Pure Land' (Jap. 'Jodo') Concept of Western Paradise in the Amida Buddhism that entered Japan in the 9th century and became popular among the Mikkoyo sects. Special villa-temples evoking the harmony of the sacred realm were built (>Byodo-in).

pourtraiture Old French word deriving from Latin *protrahere*, (the same root as portraiture), meaning to draw forth or trace. In garden design it refers to *parterres* and architecture which are adjusted geometrically to fit into and produce a certain optical effect within the landscape (> Vaux-le-Vicomte).

qanat (Persian; also *kanat*; Arabic = *foggara*) An ancient water-supply system that taps underground mountain water and brings it downhill to a settlement (or garden) by way of subterranean channels or tunnels.

quincunx The shape of a square with a centrally placed element, like a 'five' on a die; plants (trees) so planted, common in France before the classical period. Sir Thomas Browne wrote a famous discourse on the system which invested it with deep significance (> Levens Hall).

rill A small, informal channel or gully arranged decoratively in a garden (> Hestercombe, Little Sparta, Rousham, Shute, Villa Ephrussi).

rococo An 18th-century style originating as such in France in interior decoration and then in architecture (esp. in Bavaria and Austria) characterized by asymmetry, lightness, daintiness, an integrated use of white and pastel shades, and a deliberate lack of demarcation between decorative and architectonic elements. In garden design, *putti*, polychrome statuary, serpentine paths and irregularly shaped ponds, well-lit grottoes, relaxed vistas, and elaborate benches are typical.

Rousseau island Romantically planted island, perhaps with a false 'tomb', that evokes the philosopher's tomb in > Ermonville (> Wörlitz)

rubble-wall Rough, usually uncoursed wall (> Sigiriya).

ruin In baroque and rococo European gardens, artificial 'Roman ruins' were popular following the vogue for engravings by Giovanni Battista Piranesi (1720–78) of ruin landscapes that combined various Roman features in one dramatic vista (e.g. 1745) (> Schönbrunn, Schwetzingen).

scrollwork Ornamental designs using curved and twisting shapes originally in architectural or metalwork, but also applied to convoluted lawn designs (> Hampton Court Palace).

shoin (Jap.) Architectural or garden style which evokes low-lying flat planes; derived from the low-slung writing-desk of the same name (> Katsura Rikyu).

singeries (Fr. from *singe* = monkey) Humorous designs incorporating monkeys imitating human activities (> Queluz).

spugne (It.) Rough pumice-bound rendering for grottoes (> Villa Medici).

stew-pond A (small, often stone flagged) pond for keeping fish (> Hampton Court Palace).

sukiya (Jap.) Architectural or garden style of rustic plainness (> Katsura Rikyu).

sunken lawn Lawn or turf set into the ground, sometimes lined with stone (> Viceroy's Garden).

tapis vert (Fr., 'green carpet') Regularly cut, often square, stretch of turf or lawn, typical of 17th-century French gardens (> Parc André Citröen, Versailles).

topiary The art of shaping trees and shrubs (especially hedges) into elaborate geometrical or figurative designs by clipping and training (Hidcote Manor, Levens Hall, Villandry).

trencadis (Sp.) Stone, marble or enameled ceramic fragments used as rough *tessera* or mosaic facing, notably in the work of Catalan Antoni Gaudí, for example Parque Guëll (> Introduction).

tufa An often limestone-based, low-density, porous rock of volcanic origin used to dress other rocks and give them a 'rough' if uniform appearance (e.g. in a > grotto) (> Villa Medici).

wabi-sabi (Jap.) Aesthetic characterized by the appreciation of the patina and transformation brought about by aging (> Katsura Rikyu).

water chain > *catena d'acqua*.

water staircase, stairway A series of stone steps down which water flows (> Alhambra, Naumkeag, and Villas Aldobrandini, Lante and Vizcaya).

water theatre Intricate water features arranged in tiered structure with large-scale architectural and statuary elements (> Isola Bella).

water wall Decorative wall cascading with water or pierced with holes through which water is pumped (> San Cristóbal).

Wrenaissance A (slightly facetious) term covering English architecture influenced by the work of Sir Christopher Wren (1632–1723) as applied to the work of Sir Edwin Lutyens, and apparently coined by him (> Introduction).

wych elm Elm with attractive flowers and rounded leaves, *Ulmus glabra* (> Hestercombe).

ziggurat A rectangular temple tower in ancient Mesopotamia built up in a vast step-like formation (> Introduction).

Selected Bibliography

General

Adams, William Howard, *Gardens Through History: Nature Perfected*, New York/London/Paris, Abbeville Press, 1991.

—, *Grounds for Change: Major Gardens of the 20th Century*, Boston, Bulfinch, 1993.

Baumüller, Barbara (ed.), *Inszenierte Natur,* Stuttgart, 1997.

Brookes, John, *Gardens of Paradise*, New York, New Amsterdam, 1987.

Butlar, Adrian von, *Der Landschaftsgarten*, Munich, 1980.

Church, Thomas, *Gardens are for People*, New York, Reinhold, 1955.

Farrar, Linda, *Ancient Roman Gardens*, Stroud, Sutton, 1998.

Gothein, Marie Luise, *Geschichte Der Gartenkunst (II),* Jena, 1926.

Hansmann, Wilfried, *Gartenkunst der Renaissance und des Barock*, Cologne, 1983.

—, *Barocke Gartenparadiese,* Cologne, 1996.

Hirschfeld, Christian C., *Theorie der Gartenkunst*, Leipzig, 1779–80.

Hughes, Ted (tr.), *Tales from Ovid*, London, Faber & Faber, 1997.

Hunt, John, & Peter Willis, *The Genius of the Place*, London, Paul Elek, 1975.

Huxley, Anthony, *An Illustrated History of Gardening*, UK/USA, Paddington Press, 1978.

Inaji, T., *The Garden as Architecture*, London/Tokyo/New York, Kodansha International, 1998.

Jekyll, Gertrude, *Colour Schemes for the Flower Garden*, Country Life, 1914; reprinted Woodbridge, Antique Collectors Club, 1990.

Jellicoe, Geoffrey & Susan, Patrick Goode & Michael Lancaster, *Oxford Companion to Gardens,* Oxford/New York, Oxford University Press, 1986.

Kassler, Elizabeth B., *Modern Gardens and the Landscape*, New York, Museum of Modern Art/Doubleday, 1964.

Laird, Mark, *The Formal Garden*, London, Thames & Hudson, 1992.

Lyall, S., *Designing The New Landscape*, London, Thames & Hudson, 1993.

Macoubbin, Robert P., & Peter Martin (eds.), *British and American Gardens of the Eighteenth Century*, Williamsburg, VA., The Colonial Williamsburg Foundation, 1984.

The New Royal Horticultural Society Dictionary of Gardening, 4 vols., London, Macmillan, 1992.

Shepheard, Peter, *Modern Gardens*, London, Architectural Press, 1953.

Strong, Roy, *Gardens Through the Ages 1420–1940*, London, Conran Octopus, 2000.

Whalley, Robin, & Anne Jennings, *Knot Gardens and Parterres*, London, Barn Elms, 1998.

Europe

Finland

Aalto, Alvar, *The Architectural Drawings by Alvar Aalto, 1917–1939: Vol. 10 Villa Mairea, 1938–39*, New York/London, Garland, 1994.

Olsson, Paul, *Trädgårdkonst i Finland,* Helsingfors, Holger Schildts, 1946.

Pallasmaa, Juhani, Alvar Aalto: Villa Mairea 1938–39, Helsinki, Alvar Aalto Foundation and Mairea Foundation, 1998.

Pallasmaa, Juhani, *Alvar Aalto: Villa Mairea, Noormarkku, Finland, 1937–39*, Tokyo, A.D.A., 1985.

Weston, Richard, *Villa Mairea: Alvar Aalto*, London, Phaidon, 1992.

France

Adams,William Howard, *The French Garden 1500–1800*, London, Scholar Press, 1979.

Clément, G., *Le Jardin en Mouvement: de la Vallée au Parc André Citroën*, Paris, Sene at Tonka, 1994.

—, *Les Libres Jardins de Gilles Clément*, Paris, Éditions du Chêne, 1997.

—, *Une Ecole Buissonière*, Paris, Hazan, 1997.

Cohen, J.L., & B. Fortier, *Paris, a City in the Making*, Paris, Edition Babylone, Pavillon de l'Arsenal, 1992.

Hucliez, M., *Jardins et Parcs Contemporains*, Paris, Telleri, 1998.

Roger, A. (ed.), *Théorie du Paysage en France, 1974-1994*, Seyssel, ChampVallon, 1995.

Germany and Austria

Auböck, Maria, *Grün in Wien*, Vienna, 1994.

'Potsdamer Schlösser und Gärten', in *Bau- und Gartenkunst vom 17. bis 20. Jahrhundert* (exh. cat.), Potsdam, 1993.

Bechtold, Frank A. (ed.), *Weltbild Wörlitz*, Wörlitz, 1996.

Bigler, Robert R., *Schloß Hellbrunn*, Vienna, 1996.

Danreiter, Franz A., *Salzburger Ansichten*, Dortmund, 1982.

Erlach, Johann Fischer von, *Entwurff einer historischen Architektur*, Vienna, 1721.

Giersberg, Hans-Joachim, & Adelheid Schendel, *Potsdamer Veduten*, Potsdam-Sanssouci, 1984.

Günther, Harri (ed.), *Gärten der Goethezeit*, Leipzig, 1993.

Hajós, Beatrix, *Die Schönbrunner Schloßgärten*, Vienna, 1995.

Hajós, Geza, *Romantische Gärten der Aufklärung*, Vienna, 1989.

Hennebo, Dieter, *Geschichte der Deutschen Gartenkunst (II)*, Hamburg, 1963.

Jellicoe, Geoffrey A., *Baroque Gardens of Austria*, London, 1931.

Kopisch, A., *Geschichte der Königlichen Schlösser und Gärten zu Potsdam*, Berlin, 1854.

Kreisel, Heinrich, *Der Rokokogarten zu Veitshöchheim*, Munich, 1964.

Maier-Solgk, Frank, *Landschaftsgärten in Deutschland*, Stuttgart, 1997.

Ortwin Rave, Paul, *Gärten der Goethezeit*, Berlin, 1981.

Reil, Friedrich, *Herzog und Fürst von Anhalt Dessau*, Dessau, 1845.

Reisinger, Claus, *Der Schloßgarten zu Schwetzingen*, Worms, 1987.

Schaub, Franz, *Berühmte Gärten in Franken*, Würzburg, 1984.

Seiler, Michael, & Jörg Wacker, *Insel Potsdam. Ein kulturhistorischer Begleiter durch die Potsdamer Parklandschaft,* Berlin, 1991.

Streidt, Gert, & Peter Feierabend, *Preußen. Kunst und Architektur*, Cologne, 1999.

Werner, Ferdinand, *Der Hofgarten in Veitshöchheim*, Worms, 1998.

Zenkner, Oswalk, *Schwetzinger Schloßgarten*, Schwetzingen, 1993.

Italy

Bajard, Sophie, & Raffaello Bencini, *Villas and Gardens of Tuscany*, Terrail, 1993.

Chatfield, Judith, *A Tour of Italian Gardens*, London, Ward Lock, 1988.

Coffin, David, *The Villa in the Life of Renaissance Rome*, Princeton, 1979.

Dernie, David, *The Villa d'Este at Tivoli*, London, Academy Editions, 1996.

Lazzaro, Claudia, *The Italian Renaissance Garden*, London/New Haven, Yale University Press, 1990.

Masson, Georgina, *Italian Gardens*, Woodbridge, Antique Collectors' Club, 1987.

The Netherlands

Hunt, John D., and Erik de Jong, (eds), *The Anglo-Dutch Garden in the Age of William and Mary*, (De Gouden Eeuw van de Hollandse Tuinkunst), London, Taylor & Francis, 1988.
Jong, Erik de, *Nature and Art: Dutch Garden and Landscape Architecture 1650–1740*, Philadelphia, Pennsylvania University Press, 2000.
Journal of Garden History no 2/3, (special double issue on Het Loo).

Spain & Portugal

Segall, Barbara, *Gardens of Spain and Portugal*, London, Mitchell Beazley, 1999.

United Kingdom

Abrioux, Yves, with Stephen Bann, *Ian Hamilton Finlay: A Visual Primer*, 2nd edn, London, Reaktion, 1992.
Bisgrove, Richard, *The Gardens of Gertrude Jekyll*, London, Frances Lincoln, 1992.
Brown, Jane, *The English Garden through the Twentieth Century*, Woodbridge, Antique Collectors Club, 2000.
—, *Gardens of a Golden Afternoon. The Story of a Partnership: Edwin Lutyens and Gertrude Jekyll*, Harmondsworth, Penguin, 1982.
—, *Vita's Other World*, Harmondsworth, Viking Penguin, 1985.
Cooper, Guy, Clive Boursnell & Geoffrey Jellicoe, *English Water Gardens*, London, Weidenfeld & Nicolson, 1987.
Cooper, Guy, & Gordon Taylor, *English Herb Gardens*, London, Weidenfeld & Nicolson, 2000.
Daniels, Stephen, *Humphry Repton: Landscape Gardening and the Geography of Georgian England*, London/New Haven, Yale University Press, 1999.
Dixon Hunt, John, *William Kent: Landscape Garden Designer*, London, Zwemmer, 1987.
Eyres, Patrick, 'Ian Hamilton Finlay and the cultural politics of neo-classical gardening', *Garden History*, 28:1 (summer 2000).
Fearnley-Whittingstall, Jane, *Historic Gardens: A Guide to 160 British Gardens of Interest*, London, Grange, 1993.
Festing, Sally, *Gertrude Jekyll*, Harmondsworth, Penguin, 1991.
Fleming, Laurence, & Alan Gore, *The English Garden*, London, Michael Joseph, 1979.
Hussey, C., *The Life of Sir Edwin Lutyens*, London, Country Life, 1950.
Jekyll, Francis, *Gertrude Jekyll: A Memoir*, London, Cape, 1934.
Jekyll, Gertrude, *Home and Garden*, London, Longmans Green, 1900; Woodbridge, Antique Collectors' Club, 1982.
Jekyll, Gertrude and Lawrence Weaver, *Gardens for Small Country Houses*, London, Country Life, 1912; republished as *Arts and Crafts Gardens*, Woodbridge, Antique Collectors' Club, 1981.
Jellicoe, Geoffrey, *Studies in Landscape Design*, 3 vols, Oxford/New York, Oxford University Press, 1960–70.
Lawson, Andrew & Jane Taylor, *Great English Gardens*, London, Weidenfeld & Nicolson, 1996.
Richardson, Margaret, *RIBA Drawings Monographs No. 1: Sketches by Edwin Lutyens*, London, Academy Editions, 1994.
Robinson, John Martin, *Temples of Delight: Stowe Landscape Gardens*, London, George Philip, 1990.
Robinson, William, *Gravetye Manor, or Twenty Years' Work Round an Old Manor House*, New York, Sagapress, Timber Press, 1984.
Spens, Michael, *Jellicoe at Shute*, London, Academy Editions, Berlin, Ernst & Sohn, 1993.
Stowe Landscape Gardens (Guide Book), London, National Trust, 1997.
Strong, Roy, *The Renaissance Garden in England*, London, Thames & Hudson, 1979.
Symes, Michael, *Fairest Scenes: Five Great Surrey Gardens*, Elmbridge Museum Service, 1988.
Tankard, Judith, & Martin A. Wood, *Gertrude Jekyll at Munstead Wood*, Stroud, Allan Sutton, 1996.
Taylor, Patrick, *Period Gardens*, London, Pavilion, 1996.
Tooley, Michael and Primrose Arnander (eds.), *Gertrude Jekyll: Essays on the Life of a Working Amateur*, Deer Park, Wisconsin, Michaelmas Books, 1995.
Turner, Tom, *English Garden Design: History and Styles since 1650*, Woodbridge, Antique Collectors Club, 1986.
Kenneth, *The Stourhead Landscape*, London, National Trust, 1982.

Eastern Europe

Arkadia: The Illusion and the Reality (exh. cat.), Polish Cultural Institute, 1995.
Stevens Curl, James, 'Arkadia, Poland: Garden of Allusions', in *Garden History*, 23:1 (1995).

The Americas

North America

Balmori, Diana, Diane Kostial McGuire & Eleanor M. McPeck, *Beatrix Farrand's American Landscapes: Her Gardens and Campuses*, Sagaponack, NY, Sagapress, 1985.
Hilderbrand, Gary R., *The Miller Garden: Icon of Modernism*, Washington, D.C., 1999.
Hoffmann, Donald, *Frank Lloyd Wright's Fallingwater: The House and its History*, New York, Dover, 1978.
Kaufmann, Jr., Edgar, *Fallingwater: A Frank Lloyd Wright Country House*, New York, Abbeville, 1986.
Leighton, Ann, *American Gardens of the Eighteenth Century: 'For Use or Delight'*, University of Massachusetts Press, 1976.
—, *American Gardens of the Nineteenth Century, 'For Comfort and Affluence'*, University of Massachusetts Press, 1987.
—, *Early American Gardens, 'For Meate of Medicine'*, University of Massachusetts Press, 1970.
Lloyd Wright, Frank, *An Autobiography (1932)*, New York, Horizon, 1977.
Martin, Peter, *The Pleasure Gardens of Virginia*, Princeton University Press, 1991.
McCarter, R., *Fallingwater: Frank Lloyd Wright*, London, Phaidon, 1994.
McCarter, Robert, *Frank Lloyd Wright*, London, Phaidon, 1997.
McCoy, Esther. 'California Landscaping No. 9: Succulents...A Rich Effect While Undemanding', *Los Angeles Times Home Magazine* (21 April 1957), 16–17, 46.
Messenger, Pam-Anela, 'El Novillero revisited — a testimony to Thomas D. Church', in *Landscape Design*, 142 (1983), 33–35 .
Messenger, Pam-Anela, 'El Novillero revisited', *Landscape Architecture*, 73:2 (1983), 64–67.
Neutra, Richard, *Mystery and Realities of the Site*, Scarsdale, New York, Morgan & Morgan, 1951.

Padilla, Victoria, *Southern California Gardens*, Berkeley & Los Angeles, University of California Press, 1961.
Seidenberg, Charlotte, *The New Orleans Garden*, New Orleans, Silkmon & Count, 1990.
Streatfield, David C., *California Gardens: Creating a New Eden*, New York/London/Paris, Abbeville Press, 1994.
Studies in the History of Gardens and Designed Landscapes, 2:2 (2000): special issue devoted to Thomas Dolliver Church, Mark Treib (ed.).

South America

Riggen Martinez, A., *Luis Barrágan: Mexico's Modern Master 1902–1988*, New York, The Monacelli Press, 1996.
Rispa, R., Barrágan, *The Complete Works*, London, Thames & Hudson, 1996.

Asia

China

Dun-zhen, L., *Chinese Classical Gardens of Suzhou*, tr. Chen Lixian, New York/London, McGraw-Hill, 1993.
Wang, J. C., *The Chinese Garden,* Hong Kong/New York/Oxford, Oxford University Press, 1998.
Wood, F., *China: Blue Guide*, London, A&C Black; New York, W.W. Norton, 1992.

Japan

Bring, M., & J. Wayembergh, *Japanese Gardens*, New York/London, McGraw-Hill, 1981.
Keane, M.P., *Japanese Garden Design*, Rutland/Vermont/Tokyo/Japan, Charles E. Tuttle, 1996.
Masuno, S., *Ten Landscapes*, Rockport, Massachusetts, Rockport Publishers, 1999.
Nishi, K., & K. Hozumi, *What is Japanese Architecture*, tr. H.M. Horton, Tokyo/New York/London, Kodansha International, 1983.
Nitschke, G., *Japanese Gardens*, Cologne, Benedikt Taschen, 1993.
Treib, M., Herman, R., *A Guide to the Gardens of Kyoto*, Tokyo, Shufunotomo Company, 1980.

India

Brookes J., *Paradise Gardens*, London, Weidenfeld & Nicolson, 1987.
Grant Irving, Robert, *Indian Summer: Lutyens, Baker and Imperial Delhi*, London/New Haven, Yale University Press, 1981.

Turkey

Eldem, S.H., *Köskler ve Kaserlar*, vol. 1, Istanbul, 1969.
Goodwin, G., *Topkapi Palace*, London, 1999.
Ncipoglu, G., *Architecture, Ceremonial and Power, The Topkapi Palace in the 15th and 16th Centuries*, New York, 1991.

The Authors

Helena Attlee is an author and editor specialising in gardens. She has written numerous articles for magazines such as *Country Life*, *Gardens Illustrated*, *House & Garden* and the *Telegraph* Magazine about gardens in Britain and abroad. Her book with Alex Ramsay, *Italian Gardens*, has been published in a revised edition.

Andrew Boorman is a Senior Lecturer in Landscape and Garden Studies at Writtle College, Essex. He has travelled widely overseas and has brought this experience into his teaching of world gardens and landscapes. He is currently researching aspects of landscape psychology and aesthetics.

Peter Brimacombe is a freelance writer and photographer, and author of *The Pitkin Guide to English Gardens.*

Susan Chamberlin has an MA in architectural history and is a licensed landscape architect and founding member of the California Garden & Landscape History Society. She lives in Santa Barbara, California.

Peggy L. Cornett has worked at Monticello since 1983, first as assistant director of gardens and grounds and, since 1992, as director of Monticello's Thomas Jefferson Center for Historic Plants. She is author of *Popular Annuals of Eastern North America, 1865–1914*, and writes for numerous periodicals and publications.

David Crellin is an architectural historian and lecturer with a special interest in the work of Sir Edwin Lutyens. He is Director of the Victorian Society Summer School.

Patrick Eyres is Senior Lecturer in Theoretical Studies at the School of Art, Design and Textiles, Bradford College. He is also the managing editor of the *New Arcadian Journal*, which specialises in the cultural politics of Georgian landscape gardens. A number of editions (nos. 10, 15, 23, 24, 33/34, 45/46) have addressed the works of Ian Hamilton Finlay, for example The Ian Hamilton Finlay Sculpture Garden at Stockwood Park, Luton in *New Arcadian Journal* no. 33/34 (1992).

Godfrey Goodwin is Director of the Royal Asiatic Society. He has taught in Egypt and as Assistant Professor of Art and Architectural History at the University of the Bosphorus, Istanbul, 1957–68. He has written many books on Islamic art and culture of Spain and the Ottomans and has recently published a guide to the Topkapi Palace.

Axel Griesinger is an architect who lectures on garden conservation at the Architectural Association in London.

Caroline Holmes is a writer, broadcaster and lecturer on garden history and design. She lectures for Cambridge and Essex Universities, the Museum of Garden History and in the United States. She is the author of *Monet: The Man, The Garden, The Paintings*. Her book, *Small Victorian Gardens*, will be published in winter 2001.

David Jacques led the landscape teams that surveyed Hampton Court in 1982 and that restored the Privy Garden in 1995. He is Chairman of the Garden History Society and Course Director for the Postgraduate Diploma on Conservation (Landscapes and Gardens) at the Architectural Association, London. He also runs his family's traditional rural estate at Sugnall, Staffordshire.

Erik A. de Jong is Lecturer and Director of Studies at the Vrije Universiteit, Amsterdam. He has lectured and published widely in Europe and North America on the subject of garden and landscape architecture from 1600 to the present. He was a Dumbarton Oaks Fellow in the History of Landscape Architecture in 1993 and 2001.

Axel Klausmeier studied Art History, and Medieval and Modern History at the Universities of Bochum, Munich, and Berlin. He graduated in 1999 with a dissertation on the English architect Thomas Ripley (1682–1758). Since 1999 he has worked as an art historian at the Stiftung Preussische Schlösser und Gärten Berlin-Brandenburg. He has published widely on garden design and architectural history.

Marcus Köhler teaches land economy and conservation at the Fachhochschule, Neubrandenburg, Germany.

Susan Garrett Mason lives in Atlanta, Georgia, where she worked as an archaeologist and as a editor before launching a freelance writing career. She specialises in gardening and food, and is the author of *Southwinds Gourmet.*

Sue Minter is Curator of the Chelsea Physic Garden, London.

Magnus Olausson works at the National Museum of Fine Arts in Stockholm, Sweden.

Laurence Pattacini is an architect and urban designer with ten years' professional experience in landscape design. She presently teaches at Cheltenham and Gloucester College of Higher Education.

David Radzinowicz is a literature graduate of both French and British Universities. He is a freelance writer on the baroque and on 20th-century cultural topics, a translator and a lexicographer.

Jill Raggett is a Senior Lecturer in Gardens and Designed Landscapes at Writtle College, Essex, and Adjunct Professor at the Nova Scotia College of Agriculture, Canada. She has travelled extensively in Britain and abroad to study historic and contemporary gardens. At present she is completing her doctoral research on the origins and expression of the Japanese-style garden in Great Britain.

Michael Symes is a garden historian at Birkbeck College, University of London. He has written a number of books on the subject including *Garden Sculpture* and *A Glossary of Garden History.*

Jan Woudstra is a landscape architect who teaches in the Department of Landscape at the University of Sheffield. He is Honorary Editor of *Garden History*. His doctoral thesis was on landscape design and theory of the modern movement.

Index of Names

Picture Credits

The numbers listed below refer to pages where illustrations are located: **t** = top; **c** = centre; **b** = bottom; **l** = left; **r** = right.

Front jacket, main picture: Jerry Harpur; **12** UNESCO; **13** Trip/T. Bognar; **14-15** (all) Tobias Wittig; **16tl** Peter Brimacombe; **16bl**, **17t** Hugh Palmer; **17b** Liz Eddison; **18tl**, **bl** Peter Hayden: **19t**, **b** AKG, London; **20-21** (all) Alex Ramsay; **22tl** Harry Smith Collection; **22bl** AKG, London; **22bc**, **23** Michael Jenner; **24bl** Michael Jenner; **24tl**, **br** © M&J Raggett, **25** Jerry Harpur; **26-27** (all) Tobias Wittig; **28tl** Royal Library, Windsor Castle; **28br**, **29t** Liz Eddison; **29br** Hugh Palmer; **30** AKG, London; **31t** Peter Hayden; **31b** Hugh Palmer; **32** AKG, London: **33l** Alex Ramsay; **33cr**, **br** Peter Hayden; **34tl**, **cl**, **bl**, **34-35t** Alex Ramsay; **35bc** AKG, London; **36bc** Caroline Holmes; **36t**, **36-37t** Hugh Palmer; **38tl** Peter Hayden; **38cl**, **bl**, **39t**, **b** Alex Ramsay; **40tl**, **bl**, **40-41b** Hugh Palmer; **41t** Peter Hayden; **42l** Alex Ramsay: **42c** Peter Hayden: **42r** Harry Smith Collection; **43t** Peter Hayden; **43b** Harry Smith Collection; **44-45** (all) Peter Hayden; **46tl**, **cl** Alex Ramsay; **47r** Hugh Palmer; **47tl** Harry Smith Collection; **48tl**, **cl** Harry Smith Collection; **49** Trip/C. Rennie; **50-51** (all) Axel Griesinger; **52-53** (all) Tobias Wittig; **54tc** AKG, London; **54bl**, **54-55t**, **55b** Alex Ramsay; **56tl** Harry Smith Collection; **56-57b**, AKG, London; **58cl** Hugh Palmer; **58bl** Harry Smith Collection; **58 tl**, **59** Alex Ramsay; **60tl** Trip/H. Rogers; **60bc** Trip/B. Turner; **61t**,**b** AKG, London; **62tl**, **bl**, **63t** Hugh Palmer; **63bl** Harry Smith Collection; **64l** AKG, London; **65tc** Hugh Palmer; **65tr** Caroline Holmes; **65br** Harry Smith Collection: **66tl**, **cl**, **bl** Axel Griesinger; **67** Peter Hayden; **68-69** (all) Hugh Palmer; **70tl**, **71bl** Caroline Holmes; **71t** Harry Smith Collection; **71br** AKG, London; **72tl** Hugh Palmer; **72cl** Jerry Harpur; **73lr** Hugh Palmer; **74tl**, **cl** Axel Griesinger; **74bc**, **75** AKG, London; **76tl** Harry Smith Collection; **76cl**, **bl** Caroline Holmes; **77** Harry Smith Collection; **78b** Peter Hayden; **78tl**, **79** Hugh Palmer; **80tl**, **bc** Caroline Holmes; **80-81tr** Harry Smith Collection; **81br** Caroline Holmes; **82cl** AKG, London; **82-83bc**, **83tl** Peter Hayden; **83cl** AKG, London; **84tl**, **85b**, **tr** Hugh Palmer; **85tl** Peter Hayden; **86tl** Peter Hayden; **86bc**, **87** Harry Smith Collection; **88tl**, **cl**, **bl** Axel Griesinger; **89** AKG, London; **90cl**, **bl** Jerry Harpur; **90tl**, **91** Hugh Palmer; **92tl**, **tc**, **92-93t** Jerry Harpur; **93br** Hugh Palmer; **94-95** (all) Middleton Place, Charleston, South Carolina; **96bl** Peter Hayden; **96tl**, **97** Peter Brimacombe; **98tl** Hugh Palmer; **98br**, **99t** AKG, London; **99br** Hugh Palmer; **100tc** Harry Smith Collection; **100tl**, **tr**, **101** Peter Hayden; **102cl**, **bl**, **103** Peter Hayden; **104tl** © M&J Raggett; **104tc**, **tr**, **105bc** Peter Hayden; **105t** Harry Smith Collection; **106tl** Hugh Palmer; **106cr** Michael Jenner; **106cl** Harry Smith Collection; **106bc** AKG, London; **107** Harry Smith Collection: **108cl** Hugh Palmer; **108tl**, **bc**, **109** Axel Griesinger; **110t**, **b** Caroline Holmes; **111** AKG, London; **112bl** AKG, London; **112tl**, **cl**, **113** Monticello/Thomas Jefferson Foundation; **114t**, **c**, **b**, **115** Peter Hayden; **116t**,**b** Peter Hayden; **117t**, **b** Nordiska Museet, Stockholm; **118tl** Harry Smith Collection; **118b** Jerry Harpur; **119t** Harry Smith Collection; **119b** Peter Brimacombe; **120tl** Harry Smith Collection; **120tc**, **120-121tr** Hugh Palmer; **121br** Harry Smith Collection: **122-23** (all) John Glover; **124t**, **b**, **125t** Garden & Wildlife Matters; **125b** SUNY-ESF Archives; **126tl** Harry Smith Collection; **126bl** Peter Brimacombe; **127t**, **br** Harry Smith Collection; **128tl** Hugh Palmer; **128bl**, **129** Harry Smith Collection; **130tl**, cl Peter Brimacombe; **131tr** Peter Brimacombe; **131br** Caroline Holmes; **132tl**, **132-133tc**, **133bl** Hugh Palmer; **133br** Jerry Harpur; **134-135** (all) Hugh Palmer; **136tl**, **cl** Peter Brimacombe; **136bl**, **137** Jerry Harpur; **138-139** (all) Clive Nichols / Ephrussi de Rothschild, France; **140-141** (all) Hugh Palmer; **142tl**, **bl**, The Country Life Picture Library; **143** Andreas Volwahsen; **144** Hugh Palmer; **145t** Harry Smith Collection; **145bl** Caroline Holmes; **145br** Hugh Palmer; **146tl** Harry Smith Collection, **147bl** Harry Smith Collection; **147t**, **br** Jerry Harpur; **147tr**, **cr** Harry Smith Collection; **148tl** Jerry Harpur; **148bl**, **149t**, **br** Alex Ramsay; **150** AKG, London; **151t**, **b** Trip/J. Stanley; **152-153** (all) Richard Weston; **154l**, **r**, **155** Garden & Wildlife Matters; **156-157** (all) Balthazar Korab; **158-159** (all) Hugh Palmer; **160-161** (all) EWA/Tim Street-Porter;**162tl** Hugh Palmer; **162bl**, **163bc** Jerry Harpur; **163t** Hugh Palmer; **164-165** (all) Andrew Lawson; **back jacket:** Garden & Wildlife Matters; **spine image:** Alex Ramsay.

Every effort has been made by the Publisher to acknowledge all sources and copyright holders. In the event of any copyright holder being inadvertently omitted, please contact the Publisher directly.

Front jacket: Levens Hall topiary garden, see pp. 72–73.
Back jacket: Naumkeag, see pp. 124–25.
Page 2: Villandry, see pp. 134–35.

Prestel Verlag
Mandlstrasse 26
D-80802 Munich
Germany
Tel.: (89) 38-17-09-0
Fax.: (89) 38-17-09-35
www.prestel.de

Prestel Publishing Ltd.
4 Bloomsbury Place
London
WC1A 2QA
Tel.: (020) 7323 5004
Fax.: (020) 7636 8004
www.prestel.com

Prestel Publishing
175 Fifth Avenue, Suite 402
New York
NY 10010
Tel.: (212) 995 2720
Fax.: (212) 995 2733
www.prestel.com

Library of Congress Card Number: 00-111975

Prestel books are available worldwide. Please contact your nearest bookseller or any of the above addresses for information concerning your local distributor.

Editorial direction: Philippa Hurd
Glossary: David Radzinowicz
Picture research: Liz Eddison
Index: Mary Scott
Translations from German: John W. Gabriel
Translation from Swedish: Jane Zoega

Design and typesetting:
BCS Publishing, Steve McCurdy
Origination: LVD, Berlin
Production: Kluy & Kluy, Berlin
Printing: Messedruck Leipzig
Binding: Kunst- und Verlagsbuchbinderei Leipzig

Printed in Germany

ISBN 3-7913-2462-4 (English edition)
ISBN 3-7913-2463-2 (German edition)